DATE DUE

FEB 18 '81			
MAR 10 '81			
MR 17 '82			
2weeks			
GAYLORD			PRINTED IN U.S.A

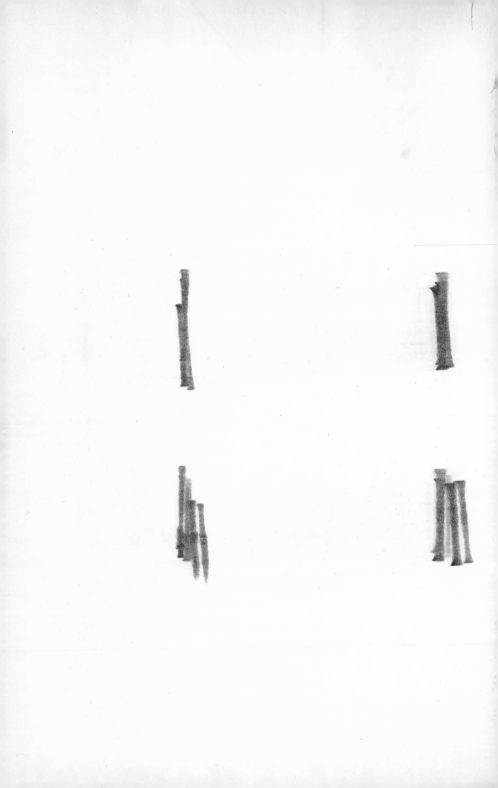

Hitting Our Stride: GOOD NEWS ABOUT WOMEN IN THEIR MIDDLE YEARS

Joan Z. Cohen
Karen Levin Coburn
Joan Crystal Pearlman

Delacorte Press/New York

26004

To our families,
for all their understanding
and encouragement

Published by
Delacorte Press
1 Dag Hammarskjold Plaza
New York, N.Y. 10017

Manufactured in the United States of America
First printing

LIBRARY OF CONGRESS CATALOGING IN PUBLICATION DATA

Cohen, Joan Z
    Hitting our stride.

    Bibliography: p. 269
    Includes index.
    1. Middle age women. I. Coburn, Karen Levin,
1937– joint author. II. Pearlman, Joan Crystal,
1941– joint author. III. Title.
HQ1059.4.C63   305.2'4   80-17203
ISBN 0-440-03656-9

Contents

Acknowledgments

We are deeply grateful to all those who have given us the benefit of their insights and experience, and to those who helped us prepare and distribute our questionnaire: Faxon Adams; Judith Adamson; Jane Anton; Jean Ashton; Sue Anderson; Harriet Avery; Barbara Barnum; Barbara Bauer; Jean Berg; Joan Bliss; Elizabeth Bohn; Jane Brownstone; Colleen Bruns; Jayne Burks; Gail Buss; Bobbi Carey; Sue Castigliano; Evelyn Cohen; Jackie Cooper; Jill Cooper; Jeanette Crockett; Mary Crowe; Bella Crystal; Elaine Crystal; Carolyn Dee; Janet Delcour; Leona Demons; Patt Denning; Ginny Dicker; Patricia DiStefano; Elinor Dopkin; Susan Dowling; Judy Dubin; Janet Eigner; Laurily Epstein; Joan Faber; Gloria Farris; Dick Fernandez; Ann Fitzgerald; Peter Forbath; Judith Frieberg; Shirley Gash; Ann Leinn Gibson; Peggy Giron; Pat Gold; Gloria Goldblatt; Mae Gordon; Linda Green; Peggy Guest; Elaine Gurian; Frank Hamsher; Ann Harris; Ellen Harshman; Beverly Hotchner; Ruth Hubbard; Barbara Huff; Carol Hunter; Marilyn Hutton; Barbara Hyett; Marion Hyson; Etta Jackson; Meg Jacobs; Beverlee Jenkins; Joyce Kaplan; Eleanor Kohlman; Lee Kohlman; Elaine Kolodny; Diane Kravetz; Kathryn Kravitz; Janet Lefkowitz; Brenda Levin; Helen Levin; Lois Levin; Shirlee Levin; Sandra Levinson; Susan Lewis; Susan Lieberman; Linda Lubell; Margaret MacDonald; Sharon Marglous; Barry McArdle; Carol McBride; Vivian McCoy; Goldie Mellowitz; Sherri Muchnick; Anna Navarro; Marion Nestle; Judy Newmark; Pat Newton; Judi Niver; Marian Oldham; Sandra Olsen; Judith Packman; Nelle Pearlman; Sandy Pearlman; Ruth Perrin; Susie Philpott; Barbara Ponse; Pat Rathbone; Shannon Ravenel; Deborah Reese; Susan Reich; Alice Reichman; Arthur Resnikoff; Cynthia Revels; Diana Richards; Ruth Rissman; Beth Rossow; Peggy Rothschild; Mel Rubenstein; Sarah Russell; Bernice Sandler; Carole Sauer; Madeline Schaeffer; Mildred Schapira; Mark Schwartz; Meg Selig; Virginia Shain; Libby Siegel; Linda Skrainka; Jackie Sloan; Sandra Slotnik; Marsha Small; Peggy Small; Gloria Smith; Leslie Smith; Weldon Smith; Abby Snay; Karin Soltes; Barbara Soule; Constance Spahn; Steve Spaner; Mary Sprague; Jayne Stake; Sala Steinback; Linda Stone; John Strauss; Freda Gail Stern; Robin Street; Betty Suggs; Jean Swenson; Josie Thomas; Nancy Jack Todd; Carolyn Toft; Madge Treeger; Susan VanMatre; Marilyn Vedebeck; Ann Wareham; Jane Wayne; Robin Wayne; Mary Weisenburg; John Whiteley; Carol Williams; Judy Wise; Savannah Miller Young; Besse Zaritsky; Raul Zaritsky; and Helene Ziegler.

We also wish to thank our editor, Betty Kelly, and our agent, Rhoda Weyr, who believed in this project from the start.

But we especially want to thank all the women who took the time to fill out the questionnaire, and those who gave so freely of themselves in our interviews with them. Except for the three women in the "Open to Change" section, we have altered descriptive details so that the women remain unidentifiable. This book is their story.

1 The Voices of Women

Today, I celebrate my fiftieth birthday. Until recently I never thought of age—ever. Even now I do not think of age, but of a number "fifty"—the fifty years that unbelievably I have lived. They passed quickly and I feel very young—mentally, physically, and sexually. I feel, too, that people do not think of me as old, or even as the age that I am. They are generally surprised when I tell my age. Occasionally, I think to myself, "Am I acting immaturely? Should I act more like a fifty-year-old?" (Whatever that means!) But mainly I'm more comfortable with being me, with all my good or bad habits, idiosyncrasies, split fingernails, and last year's hairstyle—than I've ever been. There is a serenity to this stage of my life.

I remember when my father turned fifty. I was fifteen and lay in bed and cried because he was half a century old. Now at my half-century mark, I hope I have time left to live out a few dreams. I really do believe I have enough guts to make those dreams happen. Because of the era in which I grew up (a woman's place is in the home)—and the option I took to give up personal achievement for this role, I'm only beginning at age fifty to think about how I can make my life meaningful and fulfilling beyond being a wife and mother. We have six children; the youngest is eleven and the two oldest are in college. Financial concerns hinge on providing them with educational opportunities at an age and time when my husband and I are beginning to look at changes we'd like to make for ourselves. He'd like to slow down—to phase out his dentistry practice and become a full-time farmer—something he's already started to do. I'm ready to get a job—to use some of the energy I've devoted to volunteer work at the Y in a new way. We both feel the pressure of time, and we're both excited about the possibility of indulging our fantasies at last.

—Fifty-year-old housewife from Oregon

I'm continually surprised that my youthful soul is housed in this middle-aged body. I'm not old . . . but then, I'm sure not young. And if you would believe that single-eyed monster of a TV set in my living room, most women never make it past twenty-eight. (Maybe ring-around-the-collar choked them to death.)

I scan the fashion pages and fall in love with several of the newest "looks." Sleek, slinky, the high fashion . . . and—my GOD, I'm bulging—thirty-nine years of good living have settled about six inches below my waist. So now the question: to girdle or not to girdle. I strike a blow for freedom; out go my notions of slinky silk dresses, in come the overblouse and slack look.

But when it's all finished, I wouldn't go back to

my youth. Nothing is *overly* serious now. I've lived long enough to know I can survive almost anything. I've paid my dues in almost everything and am entitled to fail occasionally. I've discovered that a staunch friend and ally (whether male or female) is worth a dozen glamorous affairs. I'm lucky to have a husband (my second) who's also my best friend. As my body gets older, my mind grows richer, my heart grows warmer, and my experiences in life get better by the minute. The young are so unfinished; I'm glad to have the patina of age.

—Thirty-nine-year-old government employee
from Texas

I think of myself as younger than I am, which means that I feel the excitement of being alive and learning in the same way as always, but with more confidence than I had when I was younger. I have a sense of realism about what is and isn't possible for me. I don't feel a frantic push to do everything, and am more able to enjoy quiet time and see such time as a source of creativity.

But sometimes I worry about being seen as a category—*old,* rather than as a person—*me.* People seem more accepting of men's aging than women's. I think older women's faces can be beautiful (look at Georgia O'Keeffe!) but that kind of beauty is not generally recognized. Even if my body gets worn with age, my spirit doesn't have to age. I have arthritis. I sure don't like it, but I have learned to live with it, and still manage to enjoy moving!

—Fifty-four-year-old-elementary school teacher
from Indiana

I think I have gained wisdom through experience. My work involves meeting and getting to know people in a small but steady stream. As a young woman, I was too shy to do this, but now I feel confident. I can handle it okay. Also, when I married at eighteen, I had very little idea of how to make a marriage work. I now live with someone else, who happens to be seven years younger than I am, and I know a great deal more than I used to about how to make the relationship a good one—which it is.

I'm sorry to admit that I am not unaffected, however, by the way our society values the eighteen-year-old female body as the pinnacle of beauty. The enormous value placed on youth and a particular kind of beauty is a curse for women in this country. In spite of all my strong feelings to the contrary, it does influence me. Older women should be shown as they can be and often are: beautiful with their wrinkles, wise with their minds, caring through their experience. I feel strongly that older women in our society are devalued for a lot of bogus reasons—which many of us accept ourselves. I hope you'll deal with this issue in your book. I feel better about myself than I ever have in my life, but this is in spite of society, not thanks to it.

—Forty-five-year-old museum staff member
from New York

This book is from women in their middle years—those whose voices you just heard, and hundreds of others who speak for themselves throughout these pages. And our voices are among them. In fact, our own feelings about middle age had a lot to do with our undertaking this project in the first place.

Before we began this book, all three of us were involved in our work as counselors and educators. The years of caring for small children were behind us. In many ways, we were feeling more competent and more comfortable with ourselves than ever before. Still, when faced with those sudden moments of awareness that *we* were now middle-aged, that *we* were no longer young, we often found ourselves feeling anything but comfortable.

Sometimes the awareness was triggered by a significant change in our lives: a child leaving for college, the death of a parent. Far more often, however, we found ourselves brought up short by nothing more than an unexpected glimpse in the mirror, feeling a little stiff in the morning, an offhand remark by a doctor or salesperson about "women *your* age." But whether the awareness was sparked by something significant or inconsequential, our initial reaction tended to be a negative one.

We noticed the same thing happening to many of our friends. Even those who were filled with the excitement of new careers, new relationships, a new sense of "time at last" for themselves were prone to self-deprecating remarks and self-conscious laughter when the subject of age came up. There seemed to be a definite discrepancy between the way most of us were feeling about ourselves and our lives, and the way we reacted to reminders that *we* were "middle-aged women."

And we saw a similar discrepancy in a great many of the women we counseled and taught over the years. Again and again we heard them make statements such as, "Oh, I couldn't do that at my age!" "I'm too old to go back to school; to change the patterns in my marriage; to start asking for what I want." But in spite of their apprehensions they did take risks, and many of them began to make changes they would never have dreamed of trying when they were younger.

We became increasingly aware of the difference between the *ideas* a lot of women have about what it means to be a middle-aged woman, and what's actually going on with most of them today.

It's certainly not hard to understand where so many of the negative feelings about middle age come from. We live, after all, in a society that has long penalized women for growing older; a society in which the media have relentlessly portrayed the middle-aged woman as "past it," obsolete, bored, and boring; someone who is losing her looks, not to mention her sex appeal; a society in which power for women has been equated with youthful beauty and having babies. And with all this emphasis on the "losses" of growing older, there's been a tendency to overlook the *gains*. So, in spite of all the exciting changes we see in mid-life women today, we also see how these negative ideas about middle age can still affect women's self-images; how they have the potential to become self-fulfilling, and to stop women from reaching out and growing as they get older.

The more we thought about all this, the more we felt that it was important to take a closer look at the discrepancy between attitude and reality; to understand the ways women are being influenced by societal messages, and at the same time, to consider what their lives are really like today. We decided that it would be valuable for women to explore the experience of the middle years together; to examine the issues that concern them; to distinguish the "real" issues of the middle years from what Susan Sontag has called an "ordeal of the imagination";[1] and above all, to find out more about what other women are feeling and doing.

We began to interview women, and before we were through we had talked at length with over two hundred of them. We also designed a questionnaire, and sent out two thousand copies to a network of colleagues and friends around the country who agreed to distribute them to a wide range of women in mid-life. We heard from women as young as twenty-nine and as old as seventy-two, but our focus was primarily on women from the mid thirties to the mid sixties, a period that encompasses in the broadest chronological sense, the "middle years" of life.[2]

The questionnaire (which you can find in appendix A) was a long one, and included both short answer and open-ended questions. Our final sample of 841 women was a diverse group: married, single, urban, rural, women from forty-two different states. Although our sample included women in every economic stratum and approximated the racial distribution of blacks and whites in this country, the women were, for the most part, middle class, with a higher income and educational level than the population in general.[3]

As we read all the replies and listened to the voices of the women, their enthusiasm and their willingness to share ideas and feelings made us feel as though we were immersed in one large conversation. Often women said that we had asked them to think about the topic of middle age in a way they had never thought about it before. They wrote about the issues of the middle years in a very personal way, especially about changes in their roles, relationships, bodies, and self-image. They acknowledged a certain vulnerability to society's attitudes, but more often than not, described their lives in ways that ran counter to the negative stereotypes that have so long been associated with middle-aged women. They talked about taking an active approach to staying physically fit and healthy. Many women who had been through menopause emphasized their new sense of freedom and increased sexual pleasure. Mothers whose children were grown claimed that the "empty nest" brought pleasures they hadn't anticipated while they were still raising a family. Single women described a growing sense of independence and capacity to enjoy life without a partner. And women of all ages and life-styles wrote about becoming more introspective and developing a clearer understanding of what was really important to them.

They reported, moreover, that they were feeling more competent and more able to cope with life than they had as young women. In fact, women in every age category chose "having more self-confidence" as one of the major benefits of being the age they were. Many also said that their new confidence had made them more willing to take risks, to try new things, whether it was starting a job, redefining a marriage, or getting involved with a younger man. They felt more comfortable with themselves, liked themselves better, and felt less dependent on the approval of others. We began to see that there was often a large gap between younger women's negative anticipation of the changes that come with age and the far more positive reality for many older women who were actually experiencing those changes.

The changes women described were not only changes within themselves, but changes in society that were affecting them as well. In a number of ways, the experience of women today is very different from that of our mothers and grandmothers. The women's movement has shaken up the status quo, and many long-standing assumptions about women have been questioned. The rules are changing, and people are starting to reevaluate what is possible, appropriate, and even "normal" for women. The definitions of success and fulfillment are also changing, and women are being encouraged to broaden their roles, to nurture themselves as well as others.

Some of the women we heard from have embraced these changes wholeheartedly; others have clung tenaciously to the rules and values they grew up with. But most, having already made many decisions about their lives before the impact of the women's movement was felt, now find themselves trying to create a comfortable synthesis of old commitments and new freedoms, of old and new definitions of women's roles, of old and new attitudes about sexuality and relationships. This is a time of opportunity, excitement, and potential growth for middle-aged women, but it is also a time of conflict and ambivalence. Most of the women we talked to, however, felt that the middle years are good years, and that this is a better time than ever before to be a middle-aged woman.

Other surveys confirm what we have heard from

women, and show that the middle-aged American woman of today is not only healthier and better educated, but also has a greater sense of emotional well-being than women of previous generations. The results of a study by Srole and Fisher of the Psychiatry Department at the Columbia College of Physicians and Surgeons reveal that the mental health of women in their forties and fifties is significantly better than that of their middle-aged counterparts twenty years ago.[4] As Betty Friedan put it, "One of the most remarkable results of the women's movement has been the unprecedented new vitality and growth experienced by millions of women who have defied the deterioration, depression, and despair that used to be considered 'normal' symptoms of aging in women."[5]

And data from the National Center for Health Statistics suggests that it is women in their middle years rather than young women who seem to be in the fortunate position of being able to make the most of changing roles and new opportunities. While middle-aged women "may be under greater pressure than ever before to 'do something' with their lives once their children leave home, they are ready and eager for the revolution in female aspirations. Broader horizons for women may have made possible a second lease on life."[6] Many middle-aged women have already resolved a number of the conflicts and decisions facing younger women today (should I get married? have children? pursue a career?). They are now approaching the next stage of life secure in the knowledge that they have lived a lot, learned a lot, and that the best may be yet to come.

Gail Sheehy's recent survey of 52,000 women in their early twenties to their late sixties also confirms the positive status of today's middle-aged women.[7] Women in her sample who were between thirty-five and forty-five reported "breaking through to a new level of sexual satisfaction."[8] And while many women in their mid-forties to mid-fifties indicated that they were concerned about what to do next as they saw their mothering role coming to an end, this same group of women also said that they were "establishing a firm sense of their own identities *for the first time.*"[9] Moreover, Sheehy states that women today often emerge from this troubled period with a regular paycheck in hand, and almost always with the knowledge that they can cope well and accomplish things on their own. Indeed, it was the women over fifty who reported greater feelings of happiness than women in any other age category who responded to her survey.[10]

Sheer numbers also make this a good time to be middle-aged. We middle-aged women comprise a rapidly growing portion of the population, and because of this we are receiving an increasing amount of attention. As the average age of the population has gone up, there has been a shift away from the relentless worship of youth. Media, advertising, educational institutions—everyone with a product to sell is showing new interest in the "mature market." There are still plenty of ads around exhorting women to look/think/act *young.* But, increasingly, mature women are being portrayed as attractive, vital, and accomplished in their own right. And while it is easy to be cynical about the economic motivation for such change, the change itself is welcome.

But it is not just messages in the media that are beginning to change: so is our willingness to be defined by those messages. Women are getting angry and refusing to accept Madison Avenue's version of what makes them valuable and desirable. The women's movement has helped us to value ourselves as women; we are now learning to value our own maturity as well.

On the whole, the women we heard from told us that they liked being the age they were, and that the benefits of being older outweighed the losses of no longer being young. In part, this response can be attributed to the fact that many of the women in our survey were above average in income and education. But this attitude was evident in women of all socioeconomic strata in our sample. Certainly, there were some women who were "stuck" in the stereotypes, too preoccupied with the battle against sags and wrinkles to look out at the world ahead, but they were a distinct minority. And certainly, there were many women in our sample who had very real problems to contend with, who were struggling or angry or scared. But with nearly all of them there was also a clear sense of, "I can cope. I can prevail." To sit surrounded by our questionnaires was often to feel surrounded by strength, by women embracing life and moving ahead—and not always under favorable circumstances. We frequently came away from our interviews with a wonderful sense of what was possible for us in our own future lives.

There is, of course, a poignancy about leaving youth behind, and no one likes the idea of moving closer to the end of life. But there is so much that we gain, so much that comes together for us in our middle years. As we move beyond the social pressures of youth and the demands of the early years of marriage and childbearing, we develop a heightened sense of personal freedom. We become more comfortable with our limitations and our strengths. As we begin to face up to the fact that we aren't going to live forever, we begin to see more clearly what really counts in life, and to develop a deeper understanding of who we are and who we can be.

2 Did You Ever Get the Feeling You Weren't Raised to Be Over Forty?

Did you ever get the feeling you weren't raised to be over forty? Well, in many ways you weren't. Nearly all the social preparation most of us received was directed at the first three decades of life. As young girls, few of us had an image of our own future beyond some hazy notion of the early years of marriage and a house full of children. Some women struck out and established lives on their own while still quite young. Most of us, however, followed the traditional pattern and moved directly from daughter to wife to mother, without giving much thought to what would happen after that. But children grow up. Or we're suddenly divorced or widowed and have to support ourselves. Almost before we know it, we are at middle age, facing the longest, least planned-for period of our lives. And it's not at all unusual—even among those of us who work—to find ourselves wondering: "What's next? How much is still possible for me? What do I want to *do* with the rest of my life?"

Not that all middle-aged women are sitting around quivering with indecision—far from it. By the time we're middle-aged, we have a clearer sense of what we like and don't like, and we're better able to accept our strengths and weaknesses. There is, after all, no better preparation for being over forty than the experience and competence we've gained in the years leading up to it. But, given all the social change of recent years, women in mid-life today will almost inevitably go through periods of uncertainty and questioning. For not only were we not raised to be over forty, it often feels as though we *were* raised to live in a world that isn't there anymore: a world that had more stability and continuity—as well as more limitations—than exist today, especially for women. The odds are diminishing that we'll make it through our middle years with our marriage still intact, or that we'll continue to live in the community in which we grew up. We have, on the average, fewer children than our mothers, and finish raising them when we ourselves are still relatively young. In fact, never before has a generation of women faced such a long span of time beyond child-rearing when they can expect to be healthy and vigorous and productive. And never before have there been so many choices and possibilities open to mature women.

So on one hand, this is a very exciting time to be considering the question "What's next?" But on the other, we may well find ourselves feeling somehow out-of-sync with current expectations. We may wonder if we made the right choices in life, or if we would make the same choices today. We are likely to swing back and forth between wishing things were the way they used to be, and eagerly anticipating the chance to strike out anew; between moments of self-doubt, and the heady exhilaration of thinking *anything* is possible.

All around us, there are reminders of the difference between the ideas we grew up with and those prevalent in the world we live in today. Supermarket magazines lure us with tales of "The New Woman: A Success at Home and in the Office," and articles about women who have gone back to work or made spectacular career changes in mid-life. We read the alumnae notes from our twenty-fifth reunion and wonder, "Am I the only one who hasn't graduated from anything since high school except Smokenders?" At times we suspect that there's a new edict for women; that we're now expected to move effortlessly from daughter to wife to mother to "Superwoman." We may be ready to reassess our priorities, to make new choices and move off in a different direction. But what direction? How far? To meet whose criteria?

One woman in her mid-forties told us that her two youngest children had recently moved out of the house, and she felt as though people were poised waiting to see what momentous things she was going to do now that she was "free":

> Sometimes I feel as though at the very least, I'm expected to find a full-time job with a snappy title, enroll in an MBA program, write a slim volume of erotic poetry, and, oh yes, run five miles a day. Me? I've successfully raised four children with whom I continue to have a good relationship, and I consider that one hell of an accomplishment. Right now, I just want to take it easy for a while, do some of the things I've never had time for, and spend more time with my husband. . . . So why do I feel so uncomfortable when people ask, "And what do *you* do?"

These days, many women are, indeed, feeling a great deal of social pressure to *perform, achieve, produce* at mid-life. But they are likely to be putting quite a bit of pressure on themselves as well. Acutely aware of the passage of time, they feel as though it's now or never to do all those things they've always dreamed about. And an increasing number of middle-aged women also feel they must prepare to be financially independent, to take responsibility for themselves and their own futures. As one fifty-two-year-old put it:

> I need to know I can support myself. It took my husband's heart attack two years ago to bring that home to me. He's okay now, but for the first time in my life, I have a full-time job, and I intend to keep it. I don't ever again want to feel as vulnerable and dependent as I did two years ago when he got sick.

Whatever decision a woman makes about what she wants to do next in life, and whatever her reasons for making it, more and more women are coming to see the middle years as a time of new beginnings, a time to try at last the aspirations that have been shelved for so long, aspirations they may only now have the time and self-confidence to pursue. A woman may relish the opportunity to stay at home and enjoy leisure activities without the responsibility of caring for children. She may choose to make a commitment to community service, or find some new, especially rewarding way in which to volunteer her time,[1] or she may combine several of these activities. But a rapidly growing number of women in their middle years are entering or reentering the labor market, or changing careers. In fact, in recent years, middle-aged women have been one of the fastest growing segments of the American labor force. Currently fifty-five percent of women between thirty-five and fifty-four years of age are employed, and by 1990, it is projected that approximately sixty-two percent of all women in this age group will be working.[2] In part, this increase can be attributed to an inflationary economy and the large percentage of women on their own. Most women work because they *have* to. But women are also working because they *want* to be productive and independent, to be challenged and have a sense of achievement, and to be recognized for their own capabilities.

Since so many middle-aged women were not prepared for careers, large numbers of them are returning to school for further training.[3] Educational institutions, from small community colleges to the largest universities, are becoming increasingly aware that a large proportion of their future students will be drawn from the ranks of mature women. Gone are the days when older students were merely tolerated. Today they are welcomed, even courted, and many services are provided specifically for them.[4]

Bernice Sandler, Director of the Project on the Status and Education of Women at the Association of American Colleges, says that the trend toward women going back to school is gaining momentum. She notes that the campus is attracting mature women who have never worked and now want to train for a career, as well as those who have been working, but now want to train for a career change: "I'm suddenly hearing a lot of women say, 'My job is all right. I like what I'm doing. But now I'm ready to try something else and move on to something better!' I'm struck by the new willingness with which women are ready to take stock of where they are regarding work, and then ask themselves if this is really what they want to continue doing for the rest of their lives. It's as if not having planned for their work life when they were young, they're eager to take the initiative to plan for their future years."

The women in our survey clearly reflected the trends Sandler and others have noted. A whopping seventy percent of those who answered our questionnaire were currently working outside the home either full- or part-time, and a little over a quarter were either full- or part-time students. Over three-quarters of the working women we surveyed had returned to the labor market after interrupting their careers to have a family. And we were most interested to see that nearly half of our respondents said they were considering making some kind of change in the next five years, either a job change or reentry into the labor market.

When we talked with women who had made the transition back to school or work, we were often struck by their enthusiasm, their pride in having taken the first step, their sense of having opened up a new world for themselves. "I like having that paycheck and knowing that, if need be, I can take care of myself," was the kind of comment we heard repeatedly. "I was scared at first, but now I feel more confident than ever before," was another.

Women talked freely about their struggles too. A number said it had been hard to start again as a novice at middle age, especially after years of being the one in charge in other situations. Some women had husbands who were very resistant to change, and their return to school or work had created a lot of tension and unpleasantness at home. ("He still expects me to be a 'traditional' wife, and refuses to accept that the traditions are changing!") And even when husbands *were* supportive, many women found themselves in the all too familiar plight of Superwoman, trying to juggle responsibilities at home and at work. There was the inevitable pressure of changing long established family patterns—pressure that went beyond the logistics of reassigning household tasks and learning to manage time more efficiently. One forty-year-old explained:

> Oh, I know all that good stuff about reducing my housekeeping standards, about taking turns with cooking and shopping and laundry and all that. It doesn't always work out the way I want it to, but I know what we *should* be doing. But what about the way I *feel* when I miss my daughter's big swim meet because it conflicts with a sales conference? Or the way we all feel when I'm home in body only, when I'm preoccupied with what's going on at the office? No, I certainly don't want to give up my job, but there are moments when I question whether or not it's worth it.

Indeed, for some women, the question is not, "Do I want to work?" It's "What are my priorities going to be?" As new opportunities are starting to open up at higher levels, these women are asking themselves how much of a personal price they are willing to pay for success, how much they are willing to give up to get ahead. ("Sure, I want to move up," said an accountant in her late thirties, "but not if it means being absolutely driven, a workaholic like so many men I know.")

Of course, the issue of being "too successful" is not the one most middle-aged women are struggling with. While it's true that some women are moving into positions of status and power, we still hold less than 5% of top management jobs. The vast majority (80%) of female workers are still in low-paying, dead-end jobs, and their earning power is substantially less than their male counterparts'. Women earn only fifty-nine cents on every dollar earned by men.[5] Age and sex discrimination are illegal, but often hard to prove. And there are few good opportunities for flexible working hours or part-time employment.

But the changes that began in the seventies are here to stay and with pressure from women will continue to evolve. Middle-aged women will keep on entering the labor force, and as they do so, create change both in the workplace and in the way families are structured. They are already attempting to create additional opportunities for shared jobs, "flexitime," and work schedules that are more humane to both men and women.[6] Women are forming both formal and informal networks in order to share information, help one another advance, and collectively apply political pressure.[7] They are becoming more informed and more willing to invoke age and sex discrimination laws.[8] They are getting more training and developing skills in management. They are entering fields and taking positions they wouldn't have considered a decade ago. A forty-year-old woman returning to law or business school has plenty of company these days. Ten or fifteen years ago, it probably wouldn't have occurred to her to take such a step. And if it had, she would have found the doors to most institutions closed to her.

The feminist movement has certainly had a lot to do with changing opportunities for mid-life women. It has affected not only the choices we confront, but the attitudes with which we confront them. But something else has also influenced women's attitudes about "What's next?" and what it means to be "over forty," and that is the concept of *adult development.*

In recent years, a great deal of attention has been focused on the idea that people can and do change considerably throughout their adult years, not just in what they *do,* but in personality and outlook and how they feel about life. Once again, however, most of us were not brought up to think in those terms. The very word "grown-up" suggests something that is all done, *fait accompli.* By middle age, surely, one is supposed to have it together, to be established and settled. But we do not, in fact, spring into adulthood full-blown like butterflies from a cocoon, and merely age, unchanged, thereafter. We go through periods of growth and development, equilibrium and disequilibrium; times when we're very comfortable with ourselves and our lives, and times when everything feels out of kilter and we wonder what it's all about. We continue, as adults, to go through stages of development.

The idea itself is hardly new; Carl Jung, Erik Erikson, Bernice Neugarten, and other social scientists have in the past formulated theories about adult development, but their work has had more of an impact on their professional colleagues than on the way most of us view adulthood. More recently, however, psychologist Daniel Levinson, psychiatrists Roger Gould and George Valiant, and journalist Gail Sheehy, with her overwhelmingly successful book *Passages,* have built on the ideas of these earlier theorists, and have begun to influence the way large numbers of people think about the adult life cycle.

The terms used to describe the adult stages of the life cycle, and the precise ages delineating each stage, vary from one researcher to another. But there does seem to be a general agreement among them about the content of the developmental stages we pass through. There is also general agreement that there are specific developmental tasks appropriate to each stage and specific points of crisis during which we are simultaneously vulnerable and have tremendous potential for growth. Levinson likens the life stages to seasons of the year—each has its own character and each is qualitatively different from the season that precedes or follows it. Yet there is change and growth within each season and transitional movement from one to the next. "No season is better or more important than any other," Levinson says. "Each has its necessary place and contributes its special character to the whole. It is an organic part of the total cycle, linking past and future and containing both within itself."[9]

There is still controversy about the theory of life stages, and we are a long way from totally understanding the complex dynamics of adult development. All of life is not a stage, and we cannot reduce what we are feeling at any point in time to some aspect of the life stage paradigm. Several researchers are now suggesting that the concept of adult life stages is too simplistic. As Bernice Neugarten puts it, "the timing of life events is becoming less regular, age is losing its customary social meanings, and the trends are towards the fluid life cycle and an age-irrelevant society."[10] (We're becoming more and more used to the thirty-eight-year-old, first-time mother, the fifty-year-old college freshman, and the thirty-year-old corporate president.) Moreover, most of the research on life stages has been done on middle-class white males, and it remains to be seen how well these patterns fit for women. There's always the danger that this research can be misused to set constricting criteria for when we should be doing what, or to show that women and minorities aren't measuring up.[11]

Rather than falling into the trap of trying to fit into a rigid model, however, we can use this current information about adult development to help us *understand our own experience*—to understand that it is natural and essential to change and grow throughout life.

What follows are brief highlights of the adult life stages. They are compiled from the writings of major researchers and writers in the field of adult development and include Sheehy's observations of the differing developmental rhythms of men and women.

Beginning to Break Ties: Ages 18–22

Whether we go away to school, get a job, or marry, these are the years during which we begin to break the psychological ties with our families, and try out the arena of adult life. We "try out" roles, jobs, potential careers, friends, and values. There may be periods of coming back home, both physically and psychically, as we attempt to create a life of our own and build an identity for ourselves in the adult world. We fear we'll be found out, that others will realize how scared we are and how little we know. So we put on a good front and surround ourselves with friends who confirm what we are—or what we hope we are. Women who move directly from a protective father to a protective husband in these years may avoid the task of forming a separate adult identity. This task, then, remains unfinished and will have to be resolved later.

Reaching Out: The Twenties

This is the period when we actually break the strong ties to home and childhood and *act* on the struggles of the preceding period. What we were trying out earlier, we are now doing "for real." We form intimate relationships and/or select our mates. Noses to the grindstone, we try to carve our niche in the world of work. We may settle down in the true establishment style, "doing it right"—forming long-term relationships, acquiring skills, building a future. Or we may keep exploring, moving—even jumping from one job to another, one experience to another, one lover to another. Whether we settle in or explore without making commitments, we are setting a pattern and style for our lives.

The main tasks of this stage are to develop intimacy and competence. It is a time when men often acquire a mentor (who guides them, helps them, and acts as a model in the world of work), an important relationship that most women just don't develop.[12] Men—and an increasing number of women—are establishing their careers at this point. Some women leave their attempts to conquer the work world until later, as they concentrate on motherhood, though a growing number are mastering the balancing act of starting both a career and a family.

The Thirty-Year Crunch: Questions, Questions. Ages 29–34

Something happens to us as we approach thirty, and it's often painful. It's a time of self-examination—of questioning and reevaluating one's earlier decisions. All that we've so carefully built in our twenties comes into question. The woman who has been home raising children may begin wanting to branch out. The urge increases as she looks around at the toy-strewn house and the squabbling children and wonders how this could have been her dream. Meanwhile her husband may be asking the same question —only he's asking it about his job, about all he's been building through his twenties, including his marriage.

The single woman who is established in the work world starts thinking about settling into a relationship. For the woman without children, the biological time clock is ticking away, and she becomes acutely conscious of the years she has left if she wants to start a family.

The tasks of this stage are to reappraise relationships, reassess decisions about career and family, and resolve the conflicts that we stir up in ourselves. We begin giving up the illusions of our youth, and either break away or intensify our commitments.

Mid-Life Crisis: Ages 35–45

Sheehy calls this the "deadline decade"; Levinson delineates the period from forty to forty-five as the mid-life transition. And if there is any stage of adult development most of us have heard of before, this is it. The mid-life crisis has become something of a cliché, the subject of parodies and jokes. ("How come I'm the only forty-year-old on the block who hasn't had a mid-life crisis yet?") We bare our feelings in some moment of extraordinary angst, only to be dismissed with "Oh, it's probably just your mid-life crisis"—though it feels like anything but "just" when we are in the throes of it.

Somewhere in this period, our mortality becomes real to us. Time suddenly seems to be running out, and we're likely to start measuring life in terms of time left, rather than time since birth. It is common to feel some sense of urgency; to tell ourselves that this is it: our last chance. For women, the physical issues of aging bring the realization that the childbearing years are over, or soon will be. Those with mentors leave that relationship behind, and start becoming mentors themselves to the new generation of young adults. Women begin to be more assertive, independent, and are reaching out, just as the men in their lives are becoming more tender, soft, and inward. This is often a time of sexual panic. Men worry about losing their sexual potency; women worry about losing their sexual attractiveness. It is also a time to question the values one has been living by so far. And at some point in this period, it is common to reach the realization that we are alone, that no other person can truly supply our security, or give us our confidence. No one can protect us from the demons within or the dangers without. As F. Scott Fitzgerald put it, "It is in the thirties that we want friends. In the forties we know they won't save us any more than love did."[13] We struggle for autonomy, but as we pull apart the illusions of our earlier years, we may feel the confusion and fear that we thought we left behind us when we left adolescence. And along with it all, we may wonder "Is there still time to change?"

If we sidestep the issues of mid-life at this time, we are likely to face them again in our fifties; they may, in fact, hit us harder then. Those who continue to avoid the mid-life confrontation altogether live out the rest of their lives in resignation. They become rigid defenders of the status quo.[14] Their familiar refrain is, "Let's keep things the way they were in the good old days." Women in this position remain girlish in behavior and attitudes, never moving beyond the dependent position of their youth. Or they turn bitter and angry, feeling cheated by the gap between their youthful illusions and the reality they face. They ignore the changes in themselves and the world, and, failing to profit from their own experience, become stuck, their development permanently arrested.

Renewal: Ages 45–60 and Beyond

For those who have faced the mid-life crisis head on, and have made peace with themselves, this is the calm after the storm. There is a deepening of relationships. Friendships, although fewer in number, become more intense and meaningful. Married couples report increased happiness now that the stresses and strains of the transition years are behind.

We have increased capacity to be comfortable with who we are—whether we're alone or with others. No longer clamoring for everyone's approval or admiration, we can now choose to do what brings us inner satisfaction.

Our experience is one of our greatest assets. With more effective judgment based on what we've learned over the years, we're better able to make decisions. We no longer need to delude ourselves. We have lived through the turbulence and crisis and have gained a sense of perspective. Researchers agree that this can be the best of times.

These stages are guidelines. They are hardly ever as distinct in real life as they appear on paper. In fact, certain psychological themes tend to repeat themselves throughout the adult life cycle in slightly altered forms.[15] We don't finish one stage abruptly and wake up the next morning to find we've moved into another. Nor do we all experience these stages with the same degree of intensity. Some people are devastated at mid-life; most are not. We may be acutely aware of a particular transition, or we may hardly notice the evolution that is taking place in us.

The whole notion of life stages and adult development is especially helpful in understanding why what is appropriate for us at one stage of life is not necessarily so at another. Past decisions that we now regret may, in fact, be the wrong decisions for who we are now, but right for who we were at the time we made them. Instead of berating ourselves with what we should have done or wish we'd done earlier, we can focus on what it is we want to do or need to do now. As we come face to face with the question, "What next?" it may help to reflect on all the coping skills we bring with us, and to see ourselves not only as people who are capable of change, but as people who *are,* in fact, changing, often in exciting ways, throughout our adult life.

Indeed, more than anything else, it was women's capacity for change in the middle years that came through to us in our survey and interviews. As women described their sense of self-discovery, and their joy at breaking out of old molds and taking risks, they vividly expressed their vitality and growth. It became increasingly clear to us that middle-aged women today are creating a whole new phase of life "over forty."

3 Open to Change

As we talked with women who were active, involved, and had very positive feelings about being the age they were, we kept asking ourselves, "What is it about these women that is so different from those who seem to feel 'stuck' in mid-life?" Good health, an adequate income, and a caring family certainly account for some of the difference. But as we listened to women in all kinds of situations, it became obvious that there was more to it than that.

There is, of course, no simple formula for a "successful" middle age. The issues we face as we get older and our individual ways of coping with them are far too varied to be reduced to the pages of a cookbook-style, how-to-do-it manual. There are, however, several characteristics, an overall approach to life, that we consistently saw in these dynamic women. They have a sense of humor and perspective about themselves and their lives. They are introspective but not preoccupied with self; their focus and energy are turned outward—toward the people they care about and the world around them. But what they have in common more than anything else, is an openness to change—in themselves, in their relationships, and in their circumstances. The women we talked to who seemed to be most comfortable with themselves and with their age were not those who clung to how things used to be, or merely coped with change, adapting themselves to the inevitable, but the women who were able to open themselves to new experiences, to grow with the changes without losing their sense of themselves.

This openness to change is apparent in the words of the three women that follow. They describe not only the ways they have responded to the predictable turning points of the middle years, but also how they have coped with the unexpected and moved beyond crises. And they share sensitive perceptions of their own evolution, of their continued blossoming in the middle period of their lives.

DEBORAH FRANKEL REESE

From the porch of her old three-story frame house in New Jersey, Deborah Reese calls out a welcome. She is a small woman, dressed in jeans and a white cotton Indian shirt; her dark curls shine like an oversized halo in the bright summer sun. At thirty-nine, Deborah is "an artist, a wife, and a mother—not necessarily in that order." Like many women her age, she is just beginning to think of herself as "middle-aged":

> Until a few years ago, I thought of myself as being very *young*, and I certainly don't feel *old* now in any sense of the word. But recently, I've found myself more and more aware of the passage of time.
>
> I suppose it was when my children became teenagers that I first began to feel my age. To begin with, their physical changes are so amazing! It's

like watching amaryllis bulbs grow, those magical bulbs that add two inches to their stalks every night. My "baby" daughter now wears a bra, my shirts and skirts—but not my jeans and shoes, because they are too small for her. I've watched my son grow enormously tall, his voice change, his moustache grow; I've watched an entire body and face I once knew so well, inch by inch, change almost overnight into a stranger! And suddenly I, who thought that I had remained in touch and very "with it" over the years, am considered totally square, out of it, by this "boy-man." All of a sudden, I am accused of never understanding, and I realize that there is a world of teenagers out there living their own lives that are very different and separate from my own. They seem so young. It's when teenagers suddenly seem so young and so different from you that you know you are getting older; that you've moved to the other side of the generation gap.

And on the other end, there are my parents who are white-haired and retired, and doing things like going to fiftieth reunions, and that also makes me aware of the passage of time.

But it isn't just that my children are growing older and my parents are growing old; there are certain changes in *me* that I can't ignore. I have to admit that I'm getting older on mornings when my back aches when I first wake up. I know it's harder to take off five pounds than it was even five years ago. I know the gray is starting to show and *doesn't* look distinguished. And, two of my fingers are already becoming arthritic, and all I can remember when they hurt is my grandmother, whose hands were so crippled that she couldn't use them.

Yet basically, I'm in good shape; I'm healthy and I feel more attractive now than I felt when I was younger. Not only that, I'm much less likely to torture myself with comparisons to tall, lithe, beautiful young girls than when I was seventeen— and that's a relief! I never had good legs. I was never limber and athletic, and my hips have always been broad. I was never one of those perfectly groomed, perfectly put together women even when I was twenty or twenty-five. I think we have to be careful as we get older not to fall into the trap of always blaming age, of saying, "Well, if I were as young as she, I'd be terrific too." I certainly wasn't any more perfect at twenty than I am as I approach forty.

But other things concern me much more than the physical aspects of growing older: roads not taken, opportunities lost, dreams deferred; facing the fact that everything is not, indeed, possible. I used to think it was. For instance, once, not too long ago, while we were driving through long stretches of farmland, I startled my husband and children by yelling out all of a sudden, "I'm never going to have one! Never! Dammit!" Since I was seven or eight years old, I had dreamed of having my own horse. It was something I always knew I would have one day. If my parents wouldn't buy me a horse and turn the yard into a fenced corral, at least I knew that I would buy myself one when I grew up, when I was my own boss. That day in the car, as we drove by a pasture full of those beautiful animals, I thought to myself, "Well, someday . . . " and then I realized that it was "someday," that I didn't have a horse, and that I probably never, ever would.

And when I think about it, I'll probably never live in the little whitewashed cottage on an island somewhere in the Mediterranean. My paintings probably will never hang in the Museum of Modern Art. And almost certainly I will never again fall in love with a man with a European accent! Some dreams die hard, but others are alive and thriving. There's the little beach house by the ocean, almost any ocean, that I want to retire to someday. I still believe in that. And the art show that I know I'll have in the city. The beautiful herb garden that I've planned in my head for years—someday it will be real. And there will be new dreams, ones I don't even know of yet. I know that my dreams will change, but I'll never stop dreaming.

All things considered, I'm happy with myself and with this time of my life. I have achieved at least some of the things I set out to achieve, and am still working on others. Learning to accept my imperfections has been one of the hardest things for me to do, but as I get older, it does seem to get easier. So I'll never be good at math and I'll probably always have a lousy sense of direction. But I've learned to use a calculator, read a map, and ask for directions when I need them. I get along fine, and have stopped torturing myself about what I can't do.

I have spent years telling my children, "you can't be terrific at everything. Nobody is perfect in all things. If you can't do that, never mind. Think of all the other things you can do well." Simplistic? Of course, but good advice nevertheless—advice I never myself followed until lately. I spent my whole life thinking of myself as a con artist. Every time someone would compliment me on something that I had done well or something about me that was good, I would think, "Oh yeah. But you don't really *know*. The real me is so awful, so inept. It's all a sham, and you just don't know. That good painting? It was an accident. I look nice? It's this skirt, not me." Suddenly, really almost suddenly, I don't think that way anymore. I'm beginning to think there is really some truth in what they say. I've always believed I was a good person; finally, I am able to perceive myself also as a competent, talented, and in some ways, important person. It's a wonderful feeling, and I think it's one that only comes with time and experience.

I feel very fortunate to be able to live my life as I am—being at home and painting part-time. But up until a few years ago, it made me very uneasy. I wasn't "The New Woman," out there being a professional or an executive or even punching a time clock. And I wasn't the sparkling floor, milk-and-cookies mama of the television commercials either. But I was—and am—lucky enough to be doing what I want to do: taking care of my family and painting.

For a number of irrelevant reasons, I had given up my art (at least on the surface) when I was seventeen. I decided to major in English in college, which left me equipped to read great literature and write critical papers! I dabbled in writing; I worked as an editorial assistant, and then I had the children. When I was about thirty, as my youngest child hit nursery school, I finally had some time for me. What I wanted after all those years, I discovered, was to paint. So, I bought new supplies, breathed in the old familiar aroma of turpentine, and began painting. I haven't stopped since.

But, as I said, it isn't always an easy decision to live with, being a part-time artist. Nearly all of my friends are heavily involved in careers, or getting the necessary degrees so they will be able to begin careers. Everyone else seems to be *out there* and I am *at home.* It's true that my studio is at home, and I say that I work at home. But I used to feel it was a cop-out to say that, especially when weeks would go by, and I would only work one day or two. I don't make a lot of money; I keep myself in supplies with a little extra. I've only had two gallery shows in the past three years, because I'm not good at the hustling part of being an artist. But I'm happy!

I also find as I've gotten older that I trust myself more. I trust my decisions about what is right for me. What other people think is becoming increasingly less important to me, whether in regard to a freaky new haircut (which my parents and more establishment friends hate and I *love*), or the quality and quantity of my art work. The only critic I really care about now, personally or professionally, is myself. My competition is with myself, not with the world. After years of uneasiness about what I wasn't doing, I've matured enough to be able to value my choices instead of feeling guilty and embarrassed about them.

I am spending more and more time painting these days. But I'm still not at a point where I can just say "the hell with everything else" and let the house fall down around my feet when I am working. When everything is in chaos, I just can't work. And since my studio is at home, it's hard to escape the chaos. I may be thoroughly immersed in the way the umber paint is mixing with the medium and dispersing into the ochre, but way back in a corner of my mind, I am also thinking about the fact that my daughter needs clean gym clothes in the morning, and I haven't done any wash for four days, or that my parents are coming to spend the night tomorrow and the house is a mess, or that there is nothing in the house for dinner!

But I am working at it, and it is getting better. I am learning that everything doesn't have to be perfect, and life doesn't have to be lived the way it is in television land or on the pages of *House*

Beautiful. I've learned that I can buy a birthday cake instead of make it, and no one will think less of me. That the sheets can go three extra days without changing, and no one will even notice. That if the roses don't get sprayed, it means we'll have spotty roses, but not a catastrophe. That if I miss a PTA meeting, it doesn't mean that I don't love my children. That I can buy cold cuts for dinner and everyone will be perfectly content. I'm learning where to take shortcuts, and learning what my priorities are. And I'm learning to respect my priorities and myself for having made them.

I also know that in five years, my children will both be out of high school and I will have more freedom than I've ever had. At that time, I will make my painting a top priority, and nothing will get in the way. Until then, my commitments will be divided and I will remain a part-time artist with full-time ambitions.

One of the best things about my middle years is sharing them with my husband, John. The caring and sharing we do will remain, I am sure, one of the finest things in my life. We have been together for twenty-one years now, and married for seventeen. Sometimes I think we will be the last remaining married couple. We have lost about ten close friends to the divorce disease . . . all trailing little children behind them. I can't really pinpoint what makes our marriage last, but I do know that the sense of "foreverness" we have is so special to us both, so much more important than Erica Jong's "zipless fuck."

Of course, in the long run, I know we're all on our own. We can give each other love, warmth, and protection as best we can, but ultimately, we have to depend on ourselves. I know that my mother and father won't always be there. And there's a good chance that eventually John won't be there with me either. Ever since childhood, the idea of losing loved ones has scared me more than anything else. It still does. The idea that *I* will grow old seems real to me now in a way it never did when I was younger. And I'm afraid of being really old and helpless myself someday. But I don't sit around and become obsessive over these fears. I live with them and with the hope that I will have the strength, courage, and maturity to deal with each situation as it comes.

In the meantime, I look forward to my own personal growth in the next decades. I have seen tremendous changes in myself and my work over the past few years. The changes are so enormous that sometimes they scare me; I don't even know where they come from. Lately, I have been painting very oversized close-up studies of open roses . . . very organic and textural. This is after years of working almost entirely with the figure. I don't know what brought the roses on, but they obviously reflect some changes within me. My work has far more authority and strength than ever before. I know that it will change and strengthen even more. And I know that I will also, for a long, long time.

KATHRYN NELSON

When Kathryn Nelson starts to speak, people turn around and listen. Her voice is resonant and her wit sharp, but mainly it's what she has to say about the issues of education and health care and other social services that commands attention. She is both savvy and passionate about the things she believes in. At age fifty-four, Kathryn's black skin is smooth and her dark eyes shine behind large glasses. Her average size seems somehow magnified when she stands up at a podium, as she frequently does, to speak to an assembled group; there is a quality about Kathryn that calls to mind the phrase "larger than life." A well-known leader in her St. Louis community, Kathryn has devoted much of her energy over the years to creating and running innovative educational programs for young people, from pre-schoolers to college students.

Kathryn Nelson is a born storyteller, and some of her best stories are about her own past. Growing up in Memphis during the Depression left her with vivid memories of "making do with very little." But at the same time, she says:

Everyone in my family learned to be creative. For example, my younger sister and I used to pick vegetables out of our garden. Instead of just selling greens, or tomatoes, we would make dinners—you know, you put together greens, tomatoes, onions, and the whole thing and go to a lady's house and sell her a whole dinner for twenty-five cents. With that twenty-five cents we bought meat to cook with the rest of the vegetables we had picked for our own dinner. So we were very enterprising and learned how to be creative even in those young days. The feeling was that there were problems to be solved and you could solve them—that was what we were taught. And my mother taught me two other things that were sort of a portent of what was to come. One was that the greatest thing I could do in this world was to get married and have children; and the other one was that it was tremendously important for me to develop whatever talent I had.

I got a scholarship to LeMoyne College and went through all four years there. And, consequently I have nothing but great things to say about some of the small black institutions like LeMoyne.

The feeling at LeMoyne was that you were

preparing yourself to give something back to the community. The goal there was to build skills and self-respect. I'm really hipped on self-respect because I believe that what you do depends on what you see when you look in the mirror and what you think about yourself. The message of LeMoyne to me was one I try to transmit in my dealings with young people. It is that what is important is the whole business of commitment to something outside yourself.

Kathryn went on to Columbia University for a master's degree. ("It was real culture shock; there were all these kids from Bryn Mawr and Smith who talked about history like they were related to the French kings.") Several years later, she married Clyde Nelson, a college boyfriend, and had four children in rapid succession.

I stayed at home with the children when they were small. I took in sewing, worked as an executive secretary for a women's organization, and did a lot of odds and ends to keep my hand in. Then I realized that if I didn't go to work, my husband was going to kill himself working—he was so determined to make a good life for us. He had three jobs; he was doing too much. So I went back to work, first as a social worker in a children's home then as a teacher. And I've been in education ever since.

Kathryn made the transition back to work when she was thirty-six. She reached another, more internal transition point in her mid-forties.

There was a period in my forties when I felt I had some kind of choice between whether I was going to be an "older person" or a "younger person."

During those years you still have a bit of shape, you haven't gained too much weight. With a little bit of coloring in your hair you can still pass for thirty, or forty. It's a time when you can decide whether or not you're going to have a "last fling," be kind of frivolous, and do some of the adolescent things you feel you missed, or whether you are going to keep on moving toward a goal, or whether you can blend the two.

I think the world as I perceived it, said, "Now you are older; now you will put your hair up and be serious." And my response was, "It is important to me to play." It is important for my husband and me to maintain some playfulness in our lives in some form or fashion, because being parents of four kids is a heavy trip, and if you don't maintain some kind of playfulness you'll die under the burden of it. So playing became a deliberate choice as the whole business of living got heavier and heavier.

I went through a real crisis kind of situation when I was forty-four. I can remember becoming so restless that I didn't know what to do with myself. It was a terrible feeling and I had great guilt about it, because, for all intents and purposes, I had everything. Now that sounds ridiculous, but you know, I had four kids; they were growing, they were learning, they were enjoyable to me. I had enjoyed them as learners; I had enjoyed their friendship. I had a nice husband who thought I was gorgeous, and so I mean, what the heck? What was I so upset about? And I remember being very restless and wanting something that I couldn't name. I really struggled with this thing internally. It was not that I wanted to go out and have an affair; that would have been so easy. It was an upheaval that was going on inside that caused me to question everything—what am I doing, and why am I doing it? I remember, we had bought a new car. We'd been to New York and Philadelphia and were in Montreal, Canada, with all four kids, traveling and spending money like crazy and really enjoying every minute of it. And I remember saying to my husband, "I've got to do something about me, I'm so restless." And he answered in true Clyde Nelson form. He said, "Don't bug me, baby. I've got problems of my own." And at that point I let go at him with a real barrage. I called him every name in the book and really let it all out. And it was over —I swear it was over with as fast as it had started. The tension melted away. I guess it had all come to a head and I took it out on him. And he's a good guy; he let me.

It was no magic or anything, but it seemed to me that after my outburst things started to fall into place in a different kind of way—or maybe I should say I started to *make* them fall into place. Perhaps the struggle of trying to get four kids into and out of college was such that I hadn't had time to think about myself. And when I took a look at what I was doing with my time and energy, I felt overcommitted, and like a victim. The pressure had built up and I needed to blow off steam. I think this kind of struggle goes on inside of every person at some point. You have to really stop and take a look at yourself and what you're doing with your energy. And so I started making some decisions about what was important, and I set some priorities. I learned to pace myself a little better. I guess that period of time was a passage to maturity. First I was young and growing and learning—and having problems, but feeling on top of things. Then I went through this middle period when I felt I was called upon to put on the mantle of being wise and solving problems for my children and my friends and the community—and I wasn't quite sure I wanted to have that role yet—as I saw it, the "emburdened" woman. I thought it had to be an either-or choice—either stay a young woman and be free and playful, or move on and be expected to be wise and solemn. I think I finally saw that I could be middle-aged and be wise and still be playful, that I had a lot of choices. The idea seems simple now, but there was that period in the middle when I had to struggle with it. I couldn't see how I could be both.

But I can be both. I *can* move from one role to another and not deny parts of myself. Somewhere along the way I have become more comfortable with my age and who I am. My feelings about getting older are not simple, however. On the one hand, I feel very conscious of time. There are a lot of things I want to do that I haven't done yet. On the other hand, I feel that learning to wind down is also important, because if you don't accept the limitations of getting older, you end up being a pretty silly person. You have got to accept the fact that you do get tired, that you forget things more easily. Some things do get harder as you get older, and you have to accept those changes. But I also think it's important not to settle in and become *too* comfortable, too accepting of getting old. Maybe the ideal balance is to be accepting but not ever to get so comfortable that you become soft and lose that edge and excitement that keep you creative. So, I both fight with change, and welcome it—all at the same time. You know, I'm a student of development and really believe that nothing happens without change, that change is inevitable and can be exciting. But I don't ever want to pick up things and join the bandwagon just because change is rolling. I want to look at things and chew them over and taste them to see if they're right for me.

I like being middle-aged. I think it's a less pressured time in many ways, it's a good part of my life. I can be myself and really enjoy it. I like that. I know more about pulling together things than I ever knew. I think the most important skill I have developed over time is that I can take a little bit from a recipe somewhere or from an experience somewhere, or from some abstraction, and put it into a whole process that I'm in the midst of working on, and come up with something that is fresh and new for me. But I had to have lived some, and had a whole series of experiences before I could choose from among them. I also know that there are doors open for me now that were never open for me before. I've established contacts in this community, I've got some skills. In a sense I'm past a lot of the struggles I used to have when I first came into conflict with the world. I can be a little outrageous and get away with it. I don't have to worry about protecting myself. I can dare to speak out and have people disagree with me and not be shattered by it. Age and experience have given me that.

I'm inspired by women who are older than I am. Women like Rose Kennedy, who are vital and involved. Actually, Eleanor Roosevelt was my first role model; she managed to get past being unattractive, past old age, past unhappiness, and she still managed to live what looked to me like such a creative life. And I look at Lillian Carter who is full of living, who believes she can do what she "durn" well pleases and enjoy it. I admire Bella Abzug because she's got brass. She dares to be who she is, so she's got something to share. More and more I've come to see that for the really vital women, there's that zest for living; they can laugh and find joy and do what they want and make a contribution to the world. It's reassuring to see them. I guess that's what I like—to be reassured. I know pretty much I can handle this stage of my life, but I like to look just a step ahead to see that what's coming next can be good too.

MARJORIE GUTHRIE

Marjorie Guthrie's small office at 250 West Fifty-seventh Street in Manhattan is filled with plaques and awards lauding her efforts to fight Huntington's disease, a degenerative, inherited neurological illness that caused the death of her famous folk-singer husband, Woody. On the walls, along with the usual family snapshots, are drawings of Woody and a framed *Time* magazine cover of son, Arlo. The large table at the side of the room is covered with pamphlets about the Committee to Combat Huntington's disease and articles about Marjorie, its founder and president emeritus.

Marjorie is a small woman with white hair, blue eyes, and a warm voice. At sixty-two, she moves with notable energy and grace, so it's no surprise to learn that she was a professional dancer for many years. Throughout Woody's long illness she supported herself and her three growing children by teaching dance, first at Martha Graham's school, and then at her own school in Brooklyn, the Marjorie Mazia School of Dance. "I've been a dancer all my life," she says. "I've loved being a dancer; I feel that's the real me." But time, circumstance, and her own will led to a whole new career and a new focus at fifty, her age the year Woody died.

Woody was in the hospital for fifteen years with Huntington's disease. I never thought about undertaking what I'm doing now, but I was suffering, hearing the words "hopeless" and "helpless" applied to him all the time. Before he died I suddenly woke up—you know, sometimes it happens that way—and I said to myself, "That's crazy. Why do I have to accept this? I don't!" So I went to the doctor in charge of Woody's ward, and we talked a little bit. He told me that *maybe* I could make a difference. Because everybody thought that this disease was very rare, the biggest contribution I could make was to find families with Huntington's. Since it is an inherited disorder, and its stigma in society is so great, nobody talked about it much.

I was in Washington to accept an award for Woody from Secretary of the Interior Stewart Udall, and he introduced me to doctors at the National Institutes of Health. I found that they didn't know much about Huntington's disease either. What I began to realize was that I knew more about it from watching my husband than many doctors, who didn't even recognize a Huntington's patient when they saw one. Too often it was misdiagnosed as alcoholism. (In fact, that's what the doctors thought was Woody's problem for a long time.) With no background in medicine I had a lot to learn. I began to look for patients. I went to hospitals and to people's homes. Little by little I found Huntington's disease patients and asked questions. Then I'd bring information back to the doctors; we began to share. Instead of being upset with the physicians for not knowing more, I became their co-worker. I think that's really what made it possible for me to get help from the scientific and health communities.

When Woody died in 1967, there was a gala concert in tribute to him at Carnegie Hall, and as his widow I was given seven thousand dollars. "Now what am I going to do with this?" I wondered. I decided to invest it in what I really wanted to do. So I took the money, hired a secretary, and got a small office. That's how the Committee to Combat Huntington's Disease (CCHD) got started. Now we're supported by many people. We have an international organization, a nationwide network of chapters in the United States, and similar organizations in nine additional countries. We provide information and work to stimulate basic biomedical research. I was chairman of the Congressional Commission for the Control of Huntington's Disease and Its Consequences. I travel around the country, speaking to medical students about the work that I do. It's a full-time job.

However, it wasn't always a full-time job. For the first five years after Woody's death, Marjorie kept up her dancing school in addition to her work for CCHD. "But," she says,

little by little, I found that my heart wasn't at the school any longer. It was a large school with a fine reputation. I had a dear friend who helped me run it; she was the secretary and took care of the money and public relations. One day she came to me and said that since we had many substitute teachers and I was doing less and less teaching myself, the instruction was no longer at the same high level. She said, "Let's go out nicely. Let's not die out." So we closed the school. And it was a good thing to do. But I must say, I'm still being rewarded for my teaching. I hear from former students from all over the country. Some have gone into medicine and have heard of me in their field, and are so surprised. It's wonderful to stay in touch with them over the years.

Other transitions in Marjorie's life have been much more difficult. She has spent a lot of time reflecting on just how she does deal with change and what it means to grow older. She is particularly aware of the invaluable support others have given her.

I've gone through a lot. But I've been fortunate. I had marvelous images of what life could be and should be from a number of inspirational sources— like my own mother, who was a writer and active to her dying day. We had a party for her when she was ninety, just two weeks before she died, and at that party we taped her message to future generations as she cut the cake. My teacher, Martha Graham, was a tremendous influence in my life. To this day, she is still out there, "doing it." I danced with Martha and taught in her school for eighteen years.

The important thing that I learned as a dancer is that one must accept physical deterioration. That's a hard thing to accept if you think you're beautiful and have beautiful movement. Suddenly your toes aren't pointing as they should, and you don't look as beautiful when you dance. I saw Martha going through that process and suffering in the beginning. Then I saw her accept the challenge, and slowly but surely find another way to express her theatricality and her desire to communicate. To this day, if Martha makes a public appearance, she may not dance, but she will stand up and speak and give a performance while she's talking that's as effective as her dancing. I've learned from her that you can use skills in different ways. I started to notice this while I was still quite young, and now I realize what I saw.

Not long ago I made a point of consciously reflecting, of going back and thinking about whom I had admired when I was younger, and why. You see, I had married again, and Martin, my last husband, had just died. That was more than two years ago. Well, that makes you think again: Where are you going? How much do you have left of yourself to go on with when that partner leaves you? That's when this little exercise of looking back dawned on me. I found that I had an understanding of myself even before I knew Martin that I could draw from. He, of course, had added his contribution to my life, but I had all these other people before him who were also part of me . . . and that made it possible for me to go on.

As I went back and thought of myself as a little girl, I began to think about whom I had wanted to be like. And I started to discuss those people with myself, to reflect why I liked that particular teacher when I was in the third grade, or the sixth grade, or the eighth grade.

Who were those people? First of all, I always wanted to be like Miss White, our music teacher in Atlantic City, who used to stand on the stage every Friday and lead the entire first through sixth grades in singing as we marched into the auditorium. She was plain; her hair was tied back in a little knot; but she had an energetic face, and I think what I liked about her was the way her hands moved, and her magic of making people sing together. When she moved those hands we *all* sang! I loved that leadership quality. Then, she had an accompanist, Miss Rich. Why did I like her? Well, she was beautiful. So I would alternate: Some days I would pretend I was Miss Rich, who was physically beautiful, and other days I'd be Miss White, whose energy was so commanding. There were four of us children in my family, and we slept together in one room at night. We used to sing the songs we had learned in school and I was the conductor. I was the one who wanted to get everyone to sing.

So I could identify with looks, energy, sensitivity. And we had a gym teacher who taught us folk dancing. I didn't like her physically, she was very mannish. But what I did like about her was her friendliness, and her way of getting everybody to dance together. She had nice qualities of smiling, of inspiring us all. I took a little bit from this one, a little bit from that one. As the years went along I continued to do that. I found all these marvelous people whom I liked and wanted to be like for *certain things.* These "things," when I put them all together, tell me something about me. It's a good test. An interesting exercise to try.

When I was in high school I was also inspired by Gandhi. I wrote a paper about him. That tells me something about the little girl who had certain thoughts. Why didn't I choose some movie actress? I didn't. I picked Gandhi. Thinking about these choices in my life has helped me develop sensitivity to understand myself better. And it gives me strength. It's good to look back and do that. It's like a reevaluation. It was unconscious at first, but now I'm very much aware of all this, and I'm using that analysis to strengthen what I do, to give me courage to do what I do. If you don't know what it is you're taking from, you just hope that things will happen, that they'll turn out okay. I don't want to hope; I want to know what I'm doing. I want things to happen because I make them happen. That's one of the strengths of being older. You can only have that perspective, that ability to put it all together, when you're older. It's there—if you use it.

Everybody is different, of course, and what is good for me may not be good for someone else. One of the things I've always felt as a teacher is that the special value of a teacher is to help people understand their own strengths and weaknesses. I feel that you're here for a purpose, and that you have to search for that. I think that people are afraid to love themselves, and that worries me. You have to build on something, and that something is who you are. I believe that everybody, *everybody*'s got something. You may have lost or submerged it. If so, you have to go back and find it. I walk on the street and I see so many sad people, people who are degenerate looking; men with no shoes, shopping-bag ladies, and I know that they were once somebody's beautiful child, somebody's dream. I always want to go up to them and say, Where's your mother? What has happened to you, or, what has society done to you? Why don't you love yourself? What is your life like? I know there is something in each one of them that is of value. I hope that those of us who can, and not everybody can, would go back and find those dreams.

If you have a handicap, I would like you to think of what you have that's special. My friends often tease me for being an optimist. I say, Why take away my rationale for living? If it helps me endure my problems, let me rationalize and be strong enough. Let me be a Pollyanna and do what I have to do. If I can't love myself, I certainly can't help anyone else.

There's a lot that works against middle-aged women loving themselves. That's why it's so valuable to look back. You didn't just descend from nowhere—you have roots just like any tree, and the stronger those roots, the easier it will be for you to hold yourself up. If you don't look back and find those roots, then you might fall over. I've always loved trees; they're my image of life itself. I think it's a great image for older people to hold onto. Look back and see who you are and what you are. The more you do it, the stronger you feel.

When I think about what society has done to older women, I don't like it. But I am beginning to see changes in that, thanks to our growing awareness. We are not weaker for living long. I love what Margaret Mead said about growing older. She loved getting older, she said, the only thing was she wished her feet didn't hurt. I feel exactly the same because my feet *do* hurt, too. But if you ask me, I have so many things going for me now, I would not want to be a teenager again, who couldn't look back. I would not want to be the suffering kid I was, who didn't know what she wanted to do with her life, who wanted to make commitments and decisions, but didn't know how or when. The first date, the first exposure to people other than my own family—so much of it was painful.

I remember eating out in public, eating spaghetti for the first time in a restaurant, and being embarrassed because I didn't know how to wind spaghetti the way one should. I remember cutting it into small pieces to make sure I would not be ashamed. That insecurity that comes from not having lived long enough—oh, you can't compare that to the joy of being an older person. Even my failures are different now. I'm able to laugh and say, "Yes, that was one lousy time." Looking back has helped me do that. Who would want to go back? The deeper the roots and the more understanding you have of your roots, the easier it is to accept the challenges we face.

Marjorie has been a woman on her own for much of her life. Her three children were still preschoolers when Woody became sick. In the day-to-day experience of living, she was on her own throughout his long illness. Her remarriage in her late fifties to Martin Stein, the vice-president of the Committee to Combat Huntington's Disease, lasted a brief two years before Marjorie became a widow again.

I've always said that we are really four-legged creatures; when we must walk on two legs it's a little harder. Man and woman walking together is like walking on four legs. If we have to walk on two, we do, but I don't put down the beauty of a good relationship with a man. I think a man is just as important and unique as a woman. But I also do like what's happening today: the attitude that a woman can make a life on her own. I love the battle and the challenge, the feeling that a woman can identify herself as a whole person, with or without a man.

Of course, no matter what, it *is* difficult to be alone. It *is* sad if you've lost a close relationship. A confused woman came to my office yesterday who'd lost her husband to Huntington's disease almost ten years ago. She's seeing another man and she's unsure of herself and afraid. I sat here and held her hand, and told her she was beautiful and a good person. She's doubting whether she should continue her relationship with this man, whether it's right, whether she should leave her sister and the rest of her family in New York and move with him to the West Coast. I told her, "Don't deny yourself possible happiness, if that's what you really want. Try it! If it doesn't work, okay, walk out." Here is a woman in her fifties, scared, shaking all over. Should she or shouldn't she? I said, "What did you do when you were a kid? You took chances, and you lived through them. That's what life teaches you. Take the chance, there's a strong possibility it'll work out, and if it doesn't, go on to the next. At least you'll know you tried, and it will give you a sense of yourself." Too often people are so afraid to take risks. But then, life is *all* risk. When I go around the country talking about Huntington's disease, I always object to the way they use the word "fatal." They say, "It's a fatal disease." And I say, "No, *life* is a fatal disease, and being born is the first symptom." The only thing in doubt is *when* you're going to die, and *how* you're going to die. It would be nice, of course, if you had someone by your side to hold your hand.

Loneliness is hard. We all need someone. If it's not a man, it should be a personal relationship of some kind that means something special to both of you. It isn't possible for all of us to have the kind of relationship we might like with a man, so you've got to find the substitute closest to it. It's harder to find that companionship when you get to my age and your friends begin to die. I know that my mother, in the last ten years of her life, was crossing out names in her address book. I've begun to do that. I say to myself, "My circle is narrowing, and I have to enlarge it with new people." It's a conscious thing. I cannot replace the people I've known twenty or thirty years, but I can hope to substitute that feeling in some way.

It's more than two years since Martin died, and I'm looking and reaching out for people I can count on, when I'm lonely or sick or want to go somewhere and share fun. They're not going to replace Martin or the old friends, but I'm consciously looking for people who like what I'm doing, people who work with me, people who open up doors. I say to myself, "Who will come back again? Who can I telephone? Who can I share intimacies with? I never want to feel like a victim. I want to have the best possible end of my life, and I have to work for it. I'm not saying it's easy, but it's conscious. I hope it works.

Of course, I've been doing that all along. There have been many endings and beginnings. As a

dancer I call that "life's rehearsals." People ask,
How did you endure all the things that have
happened? What I've learned is that after every one
of these tragedies, I always seem to bounce back. I
find a way to survive. I tell myself that old line:
"And this too shall pass."

There's another technique I use. I remember one
time when I was a young woman I had a terrible
fight with Woody. I couldn't make up my mind
whether I should divorce him. I remember going
into the woods (we were visiting someone in the
country somewhere), and I wrote down everything
that was terrible about Woody, and everything that
I loved about him. The terrible side was an awfully
long list! And the love side had only three things.
When I weighed those three items against the
twenty-five on the terrible side, there was no
question in my mind that I was going to stay
married. I remember the three things very well:
one, he was the father of my children; two, I loved
his music; three, I admired his politics. And those
items on the terrible side, I can't tell you. I've
forgotten them. I only remember that it was a long
list—personal habits, little things. How could I
compare his politics, his music, his children to all
those twenty-five petty items on the other side? I
started to laugh after I looked at it and said, "Well,
I'm sticking with him." These things were too
valuable to me. Our political activity was our
relationship to the rest of the world. Our children,
why, they were our home, our future. And the
music was something that was part of me too, the
part that I loved as an artist. So, how many things
can you ask for, from one guy?

That little piece of paper really gave me a chance
to say to myself, "What is it you really want? What
are you really talking about?" I've used it as a

device for myself many times and I've shared it with others. It isn't the length of the list, it's the quality. The same principle would work if you were to think about how you feel about getting older. The first things that occur to you are negative and superficial, and the list is likely to be pretty long. The positive things are less visible, but deeper. You have to weigh them.

Marjorie is a combination of action and reflection. Her days are long and the demands on her are many. The phone in her office rings continuously with requests for information, invitations to speak, and individual pleas for help. She is accessible; there's no glossy waiting room to keep people at a distance. When you walk into the office, you're in, and you're likely to bump into Marjorie or one of the staff just inside the door. Without a doubt, you feel welcome. She has a capacity to become interested in whomever she's talking with, not a feigned interest, but a genuine desire to know another human being. She's willing to share herself. When she talks about her work and her family, which includes an ever-increasing brood of grandchildren, she reveals the deep pleasure she gleans from both. She stops for a minute when asked what she hopes for the future.

"I don't think much about the future," she finally says.

I think about now. Martha Graham said it better than I. She said, "A dancer is a realist. Either your foot is pointed or it is not." I think about today. When I walk down the street and can't walk as fast as I used to, and my toes are hurting, I say to myself, "Is that so terrible?" Well, it's not terrible if I'm sitting, so I just keep walking as much as I can, and then I sit. I forget that my feet were hurting when I was walking.

I've faced a lot of death recently. Sometimes I do

worry about the future in terms of imposing my frailties upon others. How will I die? Will my suffering cause other people suffering? Will I need help from my children? These thoughts do go through my mind. But I don't spend much time worrying. I try to get answers. I try to ask myself, "Well, what will you do? What can you do now to take care of yourself, to maintain your independence?" Looking for answers keeps me thinking, and it keeps me positive.

There's a special feeling of continuity that I've developed from being a dancer. Dance has never been taught well from books. It has always been taught by someone who loved to dance, who learned from someone who loved to dance . . . on and on, back through time. I say I'm really two thousand years old, because all those generations went into making me a dancer. As a dance teacher I felt that I was carrying on an art form that was two thousand years old, and if I was doing that, I'd better love it and do it well. I felt a great responsibility to continue that thread, not to spoil it. In the sense of the social things that other women have done in the struggle for women, I don't want to spoil that either. I want to keep the thread going; I want to teach people to make a better world. That's what I really believe in for the future, for my grandchildren, for anybody's grandchildren.

And I'll say it again . . . I think we can all do something. I don't care what the task is. If you have women that might get that feeling from reading this book, it will have been worth a great deal. I believe in getting involved. You can't make change happen unless you are a part of the action.

Physical Issues of the Middle Years:
An Active Approach

Many of the physical changes that take place during the middle years are predictable, normal, and have little impact on our ability to function. Still, when we begin to notice them in ourselves, the initial reaction is often, "Wait a minute—it isn't time for this to be happening to *me!*" The changes—in our appearance, stamina and reproductive cycle—are irrefutable reminders that we are, indeed, getting older. Sometimes these changes are frustrating, discouraging, or downright frightening. They may make us feel vulnerable, as though we are somehow being betrayed by our own bodies. It's one thing, after all, to note a birthday on the calendar; another to feel it in your bones.

It is in our middle years that the fact of our own mortality becomes real to us. We give up the last illusions that we are still "growing up" and recognize that we are beginning the long process of growing old. It is not unusual for middle-aged women to become acutely aware of physical issues. In fact, women of all ages who responded to our survey reported that health, energy, and physical fitness were the issues of greatest concern to them in relation to growing older. But, no matter what their age, their concern was mainly about the *future* rather than the present. The majority indicated that they were *currently* feeling good about themselves physically: about their sexuality, their energy, appearance, and general health. They felt that they—and other women their age—were more active, attractive, and in better shape than they had ever imagined they would be in their middle years. "I'm in much better physical condition than my mother was at my age," was a comment we heard over and over.

In part, that discrepancy between what women thought they would be like physically in their middle years and what they are actually experiencing, is because of our changing perceptions of age as we get older. Whereas forty once loomed as a major turning point to old age, by the time we are in our middle years, it seems quite young. It's the "policemen-suddenly-look-like-kids!" syndrome.

Another reason for the discrepancy can undoubtedly be traced to the rigid age stereotyping that has so long been a part of our culture. And those stereotypes have generally provided an image of middle-aged women as static, frumpy, and shapeless—definitely "over the hill" physically. Small wonder more than seventy percent of the women who responded to our survey reported that they think of themselves as younger than their age: the stereotypes just don't fit!

However, there is also an objective basis for this sense of discrepancy. Middle-aged women *are* different today than in past generations: in attitude, health, and physical appearance. They are not only living longer, they are staying active and vital longer. And many are developing a different set of expectations about their bodies. Until quite recently, women were encouraged to take care of themselves in a fairly passive way. The emphasis was more on looking young than on feeling healthy. The goal was to "preserve, conserve, and restore" our bodies, to treat problems as they arose, rather than to prevent—or even understand—them. From the turn of the century, ads for Lydia Pinkham's famous elixirs to the older woman on TV endorsing an array of pills for the relief of tension headaches, tired blood, aching backs, and constipation, the American woman was taught to take care of herself by consuming medication. Even today, pharmaceutical ads in medical journals continue to feature the prototypic, anxiety-ridden middle-aged woman, biting her nails as she sits in the doctor's waiting room, the perfect candidate for the tranquilizers, barbiturates, and hormones that are being sold. Valium is still the most commonly prescribed drug of our day, and more than twice as many prescriptions are written for women as for men. Although tranquilizers have their place as a temporary measure, far too often they have been seen as *the answer* to a middle-aged woman's problems.

But all this *is* changing. Today a growing number of women in their middle years are taking more responsibility for their health and physical well-being. The women's movement, which has had an enormous influence on younger women as they grapple with issues of birth control, abortion, and childbearing, is now making an impact on older women and some of the physical issues that concern them: menopause, mature sexuality, and staying fit. Middle-aged women are learning to value their bodies as they have learned to value themselves, and to do so on criteria other than their ability to appear "youthful." Many are refusing to consume the latest potions and pills that promise perpetual youth and physical and emotional nirvana. They are learning about preventive measures of maintaining health; they are actively developing their bodies instead of passively conserving them. Middle-aged women in unprecedented numbers are exercising after years of little physical activity, and many report that the psychological benefits are as important as the physical.

For some it's the excitement of mastering a new skill, or meeting a challenge that once looked impossible. Some find exercise an antidote to depression or inertia. Others talk about the satisfaction of reversing what had seemed to be an inevitable process of decline. A lot of women are also learning more about nutrition and the relationship between physical and mental well-being. They are learning how to reduce the stress in their lives and are, in sum, taking a more holistic approach to health care. Women's health activists are encouraging all women to take the initiative to become more familiar with their own bodies, to detect problems early, to seek preventive medical care, and to participate in medical decisions.[1]

Women are beginning to seek out more information about the physical issues that concern them, and they are sharing that information and their own experiences with one another. And in so doing they are developing a better understanding of what is happening to them; they are becoming more comfortable with the changes in their bodies and with themselves as middle-aged women.

We cannot possibly predict, of course, what specific physical issues each of us will face in our middle years. However, two issues of interest to virtually all women are menopause and mature sexuality, and it is these that will be the focus of the next two chapters.

5 "Hot Flashes": The Good News About Menopause

Many women who were walking encyclopedias about natural childbirth and breast-feeding when they were pregnant approach menopause knowing next to nothing about it. They *are* very likely, however, to have heard a horror story or two. In fact, given all the old wives' tales about the "change of life," it's hardly surprising that a number of women told us they'd rather not even think about it until they have to.

Of course, it is hard to separate the physical and psychological aspects of menopause, and it's not always easy to separate the myth from the reality. Until quite recently there hasn't been much clear, unbiased information available. And much that has been written about menopause in the past has been demeaning and discouraging to women, as well as untrue. Books such as Dr. Robert A. Wilson's *Feminine Forever* paint a bleak picture of the menopausal woman as a pathetic, unappealing, and unattractive figure. Wilson, whose ideas were widely popularized in the women's magazines of the late sixties, views menopause as a disease that affects all older women, and proclaims hormonal supplements as the cure to return them to their "normal" feminine state. His catalogue of the physical and mental disturbances that plague menopausal women is enough to terrify any reader. His sympathy, however, seems to be more with the doctor: "What for example, can the poor doctor make of a woman who complains to him of nervousness, irritability, anxiety, apprehension, hot flashes, night sweats, joint pains, melancholia, palpitations. . . . "[1]

After dramatically scaring the menopausal woman, Wilson gallantly offers to rescue her, as well as "the poor doctor" who has been overwhelmed by her complaints:

> Despite the conspiracy of silence surrounding the subject, most women are well aware of the extent to which menopause cripples them. A show of bravery might mask their distress for several years, but ultimately not even valor offers escape from this physical reality. What we must learn is that there is no need for either valor or pretense. The need is for hormones.[2]

And Dr. David Reuben, in his well-known *Everything You Always Wanted to Know About Sex,* wrote:

> As the estrogen is shut off, a woman comes as close as she can to being a man. . . . Not really a man, but no longer a functional woman, these individuals live in the world of intersex.[3]

Many articles in medical journals also refer to menopausal women in the most disparaging terms imaginable. In an article in the *Journal of Nervous and Mental Disease,* Dr. Leonard R. Sillman wrote:

And then, after giving "the best years of her life" to raising a family and caring for the house, she finds herself reduced by the climacteric to a shriveled shell of a woman, used up, sucked dry, de-sexed, and, by comparison with her treasured remembrances of bygone days of glory and romance, fit only for the bone heap.[4]

This may sound like a voice from the Victorian age, but Sillman published this article in 1966. Most of us go to physicians who were exposed to this kind of thinking in one way or another during their training. And our own attitudes are likely to have been influenced, either directly or indirectly, by these negative views of menopause that have been pervasive for so long.

A number of writers on women's health have suggested that if men went through menopause, it would surely be studied much more thoroughly. Besides, as one woman put it: "It isn't high priority for research, because after all, nobody ever died of menopause." So, as it stands now, women may find it difficult to get specific answers to questions about their current symptoms, or information about what they can expect to experience in the future. They may even get different information from different physicians. The fact is that the female hormonal system is delicate and complex, and there is a lot that doctors just don't know about it yet. And of course, the individual differences among women produce a wide variety of experience and responses. But the information that *is* available can help to dispel many of the prevailing myths and remove much of the mystery that still surrounds this natural process.

The word menopause comes from the Greek words for "month" and "cessation." It means literally the end of menstrual periods. The whole process of changing from the reproductive to post-reproductive stage of life, including several years before and after the cessation of menstruation, is called the climacteric. The word menopause as it is used by the lay person usually refers to the climacteric.

Women are starting to menstruate earlier than they did in past generations, and they're going through menopause later. It's possible for a woman to experience a natural menopause at any time from forty to sixty. Surgical menopause occurs whenever both ovaries are removed; but a hysterectomy (removal of the uterus) does not bring on menopause unless the ovaries are removed as well. Most women cease menstruating between the ages of forty-five and fifty-five, with the average age falling somewhere around fifty. There is no way to predict exactly when an individual woman will go through natural menopause, although there is a tendency to follow the pattern of one's mother. And, contrary to popular belief, the age at which one starts menstruating has nothing to do with the probable age of the climacteric.

The ovaries decrease their production of estrogen, over a period of time, and eventually stop releasing eggs. Menstrual periods may, however, continue for a while after the cessation of ovulation. And estrogen production may fluctuate considerably even after menstrual periods stop. The estrogen level definitely drops sharply during menopause, but it's unclear whether the body eventually stops producing estrogen altogether, or whether it continues to be manufactured in limited amounts indefinitely.

How do you know if you're in menopause? The first signs that most women notice are irregularities in menstrual flow. Often brief, light periods are followed by long and unusually heavy ones. Some women stop menstruating for several months at a time and then start up again. A few women menstruate in their regular monthly patterns, and then simply stop one month—and that's it. However, most women experience irregularity in amount and duration of flow over several years. Periods become more widely spaced and eventually cease. A woman is considered to be through menopause when she has not had a menstrual period for a whole year.

Next to irregularity in menstrual periods, the menopausal symptom that women report most frequently is the hot flush—sometimes called the hot flash. When a hot flush comes on, the woman suddenly feels very warm in the upper part of her body. Her skin may look flushed and she may perspire. The whole thing usually doesn't last more than a minute, and may happen infrequently or several times a day. After the hot flush is over, the woman may feel clammy and chilly. There is considerable evidence that hot flushes are caused by the sudden drop in estrogen level that creates a hormonal imbalance and affects the dilation and contraction of blood vessels. Once the hormone levels even out, the body adjusts and hot flushes stop. Some women go through menopause with nary a hot flush; others experience them fairly often for several years with varying degrees of discomfort. A number of women recount the unpleasant experience of waking up in the middle of the night on soaking sheets, with a sense that their bodies are suddenly out of control. Others describe feeling embarrassed and self-conscious about having flushes in public. But for most women hot flushes are at worst an inconvenience—something they just learn to live with for a while. And though sixty percent of women do have hot flushes, only a very small percent find them so disturbing that they require medical treatment.

Another symptom that many women experience as a result of the loss of estrogen is that the vaginal walls get thinner and drier. Although this may cause discomfort during intercourse, local application of a water-soluble lubricant such as K-Y Jelly often alleviates the problem. And contrary to popular mythology, menopause does *not* decrease women's capacity or desire for sex. In general women who have enjoyed good sex lives before menopause continue to do so afterward. As a matter of fact, a substantial number of women told us that their sex lives had improved after menopause. They found it a relief no longer to be concerned about monthly cycles and birth control. And, for many women, menopause coincided with more freedom within the family—the increased privacy and spontaneity that the children's departure brings.

Hot flushes and thinning of the vaginal walls are the only two symptoms that definitely have been linked to hormonal changes of menopause. Other symptoms such as headaches, bloatedness, dizziness, and intestinal problems are often attributed to the "menopausal syndrome," but there is no evidence that these symptoms actually have anything to do with menopause itself.

The whole subject of estrogen replacement therapy (ERT) to relieve symptoms of menopause is highly controversial. For many years estrogen was prescribed freely—almost routinely—to menopausal women. But today the attitude of the medical community toward giving supplemental hormones is one of extreme caution. This is reflected in an article in the *New England Journal of Medicine* reporting a recent study at Johns Hopkins University:

> The clinical implications of this study directly concern the use of estrogen replacement therapy, which appears to have a statistically significant risk of uterine cancer attached to its use and thus should be prescribed cautiously only for important indications when the benefits seem to outweigh the risk. Patients receiving replacement therapy should be monitored regularly to detect possible cancer in its early, asymptomatic stage.[5]

While estrogen levels do decrease in menopause, all menopausal women are *not* estrogen deficient. (For many women the lowered estrogen level produces little or no noticeable effect.) Moreover, claims that estrogen replacement therapy will provide perpetual youth are totally unfounded. Nor is there any evidence that estrogen replacement therapy is useful in treating women who are depressed or anxious.

When depression does occur during menopause it is often tied up with negative feelings about aging in general, or with the belief that a woman's value is dependent on her ability to produce children. And a woman who is anxious or depressed before the change in hormone levels may find such symptoms exaggerated during the climacteric. Menopause may heighten a woman's awareness that she is getting older. Also, it's likely to come at a time when she is experiencing a number of upheavals in her life. Her children may be leaving home; her husband may be feeling vulnerable and in need of comforting; for the first time, friends her own age may be becoming ill or widowed; and her parents may be growing increasingly dependent. If a woman does feel depressed during menopause, it's important for her to try to understand her feelings in light of all the other things that are happening to her. That doesn't mean her depression should be brushed off as a figment of the imagination or a self-fulfilling prophesy. But, neither should it be viewed as inevitable, as a fact of life to be treated with drugs until it goes away as mysteriously as it came.

Menopause is a natural function, and if problems come with it, they should be discussed openly. The support of friends and family is, of course, valuable, and in some instances professional help from a physician or therapist is useful. A feminist therapist can be particularly effective in helping a woman to see the relationship between her individual problems and the commonly held attitudes toward middle-aged women in our society. A woman who is having a difficult time in menopause is not simply a victim of her hormones, but a person who is coping with all kinds of changes in herself and in her environment.

In her book, *The Second Season,* anthropologist Estelle Fuchs wrote:

Happily, menopause does not make women crazy. Nor need it precipitate severe emotional crises. There is no denying, however, the cultural stereotype that menopausal women are prone to depression, hysteria, etc. It's as if women cannot win—they're considered emotionally unstable and unreliable when they menstruate, and they are considered emotionally unstable and unreliable when they stop!

Among the Mangian people of Africa, when a woman reaches menopause she is described as becoming good-tempered . . . free of all the earlier restraints imposed on her because she is a woman, now free to go and act in ways previously permitted only the men. What a different picture from that of the depressed, hysterical menopausal woman, so often depicted in our own culture.[6]

Fuchs explains that "Anthropologists know that no human condition can be described as 'natural' or 'inevitable,' so long as there are human beings and societies that have differing customs and behaviors." In fact, recent studies in this country fail to show any greater risk for depression during menopause than at any other time during a woman's life span. And current research on menopause suggests that most women experience minimal difficulty either physically or psychologically. Some women experience no problems whatsoever, and for the most part the discomforts that women do have are treatable, and/or transitory.

According to Dr. Carol Williams, gynecologist and faculty member at Washington University Medical School, women today seem to have a more positive attitude about reaching menopause than women of past generations. She credits this, in large part, to the women's movement, which she feels has widened women's horizons and opportunities. "In a broad sense," she said, "it has influenced the way women feel about changing their roles, about moving beyond their child-rearing years, and entering a new period of their lives."

But to the woman looking ahead to menopause it still may seem like a rather negative, even frightening time of life. Many younger women in our sample who had not yet entered menopause expressed anxiety about what it would be like for them. They were worried about depression, about sudden changes in physical appearance, and about feeling unable to cope with their emotions. Most women who were in or past menopause, however, said that it was relatively uneventful. In fact, the majority of them described their experience in neutral or positive terms:

Since menopause I feel better physically than I have for a long time; I enjoy more freedom sexually. I feel more attractive, yet there are times when I am aware that I've left a part of life behind. (age fifty-nine)

Except for transient physical symptoms there have been no adverse effects. This surprises me because I somehow expected menopause to be traumatic. (age forty-nine)

Since menopause I can honestly say I have never felt better! After a woman has children, or a child as in our case, the rewards are great in watching them grow and mature. But as we go beyond our childbearing years the rewards of menopause are also great. Most of the women I've talked to agree that they feel better healthwise than they have in a long time. It changes some women's sex lives because they're no longer concerned about getting pregnant. (age fifty-six)

I'm finished with menopause . . . I think. I've thought so before and then found (surprise, surprise) it's still with me. Many's the cold night I've journeyed out with a light wrap, warmed by continuous hot flashes, while people stare at me and shiver! (age fifty-two)

Since menopause I feel unburdened and carefree. (age sixty-two)

Menopause was a very normal transition. No trauma. (age sixty)

Menopause affected me very little. I used to worry that I would become physically less active and thus less attractive. (I seem to equate activity with attractiveness.) I find that I am busier, happier, and feel that to those who love me I'm as attractive as ever. (age fifty-eight)

My periods simply ended. I went through menopause without even knowing it. (age fifty-one)

On the whole, the women in our sample who were going through or had completed menopause, had a much more positive attitude toward it than the women who were premenopausal. This appears to corroborate the findings of sociologist Bernice Neugarten in her study, "Women's Attitudes Toward the Menopause." The older women in Neugarten's study acknowledged some unpleasant and uncomfortable aspects of menopause, but they also talked about realizing that the discomforts were temporary, and about being more able to put everything into perspective. More specifically, they indicated that they saw the stage of life following menopause as a time of increased self-confidence, freedom, and renewal. The majority of younger women in Neugarten's study did not have these positive expectations.[7]

Neugarten concluded:

> The fact that most younger women have generally more negative views is perhaps because the menopause is not only relatively far removed, and therefore relatively vague; but because, being vague, it becomes blended into the whole process of growing old, a process that is both dim and unpleasant. Perhaps it is only the middle-aged or older woman who can take a differentiated view of the menopause; and who, on the basis of experience, can, as one woman said, "separate the old wives' " tales from that which is true of old wives.[8]

The Boston Women's Health Book Collective did a survey on menopause in 1974 that they have reported in the 1976 revised edition of *Our Bodies, Ourselves.* They, too, found that the anticipation of menopause by younger women was worse than the reality experienced by menopausal and postmenopausal women. About two-thirds of the women surveyed reported that they had had hot flashes. About half reported no change in sexual desires; the remaining half were divided equally between those who reported an increase and those who reported a decrease. In sum, the authors of this survey wrote:

> The responses to our questionnaire clearly indicate that many of us need much more accurate information about menopause. We hope that more women will do research in this area, both to improve the medical treatment of menopause and to increase our own knowledge of what menopause really is. On the brighter side, our questionnaire

definitely suggests that most women feel positive or neutral about menopause, are untroubled by the loss of fertility, and go through the two years or so with minimal discomfort.[9]

There are encouraging signs that women *are* beginning to get more information about menopause, and to share it with each other. Several books have been written recently —*by* women *for* women—debunking the stereotypes and myths long associated with menopause. Women have always talked with each other and commiserated, but in the last few years there has started to be a new openness, a new frankness in discussing "female problems." There is a growing awareness among women of the need to understand and value their own bodies and to give each other support.[10]

Menopause often causes a woman to focus on herself for the first time after many years of concern for her family. It may be a catalyst for her to take time out, to think and talk about her feelings and doubts. It can be a time of reevaluation, and of setting new goals—the beginning of a new phase of life.

6 Sex: Better Than Ever

hose of us who grew up before the 1960's can remember a time when virginity was a prerequisite for marriage, and fidelity was required thereafter; when "nice" girls were supposed to be more interested in the trappings of romance and weddings than sex, and those who succumbed to male pressure to "go all the way" were rewarded with a bad reputation and the ostracism that went with it. The information about sex our mothers gave us was likely to be cloaked in secrecy and imparted with embarrassment. We found pressed into our hands cheerful little pamphlets containing information on "what every young woman should know." We were supposed to ignore sexual longings and repress sexual responsiveness; the underlying message was, "Sex is dirty, save it for the one you love." Yet even in the marriage bed, we were to submit and acquiesce, to remain essentially passive and demure—while somehow managing in the process to have "vaginal" orgasms. Men were the ones who were supposed to know what to do, how to "turn us on," though it was unclear exactly who was to teach *them*. No wonder our earliest sexual experiences were so often disappointing, a far cry from the crashing surf and fireworks, the mindless rapture of our favorite fantasies!

Those days may not be long gone (or gone at all) in some places, but most of us now find ourselves confronting very different attitudes toward sex. After the sixties, many taboos were vigorously discarded; detailed information—and misinformation—about sex not only became readily available, it became practically unavoidable. Lyrics to popular songs were suddenly more explicit than the whispered conversations we once had with our closest friends. All at once it seemed that "everyone" was having an affair; that younger women—even our own daughters—were openly and freely exploring their own sexuality in ways we'd barely dreamed of. And within a few brief years, we, too, were expected to forget the "old" morality and become liberated, multiply orgasmic, sexual sophisticates.

Not surprisingly, many of us now in our middle years find ourselves feeling caught in the middle, as one sex therapist put it, "with one foot in a post-Victorian, sexually repressive society, and one foot in a sexually hedonistic, permissive society."[1] In many ways, the cultural changes are freeing; they give us permission to trust our own experience, to enjoy whatever feels good, to explore and experiment. So many myths about female sexuality have been exploded. We no longer accept, for instance, that our sexual needs are any less powerful than a man's, or that the only "real" orgasm, the only kind worth having, is one that occurs "vaginally" and simultaneously with our partner's, or even that having an orgasm is a requisite to enjoying sex.[2] Masturbation, we are now told, is not only "all right" in itself, but is also a means to learn about our own bodies in order to inform our partners. And those guilty fears we may have harbored about our sexual fantasies are being assuaged by information assuring us that such fantasies are not only very common, but are normal, natural, and can enhance our sexual feelings.[3]

One woman in her early fifties told us:

> When I was younger, we didn't talk much about sex, and we didn't know much about it either. I figured I was the only married woman in the world who masturbated, and I was sure I was inadequate because I never had an orgasm *during* intercourse, only before or after, and only manually. So even though I liked sex, I had some bad kind of uncomfortable feelings about myself . . . mostly out of sheer ignorance. And then the so-called "sexual revolution" came along, and there began to be all these books that said *whatever* you liked was okay, and there was only one kind of orgasm anyhow. But what made an even bigger difference was being in a woman's group a few years back where sometimes we talked about sex. I had never heard it discussed that openly and frankly before, and I found out firsthand that other women had feelings and experiences very much like my own. I can't tell you how reassuring that was! It helped me to be much more comfortable and accepting of myself, which has let me relax and enjoy sex a whole lot more.

But these same cultural changes that are, on the one hand, freeing may, on the other, leave us feeling that we have somehow missed out, that we have a lot to live up to, to get used to, not all of which feels comfortable or right. In particular, women who were virgins when they got married and have remained monogamous since, often express feelings of curiosity about the changing sexual norms and having sex with other men. And certainly more women *are* choosing to have extramarital affairs these days.[4] Still, the old ideas are not always so easily discarded.

One forty-six-year-old educator we talked to illustrated this when she described what happened at a convention she had gone to alone a year earlier:

It's a familiar story, I guess: at the meeting I met a man in his thirties whose career interests were very similar to mine. I found him really appealing in an Alan Alda kind of way, and very easy to talk to. We had dinner together and, afterwards, we sat and talked for hours. And suddenly, it seemed the most natural thing in the world for me to go to his room. Now, I consider myself a pretty sophisticated, "with it" person, but the truth is, where sex is concerned, I'm fairly inexperienced and naive by today's standards. I've been married for twenty-one years and have a good marriage that's a very important part of my life. But after twenty-one years, it's not exactly exciting all the time. So: there I was, just turned forty-five, feeling a little restless and *very* aware of the passing of time, and here's this bright, interesting, attractive younger man who obviously finds *me* very attractive, too, and we're together in a strange city . . . well, I ask you: could Erica Jong have written it better? I thought to myself, why *not?* Who could it possibly hurt? It's no big thing anymore, *every*one does it. So, armed with that overabundance of rationales, I went to bed with him. And you know, it was wonderful and exciting—and fun, really *fun.* I wondered whether I'd feel guilty about it afterwards; I expected to have a *twinge* or two. Instead, I woke up the next morning practically overwhelmed with guilt and fear. I suppose the strict Catholic upbringing I thought I'd left behind came back with a vengeance. I half expected to see a scarlet "A" tattooed on my forehead.

By the time I had breakfast, I had begun to get

back a little more perspective. In fact, when he called me later to ask when we could get together again, part of me wanted to say, "How about right now?" But a bigger part of me was still struggling with all that guilt. I didn't think I could handle letting it go any further and I just had to tell him that. He was very nice about it; he didn't pressure me . . . I think I was sort of hoping he would. It was a real tug of war, though, between all the prohibitions I've carried around with me for years about what's "right" and what's "wrong," and wanting that immediate pleasure.

At the same time that many middle-aged women find themselves struggling with changing sexual mores, they are likely to find that they are, in fact, becoming less inhibited sexually. Quite apart from the "new" morality, there is a tendency for women to throw off inhibitions as they mature, and become more comfortable with and responsive to sex. Kinsey and other researchers have shown that female sexuality generally increases in intensity in the middle years, and that women experience a greater capacity for sexual release. And this higher level of sexual functioning often continues undiminished until a woman is sixty years of age or older.[5]

The women we surveyed confirmed this positive view of mature sexuality. Over two-thirds of our respondents indicated that their *desire* for sexual activity was the same or greater than when they were younger.[6] Not only that, almost the same number said that they were *enjoying* sex more, often much more.[7] Women of all ages reported that the bonuses of maturity included feeling more open and relaxed about sex; they described a new ease in taking the initiative with partners, and a desire to try new things. Many found that they were better able to let their partner know what they liked, and that they were more orgasmic. ("I *achieve* orgasm now, I don't fake it the way I used to!")

Even when sex was not more frequent, it was often viewed as more pleasurable and intense. ("There's less quantity, more quality in our sex life now.")

A thirty-nine-year-old woman wrote one variation on a theme we heard from many women:

> The older I become, the more confident I feel about making love. I know that I can be responsive, and that wasn't true ten years ago. And I love it! I love being able to give and receive that much pleasure!

And a forty-nine-year-old interviewee said:

> During the years we were so busy raising our four kids and making ends meet, I think I considered our sex life to have been just fine. But looking back now, it didn't compare to how good it's gotten in the last few years. A combination of things seemed to come together when our last child left home. After twenty-six years of marriage, we started to really look at each other across the dinner table—we talked more about us—and discovered things that the other had been feeling and thinking that we hadn't even known. Talking more and spending more time together—just the two of us—we started laughing more, finding surprise presents for each other, finding special things to do together on weekends—and our lovemaking changed. There began to be a lovely new closeness in bed—this wasn't just "intercourse" or whatever other term you want to use—it was "lovemaking"—feeling happy and lucky to be together. Sometimes it's silly and zany, much more playful than we've ever been; sometimes it's very, very intense—totally and beautifully exhausting. A few months ago, we planned a special getaway together at a cabin in

the mountains. When we unpacked our suitcases we burst out laughing. We'd *both* brought half a suitcase full of wine and exotic little food surprises. Those three days were gorgeous—the sexiest I've ever had in my life. Needless to say, we are planning more weekend vacations.

Certainly not all women expressed such positive views about sex or their own sexual experiences, but a substantial number did, and in doing so they showed us what is possible for women throughout the middle years.

The literature about female sexuality often describes women as "peaking" sexually in their thirties, but it was clear as we talked to women that there is no magical age for sexual awakening: it is possible at any age. For some it comes fairly abruptly with a pregnancy, an affair, or a newfound ability to respond. ("My first orgasm at forty was mind-boggling!") For others, it is a gradual process. A woman in her early fifties wrote: "I was slowly opening up and becoming much freer sexually. But it's only been in the last few years that I've discovered I can totally let go and experience real passion."

One sex therapist we interviewed pointed out that "it's never too late to increase your pleasure in sex by finding new things you like. I have a seventy-three-year-old client who is just discovering her own sexuality, and trying things with her partner she hadn't known existed in her youth and middle years."

Of course, changes in our sexuality do not take place in a vacuum; sex is as much a matter of psychology as biology. We cannot isolate our feelings about it from other events in our lives, or from how we're feeling about ourselves and our relationships. We may have "boundless orgasmic potential," and still find it difficult to be sexually responsive when we're overtired, preoccupied with concerns about children or work, or when we're feeling angry or resentful toward our partner. On the other hand, we may experience a great resurgence of sexual interest when we begin a new relationship, when a long-term relationship is going particularly well, or when we are finally free from concerns about pregnancy.

It can also give quite a boost to our libidos to feel that we are being seen as sexy and desirable in the eyes of others (or one particularly important "other"). Even though we are less dependent on the approval of others as we mature, such affirmation can be very important. Ironically, as middle-aged women we're likely to find ourselves feeling more vulnerable about our sexual desirability at the same time we're feeling more confident about our sexual responsiveness. Since we live in a culture that has equated desirability for women with youth, a culture that has held up as ideal an eighteen-year-old body even most eighteen-year-olds don't possess, many of us grew up thinking that the approach of middle age—and the physical changes that accompany it—signaled the approach of our sexual obsolescence. We felt that we remained desirable only to the extent that we retained our youthfulness. And we tended to judge other women as well as ourselves by those criteria.

These attitudes have by no means disappeared either from society or from the minds of middle-aged women. But there are definite signs that they have begun to change. And the origin of that change is in women themselves: A number of respondents to our survey wrote about their changing perceptions and self-image, their refusal to buy into the unflattering stereotypes perpetrated by the media, and their growing support of one another. As women of all ages are learning to value themselves more, many are also learning to value their sexuality. No longer striving to remain "girls," they are taking full possession of their womanhood. And in the middle years, this changing self-concept, combined with a woman's experience and personal development, allows her to bring to the whole sexual arena a new strength and independence, a greater understanding and self-acceptance.

As one woman in her early forties told us:

> It seems the more I've learned to accept myself in other areas of my life, the more I've learned to accept and like my sexuality—despite my changing body! I've become generally more confident in my relationships. And I take better care of myself. I don't really know which acceptance came first, but it doesn't matter. I think both are due to the experience and confidence I've gained over the years.

Another woman reported:

> I find work sexy! That may sound strange, but when I'm working hard and feeling turned on to what I'm doing, I feel turned on sexually too. It's as though I'm in high gear in more ways than one. And the older I get, the more competent I feel—and the more I feel wanted—in the office and in bed!

There is a growing sense of separateness and self-worth that is helping many middle-aged women to define themselves as more desirable. In fact, a majority of women responding to our survey reported that one of the benefits they were experiencing as a result of being older was feeling more desirable sexually.[8]

And there are signs that mature women are also perceived as being more desirable by others. Much attention has been focused recently on the "sexual flowering" of middle-aged women. The European attitude that age and experience can enhance a woman's sensuality seems to be gaining a foothold here. The popular press has even reported that the "average age of desirability in American women seems to have risen by a dozen years or more."[9] Perhaps attitudes towards sex are, at long last, coming of age in this culture.

But if much of the credit for that goes to women themselves, some must also go to the fact that so much encouraging and positive information about mature sexuality has become available in recent years. Masters and Johnson in particular have gone a long way toward dispelling myths about sex and aging. When they published *Human Sexual Response* in 1966, they made it clear that men and women do have the capacity to be sexually active until quite late in life. There are, of course, physiological changes that cause a slowing down of some processes and responses for both men and women, but usually not until the fifth or sixth decade. However, their research shows that the ability to enjoy sex is not lost at any age: " 'There is no time limit drawn by the advancing years to female sexuality'; and for the male, too, there is, under favorable physical and emotional conditions, 'a capacity for sexual performance that frequently may extend beyond the eighty year level.' "[10]

This is well illustrated by an anecdote in a *Ms.* Magazine article on "Sexual Lives of Women over Sixty": "I am sixty years old and they say you never get too old to enjoy sex," said one woman, "I know because once I asked my Grandma when you stop liking it and she was eighty. She said, 'Child, you'll have to ask someone older than me.' "[11]

Some of the physical changes in a woman's sexual response cycle are a result of hormone imbalance or loss in menopause. Occasionally, orgasm may trigger a painful spastic contraction of the uterus, and the vagina may become less elastic. Vaginal walls get thinner and there is likely to be less—and delayed—vaginal lubrication. However, all these symptoms—reduced vaginal lubrication, vaginal constriction, and spastic uterine contractions—were found to be much less common in women who continued to have sex on a regular basis, once or twice a week. In fact, the phrase "use it or lose it" is good advice for maintaining physical comfort with sex, as well as for keeping up one's desire and interest. Indeed, Masters and

Johnson emphasize that for both men and women, regular and continued sexual activity over the years is the best way to retain sexual capacity in later life.

Much has been written in recent years about women's tendency to become less inhibited and more interested in sex at about the same time their male partners are expressing a declining interest in sex. Masters and Johnson help to shed some light on this with information about what happens to men physiologically and psychologically as they age—information that is important for women as well as men to understand. As a man moves into his late middle years, it can take him longer to get an erection, and the erection may not be as hard as in younger years. The erection can, however, be maintained for a longer period of time because the older man has less need to ejaculate —which not only allows him to remain for a longer time at the plateau phase of sensual pleasure, but also can make the older man a better, more satisfying lover. Masters and Johnson stress that if the older man ejaculates only when he needs to and not every time he has intercourse, he can most effectively retain his capacity for erection, and his ability to function well sexually until late in life.

But if a man lacks adequate information about this perfectly normal slowdown, he may start to feel panicky, even begin to worry about impotence, which can create a vicious cycle: He gets more anxious, and it then becomes even more difficult to get an erection. His "performance fear" may result in his trying to avoid sex altogether, resorting to preoccupation with work, fatigue, picking fights, psychosomatic distress, or other excuses. Worse yet, rather than feel that *he* is a failure, he may cast his partner in the role of not being desirable enough to arouse him (which may be one underlying explanation for the idea that women become less desirable as they get older).

Of course, for men as well as women, there is often more than concern about physiological factors behind changing sexual behavior: a marital relationship gone stale; worries about work, health, finances, or one's accomplishments in life. There are even those who speculate that the idea of the sheer vigor of mature female sexuality is overwhelming for some males.[12] Indeed, in the wake of all the reports of blossoming female sexuality at midlife came a spate of reports on the "new male impotence." The blame was often placed on the women's movement; the idea was that the very separateness and confidence that was allowing women to feel better about their own sexuality was "doing men in." But such an interpretation is certainly questionable. LoPiccolo and Heiman report that "many therapists and journalists think that the women's liberation movement has caused a dramatic increase in the number of men suffering from erectile failure. Our own clinical experience does not support such a theory. In terms of people who come for therapy, few cases could be seen in the light of a women's liberation syndrome. In fact, rather than necessarily threatening male sexuality, the feminist ideals of women assuming responsibility for their own sexuality and of deobjectifying and thus personalizing sex have helped take pressure off penis-centered, performance anxious men."[13]

It is also important to keep in mind the extent to which power struggles in a relationship can get played out in the bedroom. The old pattern was for the woman to withhold sex, to have a headache, or submit passively and make her lack of pleasure evident. The newer pattern is for the man's sexual interest to diminish at about the time the woman in his life is feeling more powerful and independent, both inside the home and out.[14] Nor is it a phenomenon limited to married couples. Donna, a divorced woman of thirty-nine, described with both amusement and frustration a relationship she was currently having. Three years earlier, in an attempt to pull her life together after her divorce, Donna had enrolled in a graphic arts course. Her intention was to get started on a career in graphic design, a goal she has since realized with some modest success. The instructor for the course was an attractive man, Geoffrey, about her age: "He was nice-looking in a shaggy kind of way I've always liked; he had a good sense of humor and was very warm and supportive. He took me under his wing, and we got to be pretty good friends." Geoffrey made it very clear that he would like to have a physical relationship with Donna, but at the time, she was involved with another man, so nothing came of it. After she completed the course, they met a few times for coffee and then lost touch with each other.

About eight months before we talked to Donna, the man she had been with for over two years moved to California.

We had both realized for a while that our relationship wasn't going anywhere, but I was really crazy about him, and I went through a pretty rough period after he left. I tried to keep busy, and I did go out with a few men, but nobody I cared about . . . actually, nobody I even liked. And then who should I run into at a party last month, but Geoffrey! He seemed to be as glad to see me as I was to see him. It looked like the timing was right for us this time. We made plans to get together the next night, and when we met, we had a chance to fill each other in on what we'd been doing. . . . Only it turns out that he's still doing exactly the same thing—which he still describes as "temporary"— while I have gotten on with it. I've started to establish a reputation for myself as a graphic artist; people are beginning to seek me out. And I'm also teaching a course similar to the one I took from Geoffrey—only at a more prestigious institution. When I mentioned where I was teaching, I could see he was a little taken aback. He'd seen some of my work, but he didn't know I was doing that too. Well, what can I tell you? All of a sudden, this guy who couldn't keep his hands off me at the party the night before got very cool. I mean, he was pleasant and interested, but there was a difference. I guess he didn't much like the idea of being outdistanced by a former protégé, especially a former *female* protégé, and I can understand that. But in spite of that we have gone on seeing each other: sometimes he calls me; sometimes I call him. I suppose we've been together seven or eight times over the last month. And in that time, he's scarcely touched me . . . and I *like* to be touched; sex is very important to me. The fascinating and frustrating thing is that I see us playing these incredible role reversal games: I'm the strong, self-confident one; I seem to initiate any physical contact we do have; and he's the coy virgin, the tease. Sometimes he'll be obviously seductive with me, all sprawled out on a sofa or bed, and then he'll turn away. I ask myself why the hell I bother with him, and the answer is: because in spite of everything, I like him better than anyone I've met for a long time, and he's a damned attractive man. I keep thinking he'll get over it, or we'll get past it; pretty soon he'll have "punished" me enough for my success, and he won't have to "hold out" any more. Only in the meantime, I see another game going on: I see myself regressing to the role of "helpless little girl." I find myself hiding my power so I won't be threatening. And the more I do that, the more he seems to respond. I know it's all very manipulative and unstraight, and it sure doesn't feel very good. But I've been through this before with other men where I haven't backed off at all, and I think I really scared them away. This time I'm trying to compromise—for a while anyway —and see how that works out. But eventually we're going to have to accept each other honestly and decide if we can have a relationship based on who we really *are*.

The reasons may vary, but the issue of unequal sexual desire or interest can be a problem between partners in the middle years, especially when the greater desire is the woman's. It is possible, after all, for a woman to "fake it," to go along even when she's not particularly interested. For a man, it's not so easy; in fact, the demand to perform can have disastrous results. It is a problem for which there is obviously no right answer. Some women have affairs, some masturbate, some try to talk it out with their partners, on their own or with professional guidance, in the hopes of making a change. Some are becoming bisexual and are having sexual relationships with women. And others adjust to their partner's level of sexual desire, or divert sexual energy into other activities.

For many women, it is helpful simply to understand the dynamics of what is taking place; they are less inclined, then, to interpret the situation as a matter only of their own failure or lack of desirability, or to think of it as something either inevitable or irreversible. The reality is that only a very small percentage of male impotence stems from physical causes; most is psychological in origin. Masters and Johnson point out that given reasonably good health and a willing and understanding partner, a man "can and should continue unencumbered sexual functioning indefinitely."[15]

And yet, as encouraging as all the information about mature sexuality may be, there is an important caveat: In our very goal-oriented society there is a danger of placing too much emphasis on *performance* criteria, rather than on the pleasure of the experience itself. These days, there is a tendency to equate all sexual pleasure or success with *orgasm:* how many, how often, how intense. Indeed, a number of women we heard from made a point of stating that they liked expressing their sexuality through physical closeness, holding, leisurely caressing and touching, hugging and kissing, whether it always culminated in orgasm—or even in intercourse—or not. Sex can become a chore, hard work, when we saddle it with too many expectations or set "goals" for ourselves. The greatest irony of all would be to have finally thrown off one set of "shoulds" and "oughts" and expectations about what is "good" and "normal," only to replace it with another set (as mature women, we "must" be multiply orgasmic, more desirous of sex, free of all inhibitions, and so on). Perhaps the most important thing we bring to our sexual relationships as women in our middle years is not our "unlimited orgasmic capacity," or our new freedom from inhibition—as nice as both of these may be—but our experience, sensitivity, and compassion; our understanding, and a growing sense of ourselves as separate and valuable human beings. It is these qualities that allow us to give and receive the greatest pleasure; that give sex the potential to get better and better as we mature.

7 Connections

Like so many other things, the relationships that are important to us inevitably change during the long period of our middle years. Our children grow up and our parents grow old. Friendships flourish or wither, and so, for that matter, do marriages. We may be divorced or widowed; we become grandmothers. We make new friends as we move off in new directions.

Many of our relationships deepen and grow with time; the transitions they go through serve only to enhance them, and there is a sense of shared history that gives them a special quality. As we mature, we find that we have more to bring to new relationships, more to give to old ones.

However, we may also find some of the changes that take place difficult to accept. It's not always easy to abandon familiar patterns. Sometimes we'd like to keep things the way they were when we got married, when our parents or children were younger. We do X—we've *always* done X— and we expect Y in return. Now all of the sudden, we're getting Z. What is this? Or maybe we're not willing to *do* X to *get* Y anymore. The relationship is under stress and so are we.

The situation is often compounded in our middle years by the feeling of being pulled in different directions. Having moved beyond the singlemindedness of our youth, we see the merits of diverse points of view, and feel the pressures of conflicting expectations. We may feel caught somewhere between our growing children and our aging parents; between commitments to others and a need for individual fulfillment; between the terms on which we've based a relationship for years, and the very different terms on which we'd like to base it today.

How women respond to the challenge of changing relationships varies widely of course, not only from woman to woman, but from relationship to relationship. And even from one point in life to another. Nevertheless, we did observe some fairly clear patterns in the relationships that middle-aged women are having today. And it is these patterns and the feelings they create that are the subject of the chapters that follow.

8 "Happily Ever After": Marriage in the Middle Years

Most of us over thirty-five today grew up fully expecting to marry; it was to be the pivotal event in our lives. There may have been moments when we questioned whether or not we *would* marry, but very few of us questioned whether we *should:* you just did, that's all. You grew up, got married, and had children. Fade out; the end. We gave a lot more thought to *getting* married than to *being* married.

It doesn't take long, however, to discover that marriage is considerably more complicated than "happily ever after." It's not only that we get to know one another better, revealing all our foibles after being so relentlessly charming in our courting days; it's that as we continue to develop and change over the years, the change is not always at the same pace or in the same direction as our partner's. There are times when we feel that we mesh perfectly, when our needs and interests truly complement one another's; and other times when we couldn't be more out of step.

A marriage is affected as well by the external circumstances of our lives: finances, health, a move to a new city, the demands that are made on each of us by careers or by other people. Certainly children and money are among the most frequent causes of conflict in marriage. And tragedy of any sort—illness or death in the family—can pull a couple apart just when they need each other most.

To make matters even more complicated, the whole institution of marriage is currently in flux. All around us, there is an atmosphere of questioning, of reassessing the dynamics of marriage and the role each partner plays. The general loosening-up of sex role stereotypes has changed our ideas about what behavior is "appropriate" for husbands and wives. Attitudes about commitment to marriage have been tempered by a new emphasis on individual fulfillment. It has become less likely that a marriage will be either permanent or monogamous.

And then, of course, marriage, like any relationship, changes as it moves from "new" to "old." Freshness and excitement often give way to predictable patterns and habits, passion to comfort and familiarity. We sometimes wonder as we gaze at our spouse across the room whether we are sharing a companionable silence or whether we just have nothing to say. We go through highs and lows, periods of being very turned on to one another, of being filled with warmth and tenderness, and periods when we couldn't be more turned off, when we're seething with anger or just plain bored with the routine of it all. We may feel alternately grateful and resentful, secure and trapped, restless and content.

Yet despite all the change and ambivalence and complexity that are inevitable when two people live intimately together over a long period of time, seventy-five percent of the married women we surveyed felt that one of the benefits of growing older was an improved relationship with their spouse. They especially valued that sense of shared history that can only come from long-term relationships. There is often far greater acceptance, companionability, and understanding in marriage over time. There is an intimacy that goes beyond sex—though sex, too, quite often improves. And while some changes are difficult and threatening and come about only with great effort and conflict, other changes are absorbed with relative ease as the relationship evolves and grows over the years.

In many ways, there is a better sense of perspective on the relationship. *Perspective* was, in fact, a word we heard quite often from women when they discussed marriage in the middle years. Women reported that they were more able to accept their own ambivalent feelings about the relationship, and more able to take any single experience or change in stride. The feelings expressed by one forty-five-year-old Ohio housewife were typical. She had been describing a rough period that her marriage had recently been through, during which she and her husband had disagreed violently about the way their nineteen-year-old son was conducting his life, and to what extent they should interfere. They had quarreled about vacation plans, and who should be doing what around the house:

> And we fought about nothing at all. Almost everything we said or did really got on the other person's nerves. To put it mildly, we didn't like each other much. But one night while I was doing the dishes, furious at Ray, slamming pots around and mumbling to myself—and making sure he could hear me do it—I realized that we had been through periods like this before in our marriage, and we would probably go through them again, and as awful as things were between us at that moment they *would* get better.
>
> In the early years of our marriage, I wouldn't have believed that; I didn't think you were *ever* supposed to feel so awful about each other. I had some very starry-eyed, Saturday-matinee notions

about love. Now I have more perspective on things; nothing looms so big. Of course, there are probably a lot of divorced women running around who once told themselves the same thing. But, in fact, things *are* good between us right now. I think in many ways, our marriage is stronger than ever. It's certainly more realistic. Besides, we've shared so much over the years, we have a big investment in this marriage. We care about each other and depend on each other; we can survive periods like that.

In the middle years women are likely to have a better perspective on the sexual part of the relationship as well. While a large number of women reported that sex had become more pleasurable over time ("Far more exciting than when we were young." "I have become a much better partner, having lost many puritanical hangups." "Less quantity; much better quality.") others acknowledged that sex had become "routine," "almost mechanical at times." In general, however, sex in marriage tends to go through cycles just as the relationship does.

The day after her seventeenth anniversary, a New York woman wrote to us:

> I got married in the early sixties when the pill was brand new and sex manuals were still emphasizing mutual orgasm, as though that were the only kind that really counted. I was, to use the 1950's term, "a technical virgin." That meant that before our actual wedding day, Larry and I did everything we could possibly imagine to express our love and physical desire—except have intercourse. As I look back on it now, it seems as though we were so deadly earnest about sex. We bought all the available paperbacks, read them—talked about them—and thought we were very enlightened and

progressive. In order to follow the directions in some of those books, you would have needed to take a stop watch to bed with you. I remember the one I had practically memorized before our honeymoon was called *Modern Sex Techniques.* That was an apt title because the content was totally clinical and technique-oriented, with diagrams about stages of arousal and orgasm—each bracketed and marked with the number of seconds in that particular stage. Hardly information that would help one to relax and feel sensual!

Predictably, our first few months of marriage were disappointing sexually. But right from the beginning we were able to talk about what was going on, maybe because we thought that was the enlightened thing to do. Gradually we learned to laugh at ourselves—to throw out the books, relax, and give each other pleasure. Over the past seventeen years we have developed a sex life that is more than anything else—comfortable. God, *comfortable,* there's a word that would have sent me shrieking if I had heard someone use it to describe sex when I was twenty! A comfortable sex life was certainly not what my adolescent fantasies were about. But now, at forty, if I'm honest about it, that is what I value most about my relationship with my husband—that comfortableness that has evolved over time.

Comfortableness doesn't mean dullness or sameness—although there are times when sex does seem rather dull. But there are also times when it is exquisitely tender, or tremendously exciting—times when we want to have sex very often, and other times when we are both preoccupied with other things and sex is almost non-existent for months on end. The comfortableness is a feeling that we as a couple have a sense of each other, that we can unabashedly say, "Look, I really have work on my mind and I just can't get turned on." Or we can be seductive and silly with each other and just as unabashedly say, "Hey, I am really horny." Sometimes we misread each other's signals—but most of the time we don't. Sometimes there are tears or anger, but most of the time there is warmth and joy. We experiment, but we're no longer deadly serious about the "results." Sometimes making love in a new place or at an unusual time or in a new way is wonderful and sometimes it isn't. And that's okay too. Maybe it's because of personal development and maturity, maybe it's what happens when you have a long history with one other person—I don't know what the reason is for it, but if sex isn't terrific tonight, or if I'm going through a period of little interest in sex, I know it's not going to be that way forever.

As a matter of fact, if someone were to ask me what my sex life is like at this moment, I think I'd say, "What sex life?" The truth is that both of us are flying high on work right now. We're both very busy and enthusiastic about what we're doing, and a lot of times late at night we'll just sit and talk and catch up on each other's day. And a number of my friends have told me that it's the same for them. Maybe that's because among most of the couples I know, the men are getting into positions of greater responsibility, and the women are either renewing careers, or now that the kids are finally older, they're focusing a whole lot more on their own interests and are very intensely involved.

But in spite of this period of less sexual activity— actually it's not just one period, it comes and goes for us—sex itself gets better and better. I feel freer to totally enjoy sex, and I'm not the least bit inhibited about expressing that pleasure. I also get a lot of pleasure and feel excited by seeing my husband enjoy sex. When sex is especially good, it's more intense and more exciting and more fun than I even could have imagined when I was in my twenties. I have more orgasms and that's nice, but what's really nice is that I feel like a more sexual and sensual woman.

I have always been monogamous; and although I would never make the statement that I always will be, that's the way my life is right now. Because I was a virgin when I got married, I am curious about what it would be like to have sex with other men. I'm far from preoccupied with the topic, but I *am* curious. Even though I haven't had affairs, in recent years I have developed a sense of myself as sexually attractive to men. Perhaps it's just a matter of being more comfortable with my own sexuality. Maybe that comes through to others. I'm not sure; all I know is that it feels good.

While these two women, as well as many of the others we heard from, readily acknowledged the ups and downs of their marriages, they were on balance, *positive* about the relationship and their commitment to it. Their attitude was one of acceptance and affirmation, not resignation. In this sense, they were different from a small number of women we talked to who had chosen to stay in marriages they found basically unfulfilling and unsatisfying. These women offered a variety of reasons for continuing their relationships: religious or moral beliefs, "for the sake of the children," for the status and security the relationship provided, or, as several very candidly put it, to avoid becoming "just another middle-aged divorcée." Some of these women saw their decision to remain in disappointing marriages as the compromise they were making with life. ("I figure you never get it all," one Florida woman said wryly. "And I'm willing to settle for what this marriage does provide.") Other women said they made a point of looking elsewhere for what their marriage lacked. A woman from Texas in her mid-forties wrote that her husband is a man who "works hard and loves me" but as for herself:

I was outspoken and free-thinking and a little wild at twenty, very intimidating to my parents. They sent me north to visit some relatives, and told them to find me a proper husband. I loved artists and musicians and Bohemian types. They found me a man seven years older than I was, very sophisticated and conservative—a businessman who promised to become very successful. He wooed me with flowers and theater tickets and fine restaurants, and all my family adored him. I married him three months later on my twenty-first birthday. It took him about a year to squelch any individuality or free thinking I had left in me. I became the perfect wife and homemaker and helpmate in his rise to success and fortune. I've had enormous security all my life, but have never really been in love with him. I fulfilled my family's dreams, but not my own. I have the gorgeous home, the expensive clothes, and fancy car my mother always wanted, and they mean nothing to me. My husband is an obsessive compulsive workaholic whose idea of *fun* is joining an organization, becoming its president, and getting his name in the paper for being the best worker. I am very much the opposite. We have nothing in common. I stay in the marriage because the financial security gives me the freedom to do whatever I want. My days are totally free, and I don't have to account to him for how I spend my time. I only have to look pretty and act nice at the dinners and parties we go to as part of his business. He loves to travel, so I've been to

Europe and Mexico and Canada and around the U.S. There's nothing for me to complain about in this marriage; there's his sexy, warm body in my bed every night, and plenty of money—just no one to talk to! So I have lots of nice lady friends, and an occasional warm, compassionate man friend to share my thoughts and feelings with. All in all, I sometimes think I should have held out for love instead of security, but who knows?

While security is clearly a benefit of marriage, the singular pursuit of it is a barrier to change and growth between two people. This woman seems to have written off the possibility that her relationship *can* change. We heard from other women who were reluctant even to *try* to change the relationship, because they feared more than anything else that their husbands might walk out on them. They didn't want to "rock the boat"; they were virtually immobilized by feelings of vulnerability.

As one Connecticut woman put it:

I dropped out of college to support my husband while he went to engineering school. It wasn't unusual among my friends—getting a Ph.T. degree we called it: "Putting Hubby Through." And then I devoted myself to caring for my home and raising three children. I was glad to do it—all of it. Only now I'm forty-six, the kids are independent and it's the old cliché: my husband and I don't seem to have anything to say to each other anymore. I don't think he respects me, or finds me interesting in the least. We're not really sharing a life, we're co-existing. He is polite and perfunctory with me, even in bed. He doesn't seem to want to discuss our relationship or make any changes in it, and I'm afraid to press the issue. I often wonder whether he is having an affair, and I'm terrified that he's thinking about leaving me. I feel I'm such a small part of his life, whereas I've built my whole existence around being his wife. If he leaves me now, where will I be? Middle-aged, unneeded, untrained—no college degree, no marketable skills—and alone. So I hang on and pretend everything is all right. I don't want to grow old alone.

It has now become part of the conventional wisdom that it is unwise for a woman to become too dependent on her husband for her sense of herself in the world, or to look to him for her own identity. But it was not a part of the conventional wisdom when many middle-aged women entered their marriages or made decisions about their lives. So this woman's feelings are not hard to understand. She kept her part of the bargain as she saw it, yet finds herself twenty-five years later facing a changed set of circumstances and expectations, and feeling both dependent and expendable.

But fewer and fewer middle-aged women are in this position today. Increasingly, they are reassessing their attitudes and roles in marriage and are taking advantage of new opportunities for women; they are building on changes in society, in the relationship, and in themselves, and are developing a sense of separateness and identity. And ironically, it is precisely this *separateness* that many feel has enhanced their marriage the most: the willingness to take responsibility for themselves instead of blaming or depending solely on their partners. Nora, forty-seven, learned through her own experience "how important it was for my husband and me to develop separate lives, for me to go off and be my own person, and not be a parasite, a leech, which I had been in the worse sense."

When Nora married Tom in the mid-fifties, she had been working as a nurse for several years, and he was a graduate student at a prestigious university. He planned to get a Ph.D. and pursue a career in teaching, and in Nora's mind, that was the "crème de la crème, the ultimate: to be a professor. Since I saw myself as living in the reflected glory of my husband's identity, I wanted the best, and for me that meant being married to a professor." Neither of them, however, anticipated Tom's reaction to graduate school: He was utterly miserable; his ulcer flared up, and the pressure he felt made him increasingly anxious. Eventually he withdrew from school and took a job in merchandising. Nora told us:

> And what did supportive wifey do? I heaped abuse on him; I was contemptuous. I felt he screwed me royally by not becoming my professor. How could he *do* that to me? And not only did he not become a professor, he went into business, into merchandising! I didn't like business or anything to do with it. So from that day forward, here was this guy struggling for his life, his identity, his health, his sanity, and my reaction was, "You're beneath contempt." I was ashamed to tell people what my husband did. I was apologetic about it. I gave him a very hard time.

The problem was compounded for Nora because Tom's job as a buyer required that he travel a great deal, leaving her alone in a small apartment with two toddlers.

> Those years when the children were little were really torture for me. I had so much doubt and so little confidence. It was the Spock era, and I thought I was supposed to be the be-all-and-end-all for everybody, and instead I was very unfulfilled and miserable. I felt like a prisoner, stuck in that apartment with the kids for twenty-four hours a day. There was no such thing as privacy, no such thing as developing myself. I mean, sure, I took

dance classes at night, or whatever, but I just didn't
feel together or like a person. I thought, "I'm an
unnatural mother; there's something terribly wrong
with me." I've met countless women since then who
have said the same thing, and it's nice after the
fact, but there was nobody around to tell me then.

Tom didn't understand; he was bewildered by my
attitude. He'd go off on a buying trip for three
weeks, and it was like the end of the world for me.
I felt like I was never going to see him again. I
resented him traveling all over while I was stuck at
home. And since I valued myself very little, I was
afraid he was cheating on me. So we could barely
talk to each other before he left or when he came
home, because he knew there was all that anger
and resentment and jealousy and everything just
waiting to explode . . . and it often did.

Nora tried going back to work while the children were
small, but found that it created more problems than it
solved. But as soon as the children were both in school, she
returned to nursing. She worked part-time at first, and
eventually moved into jobs that gave her more and more
responsibility:

That was an exciting time for me, my
mid-thirties; a whole new world was opening up.
And it was great for our marriage too—it was like a
miracle drug. I was becoming a separate person
again, finding out I had worth, *believing* in myself.

Nora's efforts to establish a career were interrupted several times when Tom changed jobs and the family moved
from city to city. But after their last move, with Tom's
encouragement, she returned to school, and got a bachelor's degree in nursing. In her early forties, she began
teaching at a university herself. Nora feels that she and

Tom now have an unusually good marriage, and says "it has gotten better and better as the two of us have gotten older and wiser and more mature. And I think what's enriched the relationship the most is my growing sense of myself as an independent person."

Their marriage has become a partnership of two separate individuals. Nora is now able to be supportive of Tom in a way she couldn't be earlier in the marriage when she depended on him for her own identity.

"In fact," she told us, "it's only been in the last few years that I've finally come to my senses and realized how happy I am for him that he's doing what he wants to do, and how ashamed I am for having been ashamed of him."

What happens to Tom affects Nora deeply, but it no longer defines her.

Nora's changing feelings about herself and her marriage were closely related to her return to work, but that is not always the case. We also heard from middle-aged women who were content to remain in traditional roles, and were experiencing in an equally positive way, a growing sense of separateness. Many of these women emphasized the importance of having their *own* friends. As one woman put it:

> . . . not just the couple-who-come-to-dinner-on-Saturday-night kind of friends, but friends—especially women—my husband hardly knows. They mean a lot to me, and there's a part of my life I share just with them. It took me a while to realize that I wouldn't get everything I needed from one person. I remember when I was first married, I used to think it would be fantastic if my husband and I could live on an island someplace, just the two of us. Now I think that sounds like a nightmare! And that's not because we love each other less; in fact, we have a hell of a lot more to say to each other and have more fun with each other than we used

to. But the romantic fantasy of perpetual togetherness holds no appeal. We need to have other people in our lives, and to have time away from each other.

Those "other people in our lives" can enhance a marriage. They keep us from falling into the trap of trying to be everything to one another.

Of course, having close women friends is one thing; having a close friendship with a man may be something else again. It is difficult for the relationship not to be seen as having sexual overtones—and, in fact, it often does. There's an air of sexual freedom all around us today in a way there never was when we were young and single. Suddenly it seems that more and more women we know are having extramarital affairs; newly single friends confide their sexual adventures. We may have the sense that we are "missing out." We're tantalized; we're curious; we're sorely tempted; we fantasize. We want to know that we are still sexually desirable in the eyes of others. But we're also likely to feel conflicted. Here we are, at our peak sexually, feeling more sensual and sexually responsive than ever before, and we find ourselves wondering: "How will a lover react to my changing body? Would it be worth the price if my husband found out? Would the whole thing just get too complicated?"

Confided one forty-five-year-old Westchester woman:

> Last year, I had a brief affair, my first. Nothing to put in the Guinness Book of Records, no grand passion, but nice, very nice.
>
> I had been on a committee with this man— Richard—for about three months, and we started going out for coffee after meetings and talking. And after a while, it seemed fairly obvious that sooner or later we would go to bed together. I thought to myself: "God, this is so trite; it's almost too

predictable." But there was a sense of anticipation that was incredibly exciting. I would go home after being with him and make love with my husband more enthusiastically than I had in years, partly out of guilt, and partly because I was so turned on. I had the most fantastic sexual fantasies!

Finally one night, we went back to Richard's apartment—he's separated from his wife—and started to make love . . . and he was impotent. I was lying there thinking, "Oh, my God! What have I done? What *haven't* I done?"—when I realized *he* was apologizing to *me,* explaining that he hadn't slept with anyone since he and his wife had separated, and he had been looking forward to this so much, etc., etc. I was so relieved that he didn't think it was my fault that I wasn't even disappointed. So we lay there and talked and held each other, and then I went home. And *then* I was disappointed. But a week later, we did make love, and it was wonderful.

I can't say that the sex itself was better than with my husband; after twenty-four years together, he knows all the things I like and how I like to be touched and so on. But it was different with Richard; it was new and exciting. Only after we had slept together seven or eight times, the newness was already wearing off. I still liked the way he made me feel: very sexy and desirable despite my gray hair and the ten extra pounds I'm carrying around. And I was fond of Richard. But I was getting worried that somebody would see us together. It got so, I couldn't relax. I love my husband, and I knew very well that I didn't want to risk what I had.

I suppose it was partly guilt that was making me so uneasy, some sense that I had breached a trust with my husband, but I didn't actually feel very guilty. My affair didn't really affect how I felt about my husband, only how I felt about *me*. I was forty-four years old; and until I met Richard, I had only slept with one other person besides my husband—and that had been a complete disaster—and there were things I felt I wanted to find out about myself. The whole idea that Richard continued to find me desirable was very reassuring, very confirming. But it just wasn't worth it any more, and so I started making excuses to him, and then we ended it.

We're still friends; we still occasionally go out for coffee after meetings, but I doubt that we'd ever sleep together again. In fact, he's now seeing a friend of mine who's a widow, and I'm delighted for both of them.

I don't know whether I'll ever have another affair, but I'm glad I had that one. A friend of mine once said jokingly that having an affair these days was practically a developmental task for middle-aged women. In my case, I think she was right.

While this woman's story is not unusual, we also heard from women who said they would never consider an affair, and from others for whom extramarital sex was an accepted way of life. It is clear, however, that a great many married women in their middle years are thinking and talking and struggling with the idea of having a sexual relationship with someone other than their husbands. And a surprisingly wide variety of women we talked to had chosen to do so.

On quite a different level, more and more middle-aged women are also choosing to be working wives. It is now estimated that both spouses in two-thirds of all families are working. As the phenomenon of the wife returning to school or work at mid-life has become increasingly common, it has created an increasingly common set of problems for couples.

For example, it is not unusual for middle-aged couples to find that they are simultaneously holding both old and new values about marriage and the role of each partner. They may profess belief in an equal partnership, but many discover that they have not really relinquished traditional attitudes. Change may turn out to be more acceptable in theory than practice.

Intellectually, my husband and I believe that it's perfectly all right for me to be earning more than he is. But it's so contrary to everything we learned as we grew up, that the truth is we're both finding it sort of embarrassing and threatening.

(thirty-seven-year-old accountant)

My husband and I both applied to the same fellowship program last year. We talked about how we would feel if only one of us were accepted, and we both decided that it would be disappointing but we could handle it okay. But while we were waiting to hear, I was surprised to find myself hoping that if only one of us got in, it would be him. I wish I could say it was altruism or selfless devotion on my part. But what I realized was, despite my strong, egalitarian, feminist principles, on some level it would upset me to be married to a man who was less professionally successful than I. That just wasn't how it was "supposed" to be.

(forty-one-year-old sociologist)

With inflation the way it is, Fred and I decided it would be a good idea for me to go back to work full-time. We agreed to share more of the household responsibilities, but it hasn't worked out that way. Oh, he'll help out if I ask him to, but I don't like to have to ask him to do "woman's work." I know, I know; I'm not supposed to think of it that way anymore. But I do—and I know Fred does too. Besides, it's usually easier just to do it myself than to explain it to him beforehand, and then be expected to be endlessly grateful afterwards.

(fifty-two-year-old secretary)

A related theme that ran through our interviews with women in dual-career marriages was concern about decreased time and energy for the relationship. Many women said they were so busy simply doing what had to be done (shopping, laundry, and housework in addition to working) that whole weeks would go by in which there seemed to be no real intimacy with their husbands. ("My husband complains that we've gotten to be like ships that pass in the night.") They found they had to consciously plan for time to stop and focus their attention on one another, to reestablish intimacy. Some couples had developed simple rituals such as sitting down for a drink before dinner, or taking an evening walk, or giving each other back rubs before bed. Others made it a point to go out to dinner together once a week, or to get away for an occasional weekend alone. One woman told us:

We found we had to make time for ourselves, just the two of us. When we first went away, we couldn't afford more than a weekend in a downtown hotel. But it was a revelation; it made us realize how very important it was for us to have time alone. It sometimes takes a lot of organizing and planning just to get away, but it's a salvaging thing. It doesn't matter much where we go or what we do. It's just getting away from the telephone and the kids and the briefcase full of reports waiting to be read and the leaking roof. It's wonderful to be able to talk or read books or make love without having to hurry or worry about interruptions.

In addition to the pressures of time, there is also an emotional drain on the relationship when both partners work. Energy and enthusiam that was once focused on home and family become refocused on job and colleagues. Women feel more distracted; it's sometimes hard to change gears. As one woman said:

> I notice myself doing what I always complained of my husband doing: not leaving work problems at the office. Or George will be trying to tell me about his day at work, and all the while, I'll be thinking about mine. Or what's worse, we'll be making love, and I'll find myself thinking about the meeting I have to go to the next day.

Women who were once waiting at home prepared to listen and nurture and provide an emotional safety valve for their husbands now feel the need for the same support themselves. Both partners now want time and space to decompress when they get home at the end of the day. The relationship may feel less complementary as the needs of partners become more similar.

The struggle to work through these issues is sometimes a tough one. Time takes care of some of the problem; couples get used to change gradually, discover ways to compromise, to strike a balance between old and new ways of doing things and meeting needs. It can be of tremendous value for both partners just to understand the dynamics of what is going on, to recognize the source of tension and pressure in the relationship, and acknowledge why they feel as they do.

There are also many pluses to dual-career marriages in the middle years, advantages that go beyond the financial benefits. Women who had been restless and bored at home said that the sense of satisfaction they got from their jobs had a very beneficial effect on their marriages. They felt they had more to share with their partners, and were less inclined to have unrealistic expectations for what the marriage was supposed to provide in their lives.

They found that their husbands took pride in their accomplishments, and they, in turn, had new empathy for their partners' experiences in the work world. A forty-seven-year-old social worker who had returned to work two years earlier said:

There's more spark between my husband and me these days because we're both challenged and turned on by what we're doing. He has new confidence in me, and he's proud of how I've grown over the years. And I find that I feel less threatened by the other people in his life and less jealous of his success because I have my own.

Alice, forty-two, did not go out and get a job—at least not in the sense of full-time paid employment. But as her two children have become more independent, she has gotten increasingly involved in the community. She is active in the Women's Political Caucus, and heads a local organization concerned with environmental issues.

I've even begun to think seriously about running for office myself. I'd like to be a member of the city council some day. For years, I'd show up periodically to stuff envelopes or make phone calls for some candidate or issue I believed in—I didn't have the time or self-confidence to do more. But three years ago, I agreed to head a fund-raising event for an environmental group, and then they asked me to be on the board, and this year, I'm president. I was reluctant to take it on at first; I wasn't sure I could handle it or that I'd had enough experience. But it's been fascinating; I'm dealing with issues I believe are vitally important—working for the development of solar energy, and against the development of nuclear energy.
Friends who knew me in the days when I was too

shy to speak up at PTA meetings can't believe it when they see me being interviewed on television or giving a speech somewhere. Sometimes I can't believe it myself! I feel more confident, powerful, and on top of things than I ever have. I've never been busier, but I love what I'm doing, and I'm meeting a lot of fantastic people.

My husband Ed has always been concerned about environmental issues, so I know he believes in what I'm trying to accomplish. But, I don't know; in the last year, things have just been different between us. Both of us are changing—I guess that's inevitable—but it feels like we're pulling in opposite directions.

Ed has worked hard all his life, and he's been fairly successful. He's always been ambitious and preoccupied with his career, only now he's feeling kind of burned out. He's not falling apart or anything; he doesn't want to chuck it all and move to Bora Bora, but he's really doing some serious questioning about how he wants to live the rest of his life. We've talked a little about what he's feeling, which is very unusual for him—Ed's never been a big discusser of feelings. Opinions, yes; feelings, never. The thing is, he's not feeling very good. He envies my enthusiasm for what I'm doing. I think he'd like to be starting something new too, but he doesn't know what. Besides, he's good at what he does, and when it comes right down to it, I don't think he's willing to start over—to be a novice again.

He has stopped driving himself so hard though. He gets home much earlier than he used to and he leaves his work at the office, so that when he's home, he's really home—and believe me, that's a switch. He wants to do more things with me and the kids, which is nice. But his feelings get hurt if

I'm busy or they aren't interested. And lately, I'm always busy and they're always with their friends, so there's been a lot of tension.

I'm having some very mixed reactions to all this. I feel bad for Ed; I've never seen him so uncertain; in fact, that kind of throws me. It just doesn't square with my image of him. He's always been so definite and decisive; now I'm the decisive one. But I like the fact that he is also more open these days; he's more available to us—I don't mean just physically: he listens more. Meanwhile, here I am, feeling better about myself and more involved outside the family than I've ever been. So, what do I do? I want to be fair to Ed, but I don't want to have to give up or hold back on what I'm doing. I feel like it's my turn. It's ironic, you know? For years, the children and I wanted more from him: more time, more attention, and he was too preoccupied. Now it's just the reverse.

In many ways, Ed and Alice's story is a familiar one. It's not unusual these days for middle-aged women to be moving off in new directions, filled with the excitement of new beginnings, just when their husbands are feeling the staleness of their own lives. Nor is it unusual for the mid-life male to become more aware of the expressive, vulnerable, nurturing parts of his personality, to be more conscious of his feelings, at about the time his wife begins to experience the strong, independent parts of her personality.[1] As they move beyond the most traditional definitions of "masculinity" and "femininity," they become more *androgynous.* This move toward androgyny is, in part, a function of our continuing development as adults, and in part, a response to the changing demands of our roles at mid-life, changes that free us to develop other parts of our personality.

When this pattern begins to emerge in a marriage, however, it can cause confusion and anger. There is a shift in the balance of the relationship: where is his passive helpmate? Where is her strong father/lover? If the changes are not congruent, there may be a struggle of sorts, with one partner, perhaps, wishing to realign the relationship, redefine the roles, while the other wants things to remain the way they are—or were.

But while such change brings with it the possibility of stress and conflict, it brings as well the potential for growth and movement in a relationship. Becoming more androgynous does not mean a *giving up* of anything, but a *taking on,* an increasing of one's capacity to be a fully functioning human being who has more to bring to a marriage. And that can be particularly important in the middle years as children are growing up and separating and we face the prospect of living alone together again.

Indeed, that prospect had caused a number of women we talked with to become much more thoughtful about what their marriages have to offer. "I really wonder how it will be when the kids are gone," several said. "Will I have anything to say to him or him to me?"

While some couples had discovered that the departure of children left them with no common ground, many more women told us that their marital relationship had improved. Attention and energy long siphoned off on meeting the needs of children were now redirected at enjoying one another. There have, in fact, been some studies suggesting that while marital happiness drops to a low point during the middle years of marriage when children reach their teens and begin to separate, "for couples who do not divorce, happiness increases after the children leave."[2] "It's such a pleasure with just the two of us here," said one woman a few months after her youngest child left for college. "Our conversation isn't interrupted; our thoughts aren't interrupted. We just kind of do things to suit ourselves. I hadn't even realized how much of the tension between us had to do with the children. We seem to have such a nice relationship now. In that respect, I'm happier and more content than I've ever been."

The "postparental" years of marriage are—or soon become—the preretirement years as well. Indeed, impending retirement was an issue that came up in a number of our interviews, sometimes as an event eagerly anticipated, sometimes with outright dread. There are, of course, practical problems to be faced with retirement, such as having to live on a fixed income in an inflationary economy. But in terms of the relationship itself, concerns most frequently expressed centered around wondering how *his* retirement would affect *her* life. ("I married him for better or worse, but *not* for lunch.") What would it be like to be together all the time? How could she help him feel good about himself in his retirement years?

One very active fifty-four-year-old woman told us:

> My husband's going to retire in August and I don't know how that's going to work out. I'm beginning to feel a little edgy. I'm afraid he's just going to hang around around the house reading and watching television, which would drive me up the wall! I love our togetherness in the evening, but not all day *and* all evening. That's too much for me. And he's uptight about it too, because he doesn't know how it's going to work out either. He's had so many people tell him: "Don't retire—you go downhill and everybody dies when they retire." So he's afraid of it, and at the same time, he wants to do it, because after thirty years on this job, he's had enough. So we're both at this uneasy stage.

Women who begin careers or pursue new interests once their children are grown often fear that their husband's retirement will force them to stop. Since women have traditionally married men older than themselves, there may be the out of sync feeling that *he* is winding down while *she* is still revving up. Sometimes this is coupled with the concern that the retired husband will surely need a lot of attention: "I'll have to make sure he keeps busy and still feels important," said one woman. "Over the years, his work has been his life. He hasn't developed that many close friends, and how much golf can you play? I'm afraid the transition to retirement is going to be hard on him."

In those marriages where the husband has interests apart from work, wives are understandably more optimistic about retirement. In fact, when health and finances are not severely limiting factors, the retirement years are often anticipated as a time to try new things, travel, and enjoy life together. The basic issue facing couples seems to be the need to negotiate once again a comfortable balance between togetherness and maintaining separate lives.

Grace and her husband Jim are fifty and fifty-five respectively. Since Jim is self-employed, the exact date of his retirement—or, for that matter, whether he chooses to retire at all—is up to him. Nevertheless, they find that they are "beginning to look forward to having a little more time off and doing things together." Yet Grace is aware that she and Jim have very different interests:

> Jim's an introspective, intellectual person. He enjoys sitting and reading; I'm a much more active, doing kind of person. We've always complemented each other in these respects, and we've learned to accommodate to each other's differences to a great extent. There comes a point, though, when you think: "we enjoy such different kinds of things, what sorts of things are we going to enjoy doing together when we have all that time?"
>
> We do love to travel; we get the same great joy out of wandering around different places. Sometimes we'll just take off for the day and poke around in the country, or wander around the city exploring

neighborhoods. Jim's never been able to do anything really active because of physical limitations but one hobby he's always had is photography. I've never done more than take snapshots, but I decided this year I would learn something about it. So I'm taking a course in photography at night school. Jim enjoys it so much that I figured maybe if I knew something about what I'm doing and what he's doing, I'd have more interest in it, and hopefully, that would be another thing we'd really enjoy doing together. I realize it's just one little thing; we're not going to spend our twilight years constantly snapping pictures, but it's a start.

I think it's important to plan for both things: the things you continue to do independently, and the things you do together.

The planning process, she feels, is sometimes a conscious one, and sometimes not. After so many years together, she says, "we're both very much aware of the kind of people we are. I guess there's always the possibility there may be too much togetherness at a time, but if we stay aware of each other's needs, we should be able to maintain a good balance."

For Dick and Betty of Los Angeles, the retirement years are an extension of the way of life they've shared for many years. Betty wrote to us:

I'm sixty-seven and Dick is sixty-eight. We were in our mid-thirties when we married. Both of us worked in civil service jobs most of our lives. For us, there was no worrying about being in one another's way after retirement. Rather, we couldn't wait for the blessed day to come. Seems we talked about it all our married life. We longed for freedom from routine, freedom from the alarm clock. Our lives were leading up to the day we could belong to ourselves. We retired at the same time: I was sixty; Dick was sixty-one.

We find that we're doing much the same things now we had done before retirement, only having more time to do them in. We love the symphony and the opera, and see as many plays and good movies as we can. We've always liked the out-of-doors, hiking and camping. Since we live within walking distance from Griffith Park with its fifty miles of trails, we're among the regulars who walk there nearly every day. We're on the trail at 7:30 A.M., then come back at around 9:30 A.M. for breakfast. Dick has a small workshop on the premises where he putters. He likes to work in wood, and will repair anything—or at least try to repair anything. I carry on an active correspondence, read, bake, cook, and do some volunteer work. We visit an elderly woman in a convalescent home once a week, sneaking in a little lox and cream cheese sandwich for her whenever we go. We have friends in for a meal on the average of twice a week, and in turn, are asked out frequently. Our friends range in age from thirties to seventies.

We had our differences when we worked, and we have them now. But we've never had an upset that seriously threatened our marriage. I think planning ahead, having a busy calendar—something to look forward to—contributes to our well-being. Although our life together is full, it's by no means frantic. We have lots of books and recordings, and find time to read and to listen and to be quiet. We're fairly relaxed about finances, having always had enough to satisfy our modest needs. We live on a fixed income. We buy only what we need when we need it, have no credit cards, and owe no one. We respect one another's privacy. We're not given to analyzing one another or to criticism; we know how much we need each other. I guess we've created what might be called a comfortable relationship, as well as a full life with many interests.

Betty and Dick, like all the other couples in this chapter, share a long history together. However, many women find themselves beginning new relationships in the middle years. Despite the unequal ratio of older women to older men, a significant number of middle-aged women do marry—or remarry—with varying degrees of success. Women we spoke to who had been divorced often felt they were more tolerant, more realistic in their expectations, or simply less willing to fail the second time around. Some widows said they found remarriage difficult; there was a temptation to idealize the relationship with the former husband and to make constant comparisons. On the other hand, they felt they were lucky to have companionship again, "to be a couple in this Noah's Ark society," as one put it. A fifty-six-year-old widow who remarried after two years on her own freely admitted that her decision to do so was "a pragmatic one. Harry's a nice guy. It's not ideal but it's better than growing old alone, and he provides me with a security and stability I never had in all the years of my first marriage."

"Practicality," "companionship," and "security" were three recurring themes when women discussed late (or re-) marriage. But so was the feeling that they entered the marriage with a great deal more to offer than they had had as young women. A fifty-one-year-old woman who had been divorced, then widowed, and was about to enter her third marriage put it this way:

> Okay, so I'm not as thin and pretty as I was the first time I got married at twenty-one. But I sure do know a whole lot more about life and sex and being

a wife. I have more compassion and patience and just plain good sense.

We also spoke with women who described remarriages that far exceeded any hopes or expectations. They were finding in their middle years a happiness they had not thought possible for themselves. Eleanor (fifty-eight) and David (fifty-seven) have been married for two years now. They both unabashedly announce that they've never been happier in their lives, and their pleasure in one another is apparent when you spend a few hours with them. Eleanor had been a widow for several years when she met David, who was divorced, at a town meeting:

> I've often thought that if I had met him when we were both in our twenties, we probably would have had nothing to do with each other. He's Jewish and from New York, and I'm Protestant, and from a small town in western Massachusetts. When I was younger, my horizons were much more limited. Where a man came from and who his family was seemed very important. Of course, it was a different era, too. But I just wasn't open to people outside my own little world. I married my cousin's next-door neighbor.
>
> In my first marriage, I led a very constrained life. My husband was an insurance salesman and knew everyone in town; I was the "good mama"—a class mother, PTA officer, and den mother. We were both active in our church, and spent most of our social life with people who were just like us. On the surface, everything was just fine; we were pillars of the community. We didn't fight much, but then, we didn't talk much either. And sex, right from the beginning, wasn't too great. All those years, I didn't think too much about it though. I figured that's just how things were.

My life with David is very different from that. In fact, he's *so* different, I thought it might be hard to adjust to such a contrast. But it wasn't; it was so welcome! With him, I've discovered a part of myself I didn't even know existed. We talk and talk, not just about issues and tasks, but also about our perceptions and our feelings, about our disappointments and dreams. And we're very free physically. We dance together—we try all kinds of dancing. At first, I felt a little self-conscious, you know, "at *my* age," I'd think to myself. But after a while I enjoyed it so much that my inhibitions disappeared. And the sexual part of my life is better than it ever was before. There's sensuality and fun —it's wonderful. We give each other massages—they do wonders for aching backs, as well as being a beautiful way to give and receive tenderness. Our active sex life also makes me feel good—physically and emotionally. There just really haven't been any major problems at all.

In the beginning I did worry about how all our children (his three, my four) would adjust to our marriage, even though they're all grown. But that's worked out well too. My children seem to rely on David a lot. So many people think of step families as being a problem, but they can also turn out to be extended families. At least that's what's happened with us.

David and I love to explore new places together. This summer, we took our first trip to Europe. We bumbled through conversations with waiters and bus drivers in our high school Spanish and French of forty years ago. We walked till our feet ached and tasted foods that by all expectations should have sent us to the Alka-Seltzer, but didn't. We laugh and have fun together and care for each other. I'm in love in a way I never have been before.

Part of the romance and excitement of it all is no doubt because Eleanor's marriage is still fairly "new." There is still a sense of discovery, of pleasure at having found one another and just being together. These are feelings many women would envy as they cast a critical glance at the "old shoe" comfort of their own relationships. But when the glance lingers, when women in the middle years thoughtfully assess their marriages, there is also likely to be a sense of appreciation for the stability and continuity the relationship provides. Despite the soaring divorce rate, despite all the highs and lows and the change we go through—internal, external, and social—marriage remains, for the vast majority, the preferred way to live.[3] It acts, as psychologist Judith Bardwick has put it, as a "primary existential anchor" in our lives.[4] Yet it need never be static. It can respond to change by changing itself, by deepening and growing as we do.

9 Letting Go: Relationships with Children

She is ten years old and he is thirteen, and they are whispering in the corners of our lives.

"What do you want for Christmas?" they finally ask, counting off in their heads the small amounts of allowances and baby-sitting monies stashed away in desk drawers.

What we want, of course, is that she remain ten years old forever, with her skin and hair the colors of a Renoir painting, with a mind always at work; with her sense of justice and equality, her total love of anything four-footed, and a deep, abiding concern for all whales; the way she scrambles an egg, shoots a basket, sings "My Old Kentucky Home"; the way she totally immerses herself in the lives of Jo March, Black Beauty, Bilbo Baggins and Anne Frank, and all the real people who fill the spaces of her life.

And that he remain forever a brand-new teenager, a whirling dervish of hair, teeth, shirttails and shoelaces, crumpled, crooked, undone and untied; with huge, dark eyes behind smudged aviator glasses or bird-watching binoculars; the way he plays a jazz piano even before breakfast; the way he builds a fire, sights a red-tailed hawk, and catches a baseball; his addiction to orange juice and seltzer, J.R.R. Tolkien, fishing poles and moo-shoo pork.

Or that if they insist on growing up, that their dreams come true . . . that she be toasted at author's parties, be very slender, and live by the ocean with a horse and a parakeet and practice veterinary medicine on the side; that he and his friend, famous ornithologists, live in a hand-hewn cabin in the woods and always be allowed to wear dungarees.[1]

Perhaps one of the most important qualifications for being a parent is knowing how to let go. Almost before we know it, our infant becomes a toddler, our preschooler a full-time student, the child who needed us an adolescent who frequently only tolerates us . . . until the nest is empty. Learning to release our children is one of the tasks we face as we—and they—grow older.

The process is a gradual one; we wean ourselves from one another in stages, often with a shock of awareness at the passage of time. We watch our youngest march independently off to first grade, touched by her earnestness, but startled by how grown up she suddenly seems. Our son gets his driver's license; we remember so vividly the day we got our own. Until that moment, it hadn't seemed like very long ago. We tingle with pride as our eldest receives her college diploma, all the while marveling that *we* actually have a child old enough to graduate from college!

We feel so many different things as we watch our children grow and change: there is excitement, loss, fear, relief, awe, envy; our feelings run the gamut from intense pride and love to equally intense disappointment and anger, sometimes in the same day. The difficult stages in their development seem interminable; the easier ones fly by. It's not unusual to wish we could freeze them at a stage, only to find that we enjoy them even more at the next. Perhaps no other relationship can evoke such powerful emotions, give such pleasure, or inflict such pain; no other that tempts us to become so enmeshed that we find it hard to separate their successes and failures from our own.

And so the process of letting go evokes conflicting feelings. Often we're glad to leave behind certain tasks of early child-rearing. We've had enough of toilet training, car-pooling, and being at the mercy of baby-sitters. As our children get older, we find that they are more interesting companions; it's exciting to watch them emerge as people, gaining knowledge, and developing skills. Moreover, their growing independence means more freedom for us, more opportunity to pursue our own interests and careers. But it may also mean the loss of a certain closeness, a participation in their lives, even a physical contact that we desire. "There are all those bumper stickers reading, 'Have you hugged your kids today?'" one woman said wistfully. "There ought to be one that says, 'Have you hugged your *mother* today?'" It's not the growing *up* some of us mind as much as the growing *away*.

And yet it is inevitable that our children will begin to grow away from us as they move into the outside world. We realize that learning to be independent is vital to their development; we're here to launch them, not hold onto them. Nevertheless, the process of letting go is often difficult and uneven. We find that we must continually redefine the ways in which we relate to our children. As they leave early childhood behind, we can't "kiss it and make it better" anymore; we can't protect them from the world. But along the way, we share very special times together, when both we and our children sense that they are changing, and that our relationship is changing as well. A thirty-eight-year-old woman wrote:

There are certain moments that touch me; they're often inconsequential—little things that make a big impact and leave me feeling as though I want to laugh and cry at the same time. Like when my seven-year-old daughter came to me in tears a few weeks after Christmas. She had found "Santa's wrapping paper" tucked away in the back of a closet, and all the suspicions she'd been trying so hard to ignore finally got the best of her. She threw her arms around me and sobbed, "First I found out you were the Tooth Fairy. Now I know you and Daddy are Santa Claus, and I have nothing left to believe in but the Easter Bunny!" She was *almost* ready to give up the magic. I realized I was as reluctant to see it happen as she was.

A few nights later, my eleven-year-old son came into my room long after he was supposed to be in bed. He told me he *had* to talk to me. Then with great seriousness he launched into a monologue about how he felt "stuck—stuck between being a kid and being a teenager." He told me that a lot of things he used to like to do, like play with toy cars and go sledding and watch football on TV, seemed boring all of a sudden. He asked if I'd noticed that he was "into" music more. When I assured him that I had, he immediately wanted reassurance that rock music was something *teenagers* liked. We talked for a while about school and his friends. Then suddenly he unleashed a barrage of questions: "What else do teenagers do? What did you do when you were a teenager? Is it scary to ask someone out on a date? (Clearly he didn't know the rules of the 1950's, or he would have saved that question for his father.) How long do you feel stuck in between like this?"

I was touched by his earnestness and his trust in me. And, as we continued to talk, I was flooded with memories of my own adolescence and the knowledge that this was just the beginning for him—of pain and adventure and confusion and growing. I was moved by his sensitivity and his attempt to understand himself. We hugged each other, and for that instant, he still seemed very much a little boy. I walked back into his room with him and tucked him in. As I leaned over to kiss him good night, he said, "I know I'm changing and I'm not sure what it is, but it doesn't feel good and it helps to talk about it. But don't worry, Mom. I think it's going to turn out all right." It was one of those moments. . . .

By the time our children are teenagers, they have begun to separate from us physically and emotionally. Whereas they once made constant demands on us, they now have lives that are very much their own. They are often critical of us, even embarrassed by us. As one woman struggling with her oldest child's entrance into adolescence put it:

About half of my fourteen-year-old daughter's communication with me these days consists of "Oh, Mother!" delivered in tones of ringing disdain. I think if she had her way, I would be mute and invisible in the presence of her friends, and some of the rest of the time too. I have to laugh, though, because I can remember feeling exactly the same way about *my* mother when I was her age. Nearly everything mother did embarrassed me. I wanted her to wear dowdy gray tweed suits like my boyfriend's mother, and melt into the woodwork. Once, in one of our fleeting moments of real contact and communication, I shared that with my daughter, and we laughed about it together. She obviously recognized the sentiments, and she knew I had her number. But, of course, it didn't really change anything.

Sometimes she's like a little girl, and other times, she's very grown up; the hard part is figuring out from day to day *where* she is and how to treat her. Occasionally she'll come and confide in me like she used to, and then, bang! the door slams shut. I'm "Oh, Mother!" and she's off in her own world again, a world I'm obviously considered incapable of understanding. There's a terrible irony in that, you know. I used to have to hear blow-by-blow descriptions of "Show and Tell" and what happened on the playground. Now that her stories are really getting interesting, I rarely hear anything! I know it's all part of a phase she's going through, but I do miss the closeness we used to have.

Understanding our children's changing behavior in terms of the "phases" or developmental stages they are going through, and recognizing their need to form their own identity and break away, can help us keep a perspective on the changes in the relationship. Another woman had this to say about her middle child, a sixteen-year-old son:

He is often closed and secretive, but that's okay; it's normal for someone his age. Besides, I don't need to have him share with me all the time. I'm willing for him to have his privacy. In fact, I don't particularly *want* to hear it all. I know he sometimes does things I wouldn't approve of, and I also know it's healthy for him to experiment and learn to take responsibility for himself. If he needs me, I'll be here. But I have a lot of confidence in him, and I've decided I'd just as soon *not* know a lot

of things that are going on, since I can't control
them anyway.

It is certainly true, as this mother points out, that we
exercise decreasing control over our children's behavior
and choices as they grow older. As teenagers, they are
faced with decisions about sex, drinking, drugs, educational and career choices—all of which can profoundly
affect their lives. Our authority becomes less as the stakes
get higher. What should our role be? How much should we
try to influence them? Do we really know what's best for
them? Our almost fierce desire to protect is mixed with an
equally fierce desire to know they can make it on their
own, that they can survive. "They have to make mistakes,
they have to learn the hard way," we tell ourselves, at the
same time afraid they will close doors that can never be
reopened, or make mistakes that will be devastating. What
limits should we set? How much can we let ourselves trust
them? Nearly all parents wrestle with these issues over
and over again as their children move toward adulthood.
    And frequently, our children don't know themselves
how much direction they still want. As they swing back
and forth between behaving like the children they were
and the young adults they are becoming, they vacillate as
well in what they need from us as parents. At one moment
our rules are no more than reasons for rebellion, a chance
to test us—and themselves. Other times, our children seem
perfectly comfortable, even relieved, that we have set certain limitations. What we may overlook—or fail to clarify
—is that often the rules are for our own peace of mind, our
own needs as parents, which are just as legitimate as our
children's. A divorced mother of three teenagers told us:

> I set a curfew for my kids; they have to be in by
> one on weekends, earlier on weeknights. And that
> curfew is as much for me as for them—I make that
> very clear. I don't sleep well until they're in. If for

some reason they're going to be late, I expect them to call and let me know when they'll be home. The rules aren't because I don't trust them, but because I need to know they're safe. And they understand that.

We may find, as our children mature, that their values differ from our own—to our dismay or bewilderment or admiration. They may be involved in activities we consider "immoral" or "inappropriate," or they may simply cease doing something we hoped they would always continue. One woman with five children talked about the three who no longer attended church:

> It's hard for me to accept that they don't choose to go any more. It makes me sad. It's helped me so much to have a good relationship with God. I'd like them to have that too. I never insisted that they go to church after they graduated from high school. One son says, "It doesn't mean anything to me. If it ever does, I'll go." But I wonder how they'll ever know what they're missing? I don't love them any less because of it. I don't even worry about it. I'm just so sorry they don't have what I have.

A number of women we interviewed described children whose life-styles were radically different from their own; often they respected their children's choices but were concerned about the long-range implications. ("It's all very well for him to be an usher at Radio City Music Hall *now,* but where will that leave him ten years from now?") The urge to see our children settled and safe—or, in some cases, not settling too soon for something too safe—is a powerful one for many parents. Underlying it, of course, is the whole issue of separating our own values and goals from those of our children. We can tell ourselves rationally that they are completely separate individuals who have to lead their own lives, and that times have changed since we were their age. Still, it is difficult as they grow older not to see ourselves in them. And it is just as difficult not to feel that their behavior reflects on us. If they are "successful," then we must have been "good" mothers; if they fail, then surely the failure is also our own.

The issue may be even more complicated if we feel that our children are challenging our values at a time when we, at mid-life, are questioning them ourselves; when we are wondering what's next, and what's important, and whether we have made the right decisions; when, in short, we are feeling very much like adolescents ourselves, and even seem to be facing some of the same developmental issues (changing bodies and sexuality, a changing sense of our own identity). As one fifty-year-old woman told us, "The last few years have been a real time of change for me. A lot of my energy has gone into my own development. I used to know it all, to be so darn sure about things. Now I'm questioning everything, including my parenting . . . and so are my kids."

And then, at some point in our middle years, the end of active parenting is upon us. Some mothers look forward to it eagerly; they are more than ready to move on to the next stage in their lives. For others, the thought of children leaving for good, establishing homes of their own, perhaps in other cities, is dismaying. It marks the end of the most important phase in the mothering role, a role very central to their identity. But most women seem to have somewhat mixed feelings about the idea of children departing: there is relief and the anticipation of new freedom, coupled with some sense of sadness and loss.

There has been some research indicating that the most difficult time for women is when the departure of children comes close, when it is "anticipated, but not yet realized."[2] However, the actual transition to this new "postparental" stage of life is often faster and easier than we might expect. Sociologist Lillian Rubin feels that the "empty nest" syndrome, the notion that women are plunged into depression when their children leave, is a myth, "a fabrication based on the one-sided and distorted view of women and womanhood; a view that insists that womanhood and motherhood are synonymous, that motherhood is a woman's ineluctable destiny, her sacred calling, her single area of fulfillment."[3] If this has never been an accurate description of women, it is even less so these days when so many women are moving out of traditional roles, combining motherhood with other activities, and seizing new opportunities.

Rubin studied 160 middle-aged women (average age forty-six) and found that nearly all of them responded "to the departure of their children, whether actual or impending, with a decided sense of relief."[4] The departure may be more traumatic when there is conflict or disappointment with a child, since the parent may be left with a sense of failure, regret, or a problem unresolved. But even under these circumstances, the women Rubin studied coped quite well, "for alongside these feelings there exists another powerful set of needs and emotions that helps to neutralize the pain—the longing for freedom, the wish to find and claim a well-defined and differentiated self, and the relief that, finally, this may be possible."[5]

The overwhelming majority (82%) of women in our sample who had children expressed little or no concern about children leaving home. This held true regardless of the age of the children. A third of the women who responded to our questionnaire saw the departure of their children as one of the definite benefits of being older. If we looked only at women whose children were all over eighteen, sixty percent saw children leaving home as a benefit. Marital status was not a factor; single parents expressed neither more nor less concern than their married counterparts.

In contrast with the standard stereotypes, the so-called "empty nest" period itself is frequently a very pleasant and positive one. One mother of four who has always had a very warm, close relationship with her children described how she felt the first year all of them were living in other cities, working or going to school:

> I must say, I felt guilty at first about feeling so free. It was the most gorgeous feeling in the world not to belong to all those people. I realized that had really taken its toll. Being a parent is the most marvelous thing in the world . . . and the most exhausting. It takes everything you've got. So it was great in many ways: my husband and I ate good things we couldn't afford for six but could afford for two. We went places, we did things. We rediscovered each other. It was wonderful.

A year later, however, two of this woman's children returned home to live, a pattern that is not at all unusual these days. Leave-taking is often a gradual, off-again-on-again process. Children come back periodically for vacations or visits, or decide to live at home again for a time. Just as we've begun to accustom ourselves to our renewed privacy and freedom, they return. We may discover at this point that there is a discrepancy in our expectations for the relationship: our nearly grown children may still want nurturing and caretaking from us, but they don't want to be asked any questions or told what to do. We, on the other hand, may want the companionship and contact; we want to stay close with our children, but without remaining in the caretaking role.

> My older daughter graduated from college and lived in another city for a couple of years. Then she moved back to Denver, and wanted to stay at home for a couple of weeks until she found an apartment and a job. And that was fine with me, only the "few weeks" stretched into several months. We'd had a

marvelous relationship during the time she was away, but as soon as she moved back into the house, she just became a teenager again. She expected me to take care of her again in many ways. She didn't take responsibility for things that I thought she should. We did talk about it; she knew it was happening. She said she could see it, and didn't like it, but couldn't control it. She just felt like a little girl again. And a lot of bad feeling toward me came back. And we had to deal with all kinds of sibling rivalries all over again. It was miserable. We finally decided after a few months that she just had to move out.

Bernice Neugarten has pointed out that the empty nest is not usually a problem when it occurs on time, but rather when it does *not* occur as expected.[6] Indeed, we talked to more women in their middle years who were distressed about the nest being full rather than empty.

Women who were upset about children leaving, however, often had not distinguished between the feelings they had about their children no longer being with them, and their concerns about who they were and what they would do with themselves once their children were gone. Although the two are obviously bound up together, one is a *relationship* issue, the other an issue of *role loss*. Psychologist Pauline Bart points out that the women most disturbed by the empty nest tend to be mainly those "who have no meaningful occupation or identity other than 'Mother.' "[7] Since the average woman now retires from the mothering role with some two-fifths of her life before her,[8] it is important to learn to look elsewhere for satisfaction in the second half of life, to plan for and take advantage of all the new opportunities available to middle-aged women today.

It is also true, however, that some women are quite content to remain in the role of wife and mother even after their children leave home. They continue to feel of value and to find satisfaction in their relationships and lifestyle. Others, meanwhile, are involved in careers and a whole variety of activities outside the home, and still feel the departure of their children very deeply. Indeed, while relatively few women experience more than short-term dismay when their children leave, those who do are likely to feel it very keenly, regardless of what else they are doing in their lives.

"I'm really having a hard time with the empty-nest bit," a fifty-three-year-old woman told us. She went on to describe a rich, full life, teaching, going to school, exploring new interests, participating in church and community work. One of her biggest complaints was not having enough time to do all the things she liked to do. And yet, busy as she was, she felt a big gap in her life. She very much wanted more contact with her grown sons, both in their twenties:

> One's in Texas and one's here in town. They don't call or write me very often, and that's *very* hard. It hurts; it really hurts. Sometimes I get down in the dumps and I ask myself a lot of dumb questions about why they don't stay in touch more. I have to keep reminding myself of how wrapped up they are in their own lives. Once in a while, when I'm really low, I begin thinking, "They don't know I'm around anymore, they have forgotten me." I feel I was such a good mother, why don't they reach out more? I'm still working that out; I'm not over it by a long way. No matter how I rationalize it, it's still hard.

When we talked to this woman a year later, she reported that her relationship with her sons was much improved, and that there was much more contact initiated by them. "If I had to speculate about why that changed," she said, "my guess would be that they are now more established in their own lives, and contact with me isn't as threatening to their sense of independence."

The issue, as this woman illustrates, is not just how we feel about our children leaving, but the quality of the relationship in the years that follow. We are likely to know our offspring longer as adults than we did as children. Whether they live at home or far away, whether they are settled in jobs or marriages, or moving around, continuing to try out roles and develop their own identities, it remains for us to establish a relationship appropriate for now: not just as parent and child, but as adults, human beings, and friends; to find a workable balance of involvement in one another's lives; to interact in a caring way, and yet allow each other separateness and independence.

Developing a comfortable relationship with our grown children can be a source of tremendous pleasure and satisfaction. It is not always easy, however, nor will it necessarily remain the same over time. So many variables can be involved: Our differing needs and expectations for the relationship at any given point; the satisfaction each of us is experiencing in other areas of our lives; health, finances, proximity; our ability to accept the other's life-style and choices. We don't ever completely stop being parents to our children. It always seems to creep into the relationship on our part or theirs. A fifty-two-year-old woman from Detroit, the mother of four grown children, wrote this to us:

It's still a surprise for me to realize that the children I nursed through infancy and childhood bruises, through adolescent conflicts and sophomore growing pains really no longer need "parenting." But the surprise certainly is not the result of any sudden change that came upon me unawares. After all, we did it; we raised our children and helped them to become independent adults. The surprise is that this monumental endeavor is complete; that we will never again face such a lengthy, serious, and consuming task. But the relationships that developed while they were growing up have left a most remarkable bond between us.

There is no explaining that bond to someone who has not experienced it. But I often discuss it with friends who also have grown children, and then the emotions we feel are so universal that the briefest hint can bring about complete understanding. You see it all the time when grandmothers exchange pictures. Certainly there is an element of competition in this, but more often, there is shared awareness of one of life's miracles.

As the mother of adult children, joy and pain flood through me with amazing regularity. Whatever happens to them affects me intensely. No achievement of my own could possibly bring me the same sense of pride as watching my child graduate from professional school. No physical pain I suffer can possibly match my anguish at watching one of my children being wheeled to surgery. For my husband and me, the days of standing at the door of a sleeping child's room are gone, but the shared pleasure of coming home and finding that a chore has been done by a grown child who stopped in for a while in the afternoon is equally sweet. The look we share across a room while a child impresses a guest brings the same warm feeling when that child is twenty-five as it did when he was seven.

Perhaps the most gratifying facet of the relationship with my grown children is an intellectual one. How nice to discuss art or history, music or sports with people whose interest in these things I fostered! What a warm sense of pride I feel when I discover that their interest and knowledge have grown and surpassed my own—that the roles can shift pleasantly, and I can learn from them. For me, this is what parenting is all about. It is one of life's consummate pleasures.

Pleasure, however, is not the only emotion my adult children stimulate. Three of them live in other cities, one quite far away. It hurts to see children so seldom that both we and they are taken aback by the changes in each other's appearances. The mobility of modern life provides so many opportunities for young adults, and, like most parents, I want my children to have those opportunities. But the genuine excitement and delight I feel for them is tinged with a sense of loss.

I think the single most difficult aspect of having grown children is watching them face danger. I don't care what the source of danger is: a shaky marriage, a career setback, illness—a child in trouble arouses the most incredible pain. The first inkling of difficulty hits with a wallop! Then maybe it recedes to an ache when I get caught up in the demands of the day, but it never vanishes completely. The long habit of involvement in the lives of my children is hard to break, especially when trouble looms. But now that they are grown, I often feel that all I can do is offer support. And even that can be given only when a child wants it. Sometimes I feel helpless and acutely aware of the movement of the relationship from one in which I had an enormous amount of control to one in which I must have an enormous amount of patience and acceptance.

But the pleasures I derive from my grown children outweigh the pains, and the pains make the joys more precious. Having raised four children successfully is a major accomplishment, the kind that makes me feel wise and knowing. And that's nice, even if it is mostly the work of longevity. And now that they *are* grown, my husband and I can enjoy a freedom that was never possible when they were young. The bond will never lessen; my emotions will always be tied to those four adults, but now, after all these years, I have more time for me and my husband. It is hard earned time and very special.

10 "A Daughter's a Daughter All of Her Life": Relationships with Parents

I talk to my parents practically every day," a forty-four-year-old woman from Illinois told us.

They still give me plenty of advice, but now there are also lots of things they need me to do for them, things they can't manage for themselves so easily anymore. I feel for my parents, I really do. They're always talking about how they don't want to be a burden on anyone. And yet, they expect so much of me. "We don't see you enough," they'll say after I've spent the afternoon driving them somewhere. "Can't you spend a little more time with us? We won't be here forever." I feel as though no matter what I've done or how pleasantly I've tried to do it, I haven't quite gotten it right or done enough. It's sad—but it's also very difficult.

And at the same time, I have my children making demands on me. They're not little kids anymore, but they still need emotional support and financial support. They still want my time and attention and for the house to be run the way it always has been. My husband comes home at night and he wants dinner on the table, a nice, calm house, no problems. I love my parents; I love my children and my husband, and I want to do things for them. But sometimes, I—my feelings, my work—get totally squeezed out.

As the generation in the middle, we are often caught between the needs of our children and those of our parents, trying to adjust to changes in both relationships. We may be more competent, more able to cope with things than ever before. Still, if we find ourselves in the position of caring for two generations while trying to manage our own lives in the bargain, that can be a lot to handle. One divorced woman summed it up very graphically when she said:

> I feel like I'm a battery that's discharging all the time. There's all this energy flowing out toward taking care of everything and everybody else. And there's nowhere to go to get myself recharged. I used to go to my parents for comfort and support and help. Now it's usually the other way around.

However, if being the generation in the middle is sometimes draining, it can also be a source of great pleasure. A thirty-nine-year-old woman wrote:

> There are many times when I really treasure the feeling of being surrounded by both my parents and my children. For instance, I love it when my parents come to visit us on Thanksgiving. It gives me a great sense of continuity, a sense of being a link between the generations in a very positive way. And my parents get such a kick out of being here,

out of seeing me settled and happy. They really enjoy the children, and the children enjoy them. I love watching my mother play the same card games with them that my grandmother used to play with me. (How I admire her patience!) I love hearing my father talk football with my son. He always missed having a son of his own, and they have a very special relationship. I'm willing to admit there might be some tension if we lived in the same city. But as it is, it really makes me feel good to be able to give pleasure to these people who have given me so much, just by sharing what I have.

The relationship we have with our parents evolves fairly predictably from one in which they take care of us, to one in which we interact as adults, to one in which we are increasingly likely to be called upon to care for them, to be the stronger figure in the relationship. As we move gradually from one stage to the next, it is not uncommon for us and our parents to feel a certain amount of reluctance about letting go of old roles and old ways of viewing each other.

A number of women talked about remaining in some sense their parents' "little girl" long after they had become parents themselves. A thirty-seven-year-old woman expressed her own rather mixed feelings about it like this:

In some ways, I'm still my parents' little girl. And there are times when that feels just fine, when it's nice to have someone wondering how *I* am, and wanting to look out for *me*. Of course, there are other times when I'm really annoyed by it, when I appreciate their concern, but I don't want to be treated like a child, or as though I don't have good sense. My parents are wonderful people who have my best interests at heart, but sometimes I have to remind myself that they don't automatically know more than I do about what's best for me. I guess part of me wants them to give me credit for having grown up, and part of me wishes I could still see them in a protective, omnipotent role.

That's not the whole relationship though. My parents lead a busy life and so do we. But every once in a while, the four of us—my husband, my parents and I—make it a point to do something fun together: go to a movie or play tennis and have dinner. Or sometimes we'll just sit around and reminisce, talk about what I was like when I was my daughter's age, or tell old family stories. And that's very special to me: the fact that we share a lot and can enjoy one another as people, that we can be friends. It's true that they initiate most of it, but it's not just something we *have* to do; we really like being with them. We don't have any rigid schedules for being together—like dinner every Sunday or something—none of us would like that. Instead, we stop by to see them occasionally, or they come by our house—mainly to see the kids—when they feel like it. And we talk fairly often on the phone. Our relationship is relaxed and pleasant . . . *most* of the time. I suppose that "little girl" business is really as much something I make of the relationship as something they do to me. Actually, they manage to be both parents *and* friends. I hope we can do that with our kids.

As adults, we are, of course, likely to get along best with our parents when both we and they are healthy, independent, and involved in lives of our own. As the average life-expectancy increases, and people remain healthy and active longer, the period of time during which we can interact on an adult-adult basis lengthens. However, just as we don't completely stop being parents to our children, few of us ever completely relinquish the role of child with our parents. In their presence, we may find ourselves reverting to old ways of behaving; we are surprised by the vigor with which childhood feelings and resentments persist. A very successful career woman in her mid-forties described how, on annual visits with her mother, "it usually takes about half an hour for me to regress to age twelve. It astonishes me; it amuses me; I guess it even comforts me. I don't know if I fall into it because we never learned to relate to one another any other way, or because it gives each of us something we want: I feel taken care of; she feels needed. But honestly! If the people who work for me ever heard my mother telling me to 'stand up straight!' "

While it is difficult to be objective about our parents, we do gradually come to see them as individuals, to accept that they are only human, no more perfect than ourselves. We may find that they are people we genuinely enjoy, and from whom we can gain a great deal, or we may discover that we don't really like one or both of our parents very much. We feel bound to them, obligated, deeply enmeshed in one another's lives, but we would never choose them as friends. Or, conversely, we may like them all right as people, but despair at ever having the kind of parent-child relationship we ideally want. One of the tasks of maturing is learning *not* to go to our parents for what *isn't* there, but to value and accept what the relationship does have to offer. A Chicago woman in her early forties described how, several years earlier, she had come to grips with this realization:

I've always admired my mother. She's bright and capable, and in many ways she's done a lot for me. But I've never felt that she entirely approved of me, or was pleased with what I did, or accepted me for what I was. I spent a lot of years trying to be what I thought she wanted me to be so that I could get her approval and acceptance. But it was like a carrot on a stick dangling just out of reach. Even when I did manage to please her, it always felt so conditional and temporary. She had a habit—at least with me—of picking up on the thing that wasn't okay, instead of all the things that were. You know the type: you bring home a report card that's all A's and one B, and all she says is, "How come you didn't do better in math?" And the worst part was, I always had the feeling that it was *me,* that she wasn't like that so much with other people. *I* just didn't meet her expectations. There was always just a little something wrong with my friends or with how I looked. She didn't fully approve of the man I married—naturally. You would think I would have learned by then, but that really hurt me.

I guess it was about six years ago that I went—alone—to visit my parents for a few days. They had just sold their house and had moved into an apartment. I went among other reasons to tell them that my husband Ed was leaving his job; that we were moving to Chicago, where he was going to be starting a little business of his own, and that we were all very pleased and excited about it. To my face, she was very polite, and seemed reasonably accepting about the whole thing. But later on, when we went to bed, I could hear her ranting and raving to my father. I guess she didn't realize how sound carried in that little apartment—or maybe she did. But she went on and on about what a ridiculous thing we were doing, and how could Ed be so irresponsible, and how could I allow him to do that, and so forth. Only this time, I wasn't crushed by her reaction, I was *furious!* I thought, "How can she be such a hypocrite? She has no right to criticize Ed, he's always worked hard, and is a very responsible man." I thought about going into her room and telling her what I thought, but I knew I was too angry. In retrospect, and as a parent myself, I can understand her being concerned—although I must say it didn't sound much like concern or even sadness that we were going so far away; it sounded like her usual put-down. My anger was probably way out of proportion to what she had done, but it was something that had been building up in me for years. So I got dressed and went outside to cool off, and as I walked around thinking about what I wanted to say to her, I finally realized that no matter *what* I said or did, I was just never going to get the acceptance and approval I wanted from her, and that I might as well stop trying. I had lived without it all those years, and I could go on living without it. That's just the way my mother was with me, and she wasn't going to change. I had to come to terms with that and let go. And I have. I haven't ended the relationship by any means, but I've stopped trying to make it what it isn't and never will be. I've stopped trying so hard to please her. And, oddly enough, we probably get along better now than we ever have.

A teacher in her mid-fifties, who lived most of her adult life with her mother, told us:

When I was beginning to achieve things, to gain recognition in the community, I was aware of a kind of resentment on the part of my mother. Instead of appreciating the things I was doing, it was almost as though she were jealous. I didn't understand at first how a mother could feel that way; it wasn't my concept of what a mother should be like at all. But then, a lot of things my mother did didn't fit with my concept of how a mother "should" be. It took me a long time to realize that she was just a human being who had all kinds of emotions besides the kinds I thought she should have just because she was my mother. And when I did eventually get to the point where I could accept that—I was in my forties at the time—I felt much better about the whole business. I could look at something she did that I considered not good, and not get so upset about it. I could stand up to her and fight for my right to be myself. And when she saw I was strong enough to fight for what I felt, and not be beaten down by her any more, I think that was the point at which *she* accepted *me*.

The relationship we have with our parents in our middle years is almost inevitably a complex one, rarely all good or all bad. Along with the expectations we manage to let go of, and the old feelings and needs that persist, comes a new understanding and empathy—especially for our mothers. Having established our own homes and careers, having married and had children ourselves, we have a different insight and perspective on our parents' experience. We find ourselves facing issues we remember them facing. We hear ourselves echoing their sentiments, if not their exact words. Increasingly, we see our mothers in ourselves, just as we see ourselves in our children. We catch a glimpse of her expression as we walk by a mirror. We're tempted to draw comparisons between our lifestyles, our marriages, our ability as parents, our successes and failures. ("I set out wanting to be a better parent than my mother, determined not to make the same mistakes. Now I'd settle for being half as good!") But whether we would choose to be like her or not, we carry our mothers with us. A thirty-eight-year-old woman wrote:

> My mother and I were always very close. She was lovely and warm and bright and funny. In many ways, she was my best friend. Well, no; that's not exactly true, because there wasn't anything close to

the equal give and take of friendship until the last few years of her life. I was very dependent on her; I needed her, and I think she needed me to need her. She used to talk about giving her children "uncritical love." "Nobody ever gets enough uncritical love," she'd say. She was always there for us with support and encouragement. So it was a very special relationship because she was a very special lady. But it was also hard to cut the apron strings because they were such nice strings. I'll never be as unselfish or patient or accepting a mother as she was . . . and my children will probably grow up a lot sooner because of it. In my early thirties, I still thought of her as "my mommy," for crying out loud! Talk about arrested development!

It wasn't until my mid-thirties, during the last few years of her life, that there began to be more of a give and take, that she started to open up on more of a woman-to-woman basis. She had always given of herself, but then she really started to *share,* to talk about some of the dreams she'd had; the disappointments and the unseized opportunities— and some of the moments she really treasured. She talked about things that happened when she was my age, things I could dimly remember from a child's perspective, and, at the same time, understand in a whole new way as another woman. I began to see so much more clearly why she'd given me some of the advice she had; why she had urged me to do this or warned me not to rush into that.

She'd always had such a powerful influence on my life that it was only then that I was able to see her with any objectivity at all. Oh, I had been critical enough of her as an adolescent, as all adolescents are, and I had certainly had my moments of rebellion. But this was something very different. I could accept that she had made mistakes and wasn't perfect; that she sometimes wanted for me things that she would have wanted for herself, and had transferred some of her own uncertainties onto me. None of which diminished what I felt for her one whit. I began to see that I had something to offer her, not just as her daughter, but as another adult woman—which is just as it should have been.

But as I sit here several years after her death thinking about her and about our relationship, I wonder if I really understood it this way *then,* or only *now* with the perspective of time. Did I give her anything close to what I should have given her? Did I give her what she needed—and, God knows, deserved? I'll never know. But I do know that she's still very much in my thoughts, in the way I look at life, and in the things I hear myself saying to my sister and my children. I miss her.

The empathy that we feel, however, is not exclusively for our mothers. A forty-six-year-old professional woman shared this experience:

Recently, during a very busy time in my life, my father came to visit us for a week. He tries very hard to be accommodating when he's here, and not impose, but I know he likes to spend time with me, and wishes we were closer than we are. There were a couple of times that week when I saw him sitting around talking to my husband, or reading the paper and watching TV, when my first inclination was to go off to my room and read for a while or just have some time for myself—and I'm sure I would have done that in the past, despite the fact that I had been away at work all day. But in the last year or so, I've been much more aware of my own children separating from me and not being so eager to spend time with me, which really makes me sad. And there are a lot of things about their lives I wish they'd share with me, and I know I'm not the one they want to share them with any more. And I realized that my father was in exactly the same position, only it's got to be just that much harder for him, since he sees so little of us anyway. He doesn't complain about it; in fact, he makes a conscious effort not to ask a lot of questions or make any demands, so the relationship will be a pleasant, easy one. Now I'm in a position where I can appreciate that restraint, and understand how hard it can be. So, instead of going off by myself, I'd make it a point to go in and sit down right next to him, maybe lean my head against his shoulder, and just talk for a while. It wasn't a big thing, but he was so obviously pleased and delighted when I did that it really made me feel good. Actually we both enjoyed it. It was one of the best visits we've had in years.

It can be difficult to see our parents grow old and dependent, both for their sake and our own. We resist signs of their waning powers, because their vulnerability leaves us feeling vulnerable too. One St. Louis woman said:

I don't depend on my parents in any tangible way, really. I moved away from home when I was eighteen, and haven't lived in the same city with them since. Right now, I live a thousand miles away. But the ties between us are very strong.

About six months ago, my father was in a very bad accident, and had to have emergency surgery. My mother handled all the arrangements, and stayed with my father throughout. She didn't want me to come. She felt there was nothing I could do, and coming would only be upsetting to me. It wasn't a life-or-death situation, though there were real questions about how much mobility my father would have afterwards.

I finally talked to my father several days after the surgery, and he sounded awful! So weak and out of it. It was his voice that got to me most: it's usually so deep and exuberant, and it was thin and hesitant. He sounded like an old man. I knew, of course, that when you're drugged up after surgery, you sound awful; you're incoherent and you don't remember what the hell is going on. I had surgery a few years ago, and experienced that myself. But this was my *father,* and he wasn't supposed to sound like that! Also, my father is sixty-nine years old, and I kept thinking to myself: "He'll never be the same again. He's suddenly become an old man, and I'm not ready for my father to be an old man."

To me, my father was always the Big Daddy, the one who had all the answers. We've had a very close relationship, a real sharing. Sure, I went through the usual process in growing up of discovering there was a lot Daddy didn't know and couldn't do. But even now when I'm almost forty, there is a whole lot of that old feeling left; of my father being the one I turn to for a special kind of reassurance. I only see him once or twice a year, but there has always been that comfortable feeling that he was there. I couldn't bear the thought of that coming to an end, of his being a feeble old man.

Well, as convinced as I was that he'd been permanently transformed he has recovered beautifully. His spirit is, if anything, stronger. And he still has that special way of reassuring me. A few weeks ago, after I returned from the funeral of someone who was very dear to me, my father called just to see how I was doing. He offered the usual platitudes that one says at a time like that, but it was just what I wanted to hear, and he was just the person I wanted to hear them from. It was like having him put his arms around me, and for that instant, everything was all right. It felt so good that he could still do that for me.

Of course, the day will come when he won't be able to give me that anymore. And I know now that part of me will always want it and miss it. The idea that he won't always be there is scary and sad. Perhaps on the deepest level, it makes me confront my own mortality. And this experience made me admit to myself that I wanted my father to remain healthy and vital as much for *me* as I wanted it for him.

A number of women reported that parents who were still very independent had begun wanting more attention, more fuss made over them, more evidence that their children cared and were thinking of them. Phone calls, letters, and visits had taken on an increased importance. Parents who had always been the ones to initiate contact with children began feeling hurt that their children didn't initiate more. "It's a little confusing," one woman said. "I'll be fixing dinner, and I'll get a phone call from my mother, who's upset because I haven't called her every day that week. And that's something I've never done, and have never been expected to do." It's as though parents, feeling vulnerable themselves, need some special affirmation, some reassurance that their children are there for them. Regrettably, it often comes across more as a demand or duty ("After all I've done for you . . .") than as a need, and is as likely to provoke bewildered resistance ("But *why* do I need to call you every day?") or grudging compliance as understanding.

The welfare of aging parents can eventually become a

nagging worry: Are they taking proper care of themselves? Are they lonely? Is it all right for them to continue to live on their own? Can we afford to care for them if necessary? If they live far away, we wonder whether they will ask for —or be able to get—the help they need, whether that help is financial, emotional, or takes the form of making sure there is food in the house, and someone to take them where they need to go. Surely as their children, that responsibility is ours—though we're not always proud of our reaction at being put in that position:

> When I look at my parents as they get older, I have feelings of empathy, of wanting to help, to protect them, to make things a little easier for them. But also, I feel anger. I feel: "I don't want you to get old. I don't want you to leave me. I don't want you to take up my time by being dependent on me. And I don't want you to become feeble, to stop being my parents, who I can come to even if you aren't perfect, who are between me and my old age; who are between me and death." Along with love, there are all these feelings of anger and fear and resentment. I think the anger is the hardest to deal with. My God! We're not supposed to feel that way! And then the guilt follows.

We may feel sad, impatient, even uncomfortable in the presence of elderly parents. But if our relationship with them has been a good one, it has the potential to continue to be good. There is a reservoir of positive feeling that helps us through the more difficult moments of caring for them in old age. If the relationship has been poor, it is too much to expect that it will magically improve just because our parents are older and we want to make amends, want to "get it right" with them before it's too late. We may accept the responsibility their old age imposes, but feel resentful and burdened in the process.

Some of us find that we avoid contact with aging parents as much as possible because it's difficult and threatening to accept the changes we see. We may distance ourselves from them emotionally as well as physically. Our contact with them becomes problem-oriented; that is, we see our parents mainly when something must be done for them. The effect of this can be to encourage our parents' dependence on us by reinforcing it with our attention. If they say everything is fine, we're delighted to be able to get on with our own lives; if they tell us there's a problem, we rush right over. Or, if we are very uneasy in their presence, we may find that we take on tasks they could still manage for themselves, to keep from having to be involved with them in some other way. We'd rather shop for them than sit and talk to them.

Of course, not all parents spend their later years in an advanced state of mental and physical decline; not all become needy and dependent. Only five percent of the population sixty-five and older are in institutions, such as hospitals and nursing homes. Many others need some help and support, but can live independently and are fully capable of making decisions for themselves. And quite a few remain healthy and vigorous until very late in life. A number of women described parents who were vital and active, who were still learning and growing and open to new experiences, and who were managing very well on their own. One woman wrote:

> My mother never ceases to amaze me. She's been widowed for some years, and her life has not been easy. But at seventy-five, she has more enthusiasm and energy than I do. She can still get excited about a new restaurant or an article she's read, and she can't wait to share that with other people she thinks might be interested. I turn to her often for advice and solace. I know there are times when she doesn't feel well, but she doesn't give in to it, and

rarely complains. I've watched her face crushing disappointments and see close friends and family die. And then I've seen her pick herself up and keep going: forming new friendships and involving herself in new activities. My husband and I enjoy being with her; in fact, people of all ages like being with her. I'm not saying she's perfect; she can be stubborn and opinionated, and she can talk your ear off. But whatever bitterness and remorse she feels about her life—and believe me, she's got cause—she doesn't sit around feeling sorry for herself. She keeps her life as busy and full as possible, and she enriches all of our lives. I love her, of course, but I also admire her tremendously.

A great many of us, however, have parents who have not fared as well, or who finally do reach a point where they require considerable care and attention. And with current medical techniques for prolonging life, this care can be quite long-term. We may well find ourselves dealing with problems of aging parents at the same time we have concerns about growing older ourselves. It's not unusual these days to know people in their sixties who are looking after parents in their eighties.

One of the most wrenching questions we face is what to do with parents who can no longer function independently. It can present enormous problems, emotionally, financially, and physically. In some segments of our culture, it is expected that parents will live with children when they grow old; the extended family is the norm. Others of us find that we are not at all prepared to take parents into our homes, yet we are extremely reluctant to institutionalize them. The very idea evokes such strong feelings of guilt that it is generally seen as a last resort. Nor, quite often, are our parents happy with either of these alternatives, but we may be unaware of other possibilities or unable to work out any other satisfactory arrangements for full-time care. We feel we must choose one way or the other: either they live with us, or we put them in a "home." Moreover, we know that no matter what decision is made, much of the burden for carrying it out will fall on us, since women in this society are traditionally the "kin keepers." And this is true whether the "kin" we are talking about is our own or our husband's. Dottie, age forty-two, described what happened when it became clear that her widowed mother-in-law could no longer live on her own:

My husband, Charles, never really had much of a family life. My family kind of took him in. And now Charles and I and our three children have a close family unit of our own. We spend a lot of time together, and care for each other a great deal. We've been able to build in our family what he never had as a child. Still, there has always been that void in his own background.

Charles' mother was an unhappy person who had virtually nothing to do with us. Then all of a sudden, we got a call at 5:30 one morning. I answered the phone and she said, "Let me speak to Charles." I said, "Who is this?" but all she would say was: "Let me speak to Charles!" She told him she didn't feel well, and soon after that call, she had a stroke. Charles went to Philadelphia to be with her, but before he left, we talked about what to do with her—it was obvious she wouldn't be able to live by herself. We even looked at nursing homes here in town.

I felt terrified that she would end up living with us. She was such an unpleasant person to be around, so negative. The idea of having to cope with her every day was horrifying to me. Charles had made up his mind that there was no way she was coming to live with us, but he did feel a responsibility to take care of her.

When he got to Philadelphia, he called and said, "She won't go in a nursing home. She said if we don't take her, my cousin Peter will." Well, that was the kicker; she had always favored Peter over her own son Charles. It was a classic piece of blackmail. It was like the last chance for Charles to try to get his mother's love.

Charles came home and said he wanted to bring her here to live. I understood how much his mother "had" him, and I didn't want to deny him the right to do what he felt he had to do. He kept thinking, "Now she needs me; now I'll be able to take care of her; now it will be different."

Both Charles and I had the feeling that we had invested so much time building our own family, building values and caring for each other. We felt that if we didn't take care of her, we'd be saying to the kids in effect, "Look, it's all a fraud. We're a family, but when things are unpleasant, when the chips are down, you turn your back and do what you damn please." It was a real moral dilemma. To do anything other than take her in made everything we'd done, all we'd tried to build as a family, a hypocrisy. That became the Catch-22 for us.

Anyway, Charles saw taking her in as an obligation, and I felt he needed my support. But I also felt there had to be some conditions. We agreed, first, that we'd have some meals with just the five of us; second, we'd entertain our friends without feeling obligated to include her; and third, we'd have to have private spaces and private times. And before she came, all this was made clear to her.

The children were open to her coming to live with us. They understood the situation. There was even some appeal to the idea of getting a grandmother. As for me, although I felt we were doing the right thing, part of me was screaming with rage inside. My children were twelve, fourteen, and fifteen. I had elected to stay home with them when they were small, and I had finally cut loose from that and had gotten a job. I had been starting to get some strong perceptions of myself through my colleagues as a capable person who didn't just whip up good chicken soup and bake brownies. In a very short time, I had created a viable, sound, interesting world for myself, and that was tremendously satisfying. I also saw all the time I spent with the children coming to fruition. I was really feeling good about them. My time was opening up more and more . . . and all of a sudden, I was going to be saddled with an unknown.

That's the thing about old age. It's such an unknown. With kids, you know what will happen next. The baby will get toilet trained, and will go to school by age five. A certain amount is predictable. I can look at my sixteen-year-old and know that there are only two more years that he'll be home. I have to make the most of it. But you just don't know with an old person what will happen. You have no control over that part of your life. You might have an old person living with you, not really able to care for herself, for twenty years. There are no definite time frames in old age as there are with children. I was feeling: "I've raised my children, I've put in all this time and energy, I did a good job, and I should be free now." Instead, I was getting it on the other end. I kept thinking, "Why me?"

At the same time, I felt so sorry for Charles. I decided that in fairness to him, I had to try to make him feel comfortable about what we were doing. I had to try to make the whole situation work.

Since Charles' mother did have some money, we used it to hire a housekeeper who would be a companion to her, and care for her. We also felt we needed someone on weekends so we could spend time with the kids. But even under these privileged circumstances, there were difficulties. Every day when I came home from work, the housekeeper had problems to tell me about. I was the one who was there—not Charles. Some days I just wanted to come home and have a cup of tea and be quiet. But she was always there.

I think that was one of the hardest things: There were always these other people in our lives: a visiting nurse, a therapist, a social worker. They'd come and go at all hours. I began to lose the feeling that it was my house. In certain ways, you lose control. Those are the things you never think about. All those support people make you assume the parent role. For instance, the physical therapist would say to me, "She's not making enough progress because you're not helping her." I was supposed to make her walk every day. She had decided she wouldn't walk, and here's this twenty-two-year-old physical therapist telling me off.

There also began to be some real problems with the children. My mother-in-law went through fetishes: collecting garters, safety pins. The kids wouldn't play along with it. They'd say, "She's got *thousands* of safety pins!" An adult can stand back and say, "Let's play along." My two girls just said, "She's buggy!" Only our son would play along. But then, his grandmother favored him anyway. She had a way of playing the kids off against each other and she shrewdly capitalized on his role as an ally. Our youngest child was the most hostile of the three; she felt her place as baby of the family was being usurped by Grandma.

One night we left Charles' mother with the children while we went to a dinner party. When we came back, she complained, "The kids paid no attention to me while you were gone. I asked for a drink and they didn't bring it to me." Charles got furious; he ran upstairs and woke up the kids. They said they *had* paid attention to her. I was suspicious, so the next time we went out, I told the kids, "Every time you bring her a drink, leave the glass on the radiator." Once again she complained . . . but there were seven glasses on the radiator. I said, "Look, in three hours you had seven drinks." She just turned over and went to sleep. It took some time to see through this kind of game playing.

I remember one night I came in and cleaned up her room, and tried to get her comfortable and settled for the night. Then Charles walked in and said good night, and she said to Charles, "Thank you, dear. Good night." She hadn't said a word to me. She'd look through me and thank Charles. It was a real setup.

Charles' mother also started to make constant demands on him. Her attitude was, "I want your attention and I want it now. I don't want you to pay attention to anybody else." We'd be in bed, and she'd call him in. Eventually, the sheer emotional overload got to us. The kids were becoming very disaffected by the whole thing. The whole idea of taking Grandma in and showing, "This is what we do with family" was turning ugly.

I tried to provide a way the kids could get out some of the feelings of hostility they had. My youngest wrote a poem about Grandma. In some ways, it was very bitter; we read it, we understood, and we put it up on the bulletin board. She called it "The Duchess." I thought it was important not to deny the negative feelings the kids had. I didn't want to say to them, "It will get better," because it wasn't going to. And I didn't want to say, "Well, she's old," because I didn't want to put negative connotations on being old. All old people are *not* like that.

At a certain point we felt we had to say to the children, "Look, you have resources that we've given you and that you've developed. Use them. Now's a good time to begin to call on some of those coping skills. Do you have a sense of humor? Use it. Are you frustrated? Go down and play Ping-Pong with one another. Are you hurt? Come and talk to Dad and me. Say to me, 'We used to do X and Y, and we don't anymore. Why? What can we do about it?'" The kids began to see more of the reality of making choices. It was hard, but it was a growing experience for them. We just had to make sure it didn't break down into open warfare. We had to be careful not to turn on each other.

After she had lived with us nearly a year, we went away for a month's vacation—and sent her off to stay with a relative who agreed to care for her temporarily. We came home before she did, and we all kept saying what a different house it was without her, and how different our lives were. Charles woke up one morning and announced, "When she comes back, she's going into a nursing home." We had finally reached a point as a family where we just didn't want to deal with it anymore. The advantages to her were questionable; the effect on our family life, overwhelming.

By the time she left, she didn't relate at all. She had no sense of time. She didn't react to our telling her about going to a nursing home. She was really in a sort of no-man's-land. She didn't seem to realize what was happening to her. She was lucid in talking about the past, totally confused about the present.

Watching that is terrifying. Talk about

"intimations of mortality"! It made me very nervous. I could see myself in it; the indignities, the things that would bother me, I transferred onto her. For example, I never bathed her. It seemed like such an invasion of her privacy. And it struck me that I like my food in certain ways. I thought to myself, "She may be eating food prepared in the way I like to prepare it, and may not be able to communicate to me the way *she* likes it. She's really at my mercy in so many things." After a while, I don't think she felt she had any control.

I do think the whole experience made me much more sensitive to older people. I want the kids to see *my* parents more, and to experience my aunt Mary, who is old and terrific. I want them to enjoy these other old people in their lives. I also want them to realize that life is very finite, and we have to take advantage of the time we have.

I actually did take my daughter, Annie, to Philadelphia to see Aunt Mary for a long weekend this fall. She's a very special person and she won't be around much longer. I wanted Annie to have an opportunity to enjoy her while she was still vibrant. I also wanted to disassociate aging with something awful. Aunt Mary is so much fun, and shared so much of her present and her past with Annie. And, of course, it also helped me, too. I was consciously looking at her as an image of how one *can* grow old. She is a living example of that line of poetry, "Do not go gentle into that good night. . . ." She'll be a fighter until the end, and I'm cheering her on. I hope she goes out in a blaze of glory. I like to think I'll be like that.

People ask me if I would do it all over again. I think yes, although Charles says no. I wouldn't put her in a nursing home without trying to take her in first; I wouldn't want someone to do that to me. The sad thing is, I don't think a nursing home is the answer. They're so impersonal; there's such an insensitivity to life, because they're so used to people dying. And we put Charles' mother in a "good" one. On the other hand, it works for some people. Some of the women in the home did reach out to one another, and support each other. . . .

One of the things Dottie realized from her experience was how little she and Charles knew at the outset about the behavior and needs of the elderly. She was unprepared for the extent to which bringing someone to live in their home would upset the balance of family life. "We were totally unaware that we'd ever have a problem of that magnitude to cope with. We were whistling in the dark." They knew nothing about costs or available resources. When they began looking into it, they discovered that although there are no easy solutions when it comes to caring for aging parents, there are now a great many services and resources for older people in most communities. Finding and using them can help to ease the burden. Many of these resources are, in fact, designed to help older adults continue to live independently in the community, either in their own home or in housing units which provide a range of supportive services.

However, most of these resources involve someone coming in, performing a service, and leaving; they are generally *not* adequate for the elderly person who requires a full-time schedule of care. So while nursing homes are not always the only alternative to bringing parents to live with us, there are times when they are the most appropriate and feasible one. Unfortunately, understanding this intellectually does not keep us from feeling torn apart with guilt when we do put a parent into a nursing home. Instead of seeing it as the best, safest, least destructive course open to us, we castigate ourselves for having "abandoned" someone we love to a fate we feel we wouldn't want for ourselves. Indeed, our own future is likely to be very much in our thoughts as we make decisions about our parents. Carol, age fifty, talked about the experience of placing her mother-in-law in a nursing home, and bringing her father-in-law into her home to live:

> The whole situation was very difficult because we were trying to do what we thought was best, and realized that it was in conflict with what the parents thought was best. Alan's mother had gotten to the point where she couldn't handle herself, and his father was going physically downhill trying to care for her. We knew that if he continued in that vein, he would die very quickly, and yet caring for her was a thing that really kept him going. So we were caught in this terrible bind of having to make a decision for a man who still had all his faculties. But there was a point when he had to go into the hospital for a short time, and she came to stay with us, and we realized in spades how difficult it was to look after her. It became very apparent then that we had to put her in a nursing home, and bring him to live with us. It was a sort of "damned-if-you-do-damned-if-you-don't" situation, because we knew that by taking the responsibility of caring for her away from him, we were in a way taking away his reason for living. But, on the other side, we knew he couldn't take the physical strain of caring for her either. We also realized that he was going to have some feelings about coming to live with us, because he'd been a very independent kind of person.
>
> We did feel there was a kind of inevitability about it all. In fact, we'd talked about it many times before it actually happened. There are certain members of your family you know you can live with, and others you know you couldn't ever live

with. And we knew he was a person we could have in our house. Had it been the other way around, it would have been much more difficult; neither of us could have handled his mother. But as it was, my father-in-law lived with us for nearly a year until his death, and it worked out reasonably well for all of us.

One thing that I find happens in this situation is that you are never without some feeling—maybe not on the level where you're acting, but very shortly below that level—where you realize that you're getting older too, and you are acting as a role model for your own children on how to treat aging parents. I think it would be dishonest to say it doesn't affect how you feel and act.

I find that working is something of a lifesaver. I think if I weren't working, it would be very easy to spend my life either taking my mother shopping, or visiting Alan's mother in the nursing home, or, you know, getting so totally involved that it wouldn't be a terribly healthy thing. So in a way, I work because it's satisfying to me; it feels good to earn money, and to know I'm worth something to somebody else. But it's also very convenient, because it helps me to set some limits. I can say, "I can only spare so much time this afternoon," and they'll understand that, they'll accept that. It sounds a little cruel, and in a way it may be, because you are taking time away from people who need you. But it's the only way I think you can keep your own sanity.

It is important, as Carol points out, to set limits on the extent to which parents' needs affect our lives. That is often much easier said than done, but no matter how much we love our parents, no matter what the circumstances, we need to maintain time and energy for ourselves and our other relationships. There are bound to be moments when we are resentful about what we are doing, and guilty about what we are not. "But," said one counselor who works with families of aging parents, "the key is to ask ourselves how much we can give and still feel good about. When we reach the point where what we're feeling is mainly resentment, we should stop, and establish some limits for ourselves. Sometimes offspring take on too much responsibility for parents. We treat them as children instead of as older adults. Yes, they may need help and love and caring, but only a small percentage are incapable of making any decisions for themselves. There's a line between support and responsibility. We can help *them* generate options, find resources, and get care: visiting nurses, home care, alternative housing, meals on wheels. To be sure, this society is a *long* way from providing adequate services for all our elderly, but there are many things available if we seek them out. When we set reasonable limits, we're able to spend good time with our parents . . . not just when something goes wrong."

Part of the difficulty we have in dealing with aging parents stems from the stereotypes—if not outright ignorance —many of us carry around about old age. Too often, we're inclined to classify the elderly as cookie-baking saints, irascible harpies, or senile vegetables; we romanticize them or dismiss them as useless. In either case, we are ignoring the complexities, glossing over the reality of them as human beings. There *are* things that happen with the aging process, changes in our parents that we must accept. But not to look beyond those changes is to lose sight of all our parents really are. Eve and Martin, a biracial couple from Pennsylvania, are an excellent example of people who were able to accept and value aging parents, and in the process, accept the end of life as well:

When I was thirty-two, my husband, Martin, was forty-six, and our daughters were three and five.

But my husband's parents were already in their eighties. Their health was failing. Mama had diabetes and bad eyes and couldn't walk well by herself. Daddy felt uneasy about taking care of her. They were both a little afraid. All the children knew something had to be done, but no one was sure quite what. It seemed as if there were just two choices: either they had to go into a nursing home or live with one of the children. And it didn't seem right to put them in a home.

Martin and I decided that we would take care of them. We knew it would be a big change for them to live in a northern white community when all their lives had been spent in a southern black community. But they had always enjoyed visiting us, so we thought it would work. Some nephews brought their furniture, and, after we had arranged it and made a kitchen upstairs for ourselves, they came. We made the kitchen so we could have some separation between the upstairs and downstairs. A daughter gave up her job in New York and moved downstairs with them. She did their cooking in the way they were used to, and took care of Mama. We didn't want to block off the upstairs because we wanted Mama to hear the sounds of the children. Mama couldn't climb stairs anymore, and we hoped the children would go down to visit often. For sixty years, Mama had been raising someone's child. I felt lucky indeed to have her help too.

It seemed natural, having them with us. It was a wonderfully happy time for us. They added stability through their experience, patience, tolerance, forgiveness. They talked to us about their lives, so we learned from them. And they were wonderful company for me. I was home alone raising children, and they were someone to talk to. They gave much affection to me and the children. They enjoyed the children with me. Since I had waited longer than most of my friends to have babies, most of my friends were already out working. With Mama and Daddy there with me, I was deeply reinforced in my value as a mother. They thought I was a good mother and had smart children. That mattered to me.

The children would sneak Mama a sweet or a piece of bacon after the doctor had banned those pleasures. They learned how to take her hand and guide her when she went blind. They learned how to take care of her by imitating us. They loved to help bathe her, and she didn't mind. When she began having small strokes, the children were never afraid or repulsed. They felt needed; after all, they didn't see adults as frail and vulnerable, but Mama was.

We had two good summers while Mama was healthy. We sat outside with her while she snapped beans for me to freeze. I did more freezing with her than I ever have since. She was a good influence. Daddy kept busy with keeping the walks and yard neat and going to the store. In the winter, he made a fire every day, and taught Martin how a good fire gets going.

Mama had a bad stroke after two years and died in the hospital. Daddy missed Mama so much. About six months later, his prostate metastasized. I took care of him during the day now that he no longer went outside. After a couple of months, he didn't leave his room, and he lost strength slowly. A visiting nurse came once a week to bathe him. She said there wasn't much we could do except take care of him the way we were. Once he took an overdose of his pain pills. When I found him, he kept asking, "Is I dead? Is I dead?" I smiled at him and replied, "If you're dead, then I must be an angel." He chuckled and he came around and he often talked about the incident, saying he had tried to decide the Lord's work. But he seemed ready to die.

Taking care of him so intimately, I grew to understand the importance of talk when the circle is starting to close. And the importance of admitting that the circle was closing. Daddy helped me to see that death was not something to fear or fight when life has been full. Having him die at home was a good experience for all of us, akin to the experience of prepared childbirth for me. It wasn't horrible or repulsive. Caring for him every day helped prepare us. He got so thin and dehydrated. When you see a person every day right at home, the changes are natural and gradual, not too bothersome. And when you're doing all you can to help, you don't feel so bad when death comes. We were all quite worn out the weekend he died. Turning him in the bed, cleaning him, coping with the diarrhea, and feeling sad can take a toll.

The morning he died, he kept shouting to us that "the fire" was coming, that we should break a window and get the children out. I sat in his chair while he gradually calmed down, and watched him close his eyes and go to sleep. Martin had taken the children to their dancing lesson; my sister-in-law had gone out shopping; and I went upstairs to rest and read. When they all returned, he was gone. He was still warm, and his spirit was very much alive. We opened his door, relit the fire in his room, and all of us sat in there with his spirit and talked about him and Mama. A family priest came for prayers. The girls combed his hair, kissed his forehead, and folded his hands. We didn't call the doctor or the undertaker until we were ready to let him go. We were very fortunate to have that quiet time. I sometimes wonder if I'll be so lucky in my old age, surrounded by children and grandchildren, allowed to die in my own time, not rushed or pushed into a place that will hope I die on their terms.

When I ask my children if they will take care of me when I'm old, they say matter-of-factly, "of course!" I have taken them with me often to a nursing home to visit the ladies. They are at ease with old people. They aren't scared of aging in people or death. They visit the white ladies and the black ladies. So Mama and Daddy left us with quite a legacy: besides the traditional values, the strong culture, the storytelling, the sense of their own value as individuals, they left our children a perspective on color and a veneration for people of age, whatever the shade of skin.

My interest in older people was so awakened that I got a master's degree in gerontology, and, after volunteering for two years in a nursing home and several senior centers, I am now working as a field representative for the National Council on the Aging. I could not have been prepared for this without the help from Mama and Daddy. I knew that I was at ease with the idea of having them live with me, but it did not occur to me that they would help me define clearly what I could do well, and wanted to do. But that's how it turned out.

11 On Our Own

Today, roughly one out of every five middle-aged women is single.[1] And the number of women on their own is increasing: women who are separated, divorced, widowed, or who never married; women not in a one-to-one relationship they consider permanent whether they live with others or not. There have been more widows each decade (widowhood happens to three out of four married women, and the median age for "new" widows is fifty-two[2]); the divorce rate for long-term marriages has soared, and more women are deciding not to marry. All of which means that a growing number of us can expect to be on our own for a substantial part of our adult lives.

And yet, relatively few of us over thirty-five are really prepared to be on our own. We grew up vaguely expecting to marry and be "provided for" forever after, to have our identity tied up with our husband's, and our social life revolve around being part of a couple. The prospect of being on our own is, for most women, a disturbing one; we prefer to think that it won't actually happen to *us*. And then, suddenly someone we know is widowed or divorced, and we can't help wondering, "But if it *does* happen, will I be able to manage? Can I survive financially? Will I be too old to attract another man? Will I be permanently *alone?*" Quite apart from how we might feel about no longer being with our partner, the idea of single life at middle age can be frightening in itself. Indeed, a number of married women who responded to our survey expressed concern about the possibility of being alone in the future.

Although most middle-aged women do not come to be alone by choice, the number of women who are *choosing* to be single is growing, in part because more opportunities are opening up for women; in part because it is now easier legally and more acceptable socially for a woman to end a marriage. Then too, with all the recent emphasis on individual freedom and taking responsibility for one's own happiness, more middle-aged women are finding the strength and support to get out of unsatisfying relation-ships and start over, to try to find something better for themselves.

But whether a woman is alone by chance or by choice, there is definitely less stigma attached to being a single woman these days. References to spinsters and "old maids" are fading; women on their own are less likely to be seen as deviant or pitiable—and they are less likely to see themselves that way. In fact, among the women who answered our questionnaire, those who were single, sepa-rated, or divorced had a somewhat more positive self-image than women who were currently married. They reported having more self-confidence, more sense of pur-pose and adventure, and they felt more attractive than their married counterparts—even said they had more zest for life.

Moreover, nearly all the women we interviewed who were on their own in their middle years conveyed a sense of strength, humor, and resiliency. They were proud of their growing competency and autonomy. They were not simply "on hold," marking time until someone came along to rescue them or make it all right; even those who wanted very much to marry—or remarry—eventually were building lives for themselves here and now. They were establishing new social networks and support systems. Many recognized that being on their own had forced them to grow as independent human beings in ways they might not have grown in other circumstances. They didn't claim that being a "middle-aged single" was a bed of roses, but most did state that they were finding themselves a lot more able to cope with being alone—and to enjoy their lives as independent women—than they had ever anticipated.

There are, of course, a number of factors that contribute to how a middle-aged women feels about being on her own. For example, is she newly single, or has she been on her own for some time? Does she have adequate financial resources and marketable skills? How is she getting support and establishing intimacy in her life?

The most pressing issue facing almost all single women is the financial one. Women who have chosen never to marry are more likely to be in a position to support themselves in middle age. Unfortunately, many women who emerge from marriage in the middle years find that they have neither marketable career skills nor an adequate income. Those who have not worked in the past are suddenly faced with earning a living, which may mean getting training or education after years of being at home with children. Those who have worked all along discover that a salary they considered all right when combined with their husband's is often far from enough once they are on their own. Besides the fact that most women continue to earn substantially less than men, widow's benefits are minimal, alimony is becoming a thing of the past, and a great many men default on child-support payments. Whatever their other differences, one thing women on their own often have in common is an ongoing concern about financial security—or, for that matter, financial survival.[3]

Then, too, women who have children find that the responsibility for raising them alone can be overwhelming at times, not only financially, but physically and emotionally. Often there is no respite, no one to share daily decision-making, no one to take over when the single parent needs a break. True, more men are now taking on or sharing custody of children, but it is still women who carry much of the burden of child-rearing. And, no matter how much we love our children, no matter how much pleasure and fulfillment they bring into our lives, there are times when raising them alone feels like precisely that: an awesome *burden.*

Besides, in a society that has held up a Norman Rockwell vision of ideal family life (Mom, Dad, and a couple of freckle-faced kids on the way to Grandma's house), the woman on her own is susceptible to the fear that she's not doing it right; that the picture is incomplete; that her children are being deprived of a normal upbringing, even if family life has never been more pleasant. Should she marry again so that there will be a man around the house? How much should she do for her children's sake, and how much for her own? All mothers struggle with that question at times, but the woman alone is particularly subject to feeling guilty about putting her own needs first—and resentful about putting them last. In fact, one of the ongoing tasks many single mothers face is finding ways to maintain a comfortable balance between taking care of children's needs, and taking care of their own.

Despite the difficulties of being a single parent, however, many women stressed that their children were especially important to them as women alone. If they were a worry at times, they were also a great source of joy; if they limited privacy and freedom, they also provided structure and meaning to life. A number of women described a special quality of friendship and companionship, a sense of unity that had evolved between themselves as single parents and their children. And yet they found, too—in spite of fears to the contrary—that when the time came for children to depart, they were ready to let go and refocus on their own lives.

Certainly one of the strongest needs most women on their own have is for a sense of *connectedness*—for intimate adult relationships that provide emotional support, companionship, and physical closeness. It's relatively easy, many women have told us, to find casual sexual partners; the hard part is finding someone they care about and enjoy as a person, and with whom they can be emotionally intimate. A lot of women compound the problem by holding on to a fairly rigid set of criteria for candidates for intimacy: *"Wanted:* Single male; very close in age; preferably taller, smarter, as well or better educated; of equal or superior social status. Object: Matrimony—or at the very least, a 'meaningful' long-term relationship that includes commitment and exclusivity." But while that may be what many middle-aged women would prefer—or what they have learned to expect for themselves, it is *not* the only possibility for achieving intimacy. It is not even the most likely one. The reality, of course, is that the older one gets, the larger the ratio of single women to single men, and the smaller a woman's chances of finding a partner—let alone one who meets all of her ideal criteria. Nor does the search for Mr. Right preclude finding other sources of support and intimacy. Learning to be open to other options (active, supportive relationships with other women; relationships with younger men, friendships with men with whom they will not be romantically involved, and seeking out people of all ages with similar interests) is another of the tasks single women face as they build a life for themselves in middle age.

Fortunately, there are a growing number of opportunities these days for mature single women to meet other people—and a decreasing number of social taboos restricting them. It is far more acceptable now for women to go places and do things on their own; single women are feeling much freer to initiate social contacts and to involve themselves in all kinds of activities—including a whole array geared specifically for singles—no matter what their age. After growing up in an era when women were taught to be fairly passive socially, quite a few women did tell us that they found it difficult at first to take the initiative. But most soon learned to take risks and reach out for intimacy, and to reach out in more than one direction. They had formed connections with a variety of new people by involving themselves in everything from politics to disco dancing, from running in marathons to going back to school or work. If they had not completely conquered loneliness, they often reported that they had broadened their interests and increased their self-confidence as well as their circle of friends. Some also pointed out that, in the process, they had come to value the spontaneity and greater freedom single people have to do *what* they want *when* they want with whomever they choose. Quite a few women commented that it would now be hard to give up their freedom in favor of intimacy with just one person.

Regardless of other sources of companionship, nearly all the women we talked to emphasized the value of developing friendships with other single women. There was a tendency to drift away from married friends and form close ties with women in similar circumstances, whom they saw as an especially important source of understanding and support and caring, as well as fun; someone they could call on at any time, who shared their needs and interests.

The whole issue of finding *physical* intimacy as a single, middle-aged woman was viewed as something of a mixed bag. There were some women who had relegated sex to a relatively unimportant place in their lives; a few even said that they were glad to put "that part" of their lives behind them. There were a great many more women who celebrated the sexual freedom single life at middle age provided. They were delighted with their increased pleasure and interest in sex, and with the opportunity to explore it on their own terms. Some described having satisfying sexual experiences for the first time in their lives, and found that they felt more confident about their sexuality and desirability than ever before.

Most of the single, middle-aged women we talked to, however, viewed the subject of physical intimacy with more than a little ambivalence. There were times when sex seemed terribly important, and times when it wasn't at all. There was the excitement of newness, the sense of possibility and discovery, and yet there was the desire for physical relationships that were secure, familiar, and continuing. And there was also concern about their ability as "older women" to continue to attract sexual partners.

But the real issue for most women was finding someone with whom they could combine physical intimacy with emotional intimacy and companionship. "If all I want is sex, that's no problem," one woman told us. "I can usually find *some*one—most women can. But that really loses its appeal fast. Or I know men I like a lot, but there's just no chemistry at all. What I really want is to have someone I care about who cares about me; someone I like and respect, that I enjoy talking to and laughing with, as well as making love with. And just as important as the sex itself is all the other touching you do: the hugging and snuggling and reaching out and knowing someone is there. That kind of relationship is so much harder to find—and so much better when you find it!"

Some newly single women described going through an initial period of "indiscriminate" or "excessive" sexual activity ("Lots of sex for the sake of sex . . ."), sometimes in reaction to a repressive marriage, or out of a need for reassurance that they were still desirable; sometimes as an attempt to avoid being alone. Others reported, however, that they felt very awkward and uncomfortable about the whole subject of sex at first. There they were, beginning the dating game again, only at a much older age, and with a whole new set of rules. The idea of casual sex seemed unappealing or immoral; even sex with someone they cared about wasn't always a comfortable prospect. They could hardly pretend to be blushing virgins, but after years and years of marriage—often to the only man they'd ever slept with—they didn't exactly feel like great sexual sophisticates either. "I found myself feeling more adolescent than my own adolescent daughter," one divorcée recalled. "There I was, a forty-five-year-old mother of four, wondering how far to go on the first date, and worried to death about what he would think of me! I didn't want to look like a prude, but I didn't want to look desperate or 'easy' either."

It takes time for most newly single middle-aged women to work out comfortable ways of handling issues of sex and intimacy—and they are issues that may never be permanently settled. But then, it takes time in general for women to adjust to being on their own. One feminist therapist we talked to, Dr. Alice Aslin, said that women tend to go through a *process* in making that adjustment. And while that process varies from one woman to the next, for most, she finds, it includes a "fairly scary period" of trying to make sure they can take care of themselves. The scare is particularly strong if they feel they have no choice, that they were forced into being on their own.

> What I try to do when they're at that stage is to get them to focus on reality issues: legal and financial matters, finding some initial employment if necessary, and then later thinking in terms of what they might like to do in the future. I encourage them to look at things from the perspective of their need to learn to take care of themselves, to stand up for themselves. That doesn't mean they have to have it all together initially, or go around pretending that they do. Women probably won't feel confident right away, and it helps to

accept that. It's okay to get support and information; in fact, I encourage women to do that: to ask for help from people who know what they need to know, and to spend time with other women who are going through the same thing, particularly women at other stages in the process. Of course, that tends to happen automatically. Women in similar circumstances tend to connect; they begin to recognize a need for companionship with other women.

Dr. Aslin stresses that the process of adjustment is a long one—often as long as three to four years.

Maybe at the end of a year or a year and a half, women are feeling less frightened, but to feel really confident is a much longer process, and it sometimes helps to know that.

A big part of the process is adjusting to the loss of the role as wife, because that affects women in a number of ways: legally, socially, as a parent. The trauma for many women, as I see it, is really around the loss of that *role* versus the loss of that *person.* I've heard women say over and over again that they don't miss Herbie, they miss the security of marriage, and the security of being a wife. In subcultures where it's taboo to be divorced, the loss is even greater, but widows go through the same thing.

Initially a lot of women are scared to death they won't remarry. The underlying belief is that if they get a chance, they will. Most women don't plan on always being single. Many of them never give up the fantasy that they're going to meet someone— Prince Charming—and marry. And I don't think it's necessary for them to give it up *if* they can go ahead and really be involved in their life as it is—

single—and if they have a real commitment to making their life happy. You can have all kinds of fantasies, and they don't have to get in the way. But there are women who tend to rely so much on the fantasy that they're not functioning, they're not taking care of their lives now, and that's when it becomes a problem. I feel it's important for women to reach a point where they view remarriage as a choice, an option, as something they really want, not as a "solution" or something they just expect for themselves. It's important for them to realize that they *can* take care of themselves: "If I remarry, fine; if not, I'm building a life for myself."

One thing I point out to women is that they don't have to like living on their own all the time. I think that's one of the myths. A lot of women get scared when they don't like it at times. But there are times when you don't like *any*thing—I don't care what it is. A woman needs to look at her expectations and the things about living alone she doesn't like. For a lot of women, it's weekends and holidays—those are the really hard times. I suggest that they identify the points when it's stressful, and make plans to take care of themselves particularly at those points.

Most women don't even imagine continuing to do the kinds of things they enjoy just for themselves. If they've always liked preparing a nice dinner on Sunday or fixing up the house, or going to a certain place on vacation, it may not enter their minds to keep on doing that once they're alone. I try to point out that if there were things they enjoyed before, they can re-create them, whether it's their home that's important, or celebrating holidays—whatever it is. And most women will say, "Well, I can't decorate or cook because there's nobody to do that for." And I say: "But there *is* somebody—there's you!" And I try to reinforce that she's important enough to nurture and take care of. That's very hard for some women; they can't even imagine doing that. Sometimes to get them thinking in those terms, I'll ask: "If you were with a man, what sorts of things would you like to do? Could you do those things for yourself? Could you do them now, even though there's no man involved in your life?"

Of course, once a woman has gotten her own self-esteem and independence, the process of deciding to marry or live with someone again can present new identity problems. She has to learn to reconnect to someone without losing herself to him. Often there's a fear that "I'll lose me." It may be seen as a choice between independence and dependence. Women often have the image that you're one or the other, whereas most of us are really some combination, and we each need to find a balance of the two that's good and comfortable and productive.

Frequently women go through a period where they feel they have to be self-sufficient to the extreme. And that's a very natural part of the process as they grow. After the "scare" dies down, there's a sort of flamboyant "I'll do everything." It's a way to test limits and self-confidence. I see women who come in and they've just put up a door or installed plumbing or something, and they're just ecstatic about it. They may never do it again in their lives, but they know they can. They learn and gain confidence, often by doing very difficult kinds of things.

The process of adjusting to being on your own is not an easy one; there are good times and bad times. But that's what life is all about; it isn't just "happily ever after." The exciting part for me is watching women bloom; watching their personalities come alive in all kinds of ways; in careers, in creative activities; in relationships. A sense of humor they haven't expressed in a hundred years—or *ever* maybe—comes out. They really come into their own as people.

Our interviews with women on their own left us with impressions very similar to Dr. Aslin's: that most of the women had, indeed, grown a lot. In circumstances many might not have chosen for themselves, they were not merely surviving, but *prevailing,* and yes, often "blooming." Was it simply a matter of having no choice? That "one does what one has to do"? Perhaps in part. Why, then, when men have been more prepared to function independently, when they have more financial security, more societal permission to pursue companions and sexual partners —why has research shown that *women* tend to fare better on their own?[4] It may well be that the qualities we have been encouraged—and inclined—to develop, such as empathy, sensitivity, and adaptability, not only allow us to form close connections but give us a particularly strong sense of perspective and experience that stands us in good stead as women on our own in the middle years. Certainly this seems to be true of the six women who follow.

JENNIE

Jennie, forty-three, is a slim, chain-smoking strawberry blonde who lives with two of her three children in a suburb of Atlanta. As she talks, Jennie smiles frequently, and gestures with great animation, but every once in a while there's a wistful quality about her. She is a down-to-earth woman who openly discussed her feelings about suddenly finding herself a "woman on her own":

> My husband walked out on me after nineteen
> years of marriage. He just came home one day and
> announced that he was in love with someone else

and he wanted a divorce. Just like that. When I tell people, they always say, "Oh, come on! It never happens out of a clear blue sky. You must have had *some* idea!" But I really didn't. Maybe I just didn't want to know.

We got married when we were both twenty-two. I stayed home and took care of the house and kids, and that was fine with me. I never had any desire to go out to work, and Jack always said he didn't want a working wife anyway. Besides, we always managed all right on his salary, even though we couldn't save much. Our house is in a neighborhood full of families just like ours—or just like ours *was*. I had good friends, I kept busy; I figured Jack and I got along as well as most couples. My life revolved around him and the kids. I thought everything was fine.

So when Jack first told me he wanted out, I was completely stunned. I just couldn't take it in. I kept saying, "You can't do that! What did I do wrong?" I figured somehow I could talk him out of it; find out what the problem was and fix it. And then I saw that he really was leaving, and I panicked. I thought, "Oh my God! What will happen to me? What will people think? How can I manage alone with three kids?" I never thought of myself as a clinging vine, but suddenly, I felt completely helpless. Paralyzed. My whole life was falling apart in front of my eyes, and I'd come out with some stupid thing like, "But what will I do about the storm windows?"

In the first couple of months after he left, I think I felt more strong emotions than I ever had in my life: I was so angry and hurt and resentful and scared. But more than anything else, I was humiliated. Jack left here and moved right in with his girlfriend, and they got married about thirty seconds after our divorce was final. I felt like it had been publicly announced that I was a failure as a woman. I really hated him for that. God, how I hated him . . . and loved him and missed him . . . and you name it, I felt it. There were times when I actually thought to myself "I wish he had *died* instead!" I was a mess.

By the time we signed the divorce papers, things had gotten pretty nasty between us. We had never argued much about money in nineteen years; now we were at each other's throats over every nickel. I ended up with custody of the children, the house, and not much money.

That was almost two years ago. And it's really only been in the last few months that I've started to feel like myself again. I didn't want to move out of the house because of the kids, but living in a suburb where everybody's a couple and you're that woman whose husband left her for another woman is horrible. I'm only now getting over the embarrassment. But in the process, I'm changing a lot too. I'm doing things I never even thought about doing before, and not just around the house. I'm taking a yoga class and I'm going bicycle riding with a whole group of people on Sundays. I even play on a volleyball team. And I do things Jack never wanted to do, like go to concerts and eat Chinese food! I've lost fifteen pounds and I pay a lot more attention to how I look. So now people's reaction isn't "Oh, there's poor little Jennie," it's: "Hey, Jennie, you never looked better!"

I've started to *feel* a lot better too. I've been going out a little. Not with anyone I especially like, but it's companionship, and it's been good for my battered ego. I've discovered that people really do enjoy being with me, and that I feel much freer to be myself without Jack around. But I have to admit all that "getting to know each other" stuff you do with men does feel pretty awkward at my age.

And sex: it seems like if you and a man don't actually *dis*like each other, he expects you to go to bed with him, and the idea of casual sex doesn't sit so well with me. I have had a couple of sexual experiences though; one was very nice, and it gave me back some of my confidence; the other was disappointing. But I have found that as time goes by and I feel better about myself, the idea of making love with a man I care about really sounds good to me. Of course, that's easier said than done. I don't know if I'll be able to find someone I can trust and respect and love. Especially trust. It's going to be damn hard for me to trust a man again.

Jennie pauses for a moment, scowling and lost in thought. Then she shakes her head, lights another cigarette, and almost visibly changes gears:

I do have my first decent job! I realized right away that I would have to work, but obviously I wasn't too skilled. People weren't exactly falling all over themselves to hire a forty-one-year-old lady who hadn't worked for twenty years. I had been a secretary for a couple of years before I got married, but I'd hardly touched a typewriter since then. So I started off with a job I hated as a sales clerk. I quit after a month because it didn't pay enough and besides, I was in such bad shape at the time that having to deal with people all day and be pleasant and polite was more than I could manage. I'd go home and fly off the handle with the kids and cry. Some friends of mine encouraged me to take a refresher course in secretarial skills, which I did, and now, after trying out a couple of jobs, I've got a pretty good position as a secretary at a corporation not far from where I live. My salary is still not terrific, but the company has good employee benefits, and I think it's a secure job. I like the man I work for; I *don't* particularly like working, and I don't think I ever will. I really miss the freedom I used to have.

I worried a lot about how the kids would take the divorce, and they were upset at first—and I think embarrassed by the whole thing—but not as upset as I thought they'd be . . . at least not outwardly. Still, there are times even now when they're angry because Jack's not here, and they take it out on me. Here I prepared all these nice, helpful things to say when they criticized their father, and instead, they criticize *me!* Maybe it's because I'm around and he's not, and I'm the one who has to make the rules and enforce discipline and say, "No, we can't afford it."

I really had a hard time with my older son. After he graduated from high school last year, he didn't know what he wanted to do with himself, so he wasn't doing anything except hanging around and using drugs. He expected me to support him, but he didn't think he had to listen to me or obey any rules. We fought all the time. And Jack was no help at all. He'd say, "What do you expect *me* to do about it?" About six months ago, things came to a head, and my son said if I didn't stop bugging him he'd move out. Well, I called his bluff, and said maybe that was a good idea, because as bad as I felt about the way he was messing up his life, he was really starting to pull all of us down with him. I wasn't sure what was going to happen; I was afraid we'd never see him again. But he moved into a house with some friends, and got a job and is talking about going back to school. He comes around fairly often to see us, and as worried as I was about it, I think it's turned out to be the best possible thing for all of us.

And things between me and the younger kids are better now too. There used to be a lot of resentment about the change in our standard of living, and it wasn't just that *they* resented it; *I* resented it too. A lot of things we took for granted just aren't possible anymore. But now that they're older—my daughter is sixteen; my younger son is fifteen—we all try to figure out ways to manage. They're getting better about doing chores around the house, and they earn their own spending money. Instead of complaining about our "budget" meals, we've learned to make an occasion out of the good ones. I wish I *could* do more for them, but that's not how it is, and I think they understand that now. Basically, they're good kids, and I'm proud of how they've handled themselves.

I think they're proud of me, too: the fact that I've pulled myself together, and learned to be independent. I've also changed from trying too hard to protect them and to be both mother and father, to letting them take a lot more responsibility for themselves. It would have happened anyway, but not this soon or this much. I haven't stopped being "mother," but I do treat them more like adults and friends. In some ways, I think we have more in common now than we used to. Being single again after twenty years of marriage is a lot like being thrown right back into adolescence. At times, I feel like I'm struggling to grow up all over again. If I had the choice, it's a struggle I'd just as soon not make. But nobody asked me. It's something I've had to do, and it's been a long haul, but, you know, I kind of like what I'm finding out about myself.

JO ANN

Jo Ann is a sedate, sixty-two-year-old woman, who was widowed at fifty after a long marriage. She remembers clearly her early struggles with the day-to-day realities of being alone:

When Dick was alive and the kids were at home, I always made sure I was well stocked with their favorite foods. I guess most of us shop that way. For example, Dick loved those fat kosher dill pickles, and so I always kept a jar of them in the refrigerator. I remember going grocery shopping one day a few months after he died, and as I walked past those pickles, I started to pick up a jar and put it in my basket. And then I thought to myself, "Wait a minute. You don't even *like* pickles," and I put them back. It really hit me then: I didn't have anybody to buy things for anymore. The kids were grown; the only one I had to please was me. I stood there in the aisle in front of those pickles and burst into tears.

It was the little incidents like that one that got to me. The truth is, my marriage hadn't been a good one at all. But I felt lost without it. It seemed it was better to have someone to fight with than no one at all. I missed the structure that I'd been used to all my life. First I was somebody's daughter, then somebody's wife and somebody's mother. Certain things were expected of me. Not having that anymore left me feeling so alone and at loose ends.

One night, not long after the pickle episode, I was downtown shopping. As I walked out of a store at closing time, I started thinking: "I'd better hurry home and get dinner started." Only there was no one at home waiting for me. Not a soul in the world cared if I cooked dinner or not. I was standing there in front of the store trying to decide whether to go home and cook something for myself or go alone to a restaurant when some old friends happened to walk by, a couple I hadn't seen in years. We got to talking, and they asked me to have dinner with them. I went, and, you know, I felt exhilarated. It was as though all of a sudden I was liberated, and I loved the feeling. I could go with them, I could do whatever I pleased. I didn't have to worry about anyone else. For a while, I went from one extreme to the other like that: feeling lonely, confused and unneeded, and feeling thrilled with being able to make my own plans, to make my own choices. It took me some time to find a balance. I discovered that it was very important for me to have structure in my life, and that was something I had to learn to do: make my own structure.

That meant having regular work hours and planning in advance in ways I never had before, especially planning times for social companionship. I set up regular dates with friends—you know, the Wednesday night bridge club, that sort of thing. I learned to plan my weekends so that I'd have someone to be with and do things with for at least part of the time. I found if I didn't take the initiative to call friends to go to dinner or to a movie, the time between Friday night and Monday morning was interminable. It's an effort you don't have to make in the same way when you have a family. Then there are all kinds of tasks and demands that provide structure and people around you everyday. Like it or not, you have a *reason* to get out of bed in the morning. Now I have to make my own reasons.

GAIL

Gail is an attractive forty-year-old divorcée, who lives in Cincinnati with her eleven-year-old son. She is a very frank, self-assured woman. "But," she says, "I went through thirteen son-of-a-bitchin' years to get where I am today, to be a 'now' woman. Now that I am, I'm enjoying it, but back then, I sure wouldn't have chosen it for myself."

By the time she was thirty-four, Gail had been through three disastrous marriages. The first, at twenty-four, was "to a man I didn't really love, but I figured that was what you were supposed to do: get married. So I did." That marriage lasted six months. The second, several years later, was to the father of her child, a man she loved very much, who was twenty-two years older than she. Gail never minded the age difference, but he found it increasingly difficult to handle. He began accusing her of playing around, and eventually insisted on a divorce. Alone with a small child and virtually penniless, Gail plunged into a third marriage. "Joe was the rescuer I thought I needed. He wanted to get married and that meant money. It meant security—aside from the fact that he was an alcoholic. Still, it was a roof over our heads, and a father for my child, who desperately wanted one. And crazy and drunk as Joe was, he loved my son." But after a year, Gail couldn't take the drinking any more, and divorced Joe. "I figured anything had to be better than living like that."

So at thirty-four she was alone again, this time in a strange city where she knew practically no one. "I felt really desperate then. I had nothing: no job, nowhere to live. I got more and more in debt." To bail herself out, Gail ended up taking a relatively low-paying job in a rough part of town. She and her son, Teddy, moved to a small, unfurnished apartment near work, and spent a miserable, lonely year.

It was the pits. Horrible. Living on a busy, dirty street right next to the firehouse. I didn't even dare let Teddy go out to play. We had no friends, no car, and practically no furniture. It was tough. There wasn't enough money to take Teddy to McDonald's if he wanted a hamburger. But I realized that another marriage was not the answer; that I had to pull my own life together. I don't think it was until then, when I was thirty-five, that I really started to become an adult and accept responsibility for myself.

At first I was so lonesome, I hated it. I didn't feel I could cope with things on my own. It was always much easier to let somebody else do it. I guess that's one reason I kept getting married . . . only it turned out they never did do it.

Anyway, after a while, I adjusted to being alone, and I found I didn't mind it so much. In fact, I kind of liked it. When you really have to stand on your own and learn that if you have a drip in the faucet *you* have to fix it, you do it. I *had* to do it on my own, and in doing it, I discovered it wasn't so bad.

After we'd been there about a year, a relative of mine came through town. She took one look at the way we were living, and offered to give me the airfare back home to Cincinnati, and help us find a decent apartment there. I had just learned that the company I was working for was going into bankruptcy, so I was going to be without a job again, with very little means of going to look for one. I figured, "What's the difference if I die here or there? It just doesn't matter at this point." So I came home, again without a job, and still in debt. But the people I worked for who were closing down agreed to say they had fired me so I could collect unemployment, and that gave me something coming in for a while.

As it turned out, we found an apartment in a very nice neighborhood near a good school. By then Teddy was in school all day, and was old enough to stay by himself if he had to, so I no longer had to worry about a sitter. I was just worried about eating. But I was really lucky, and within a month found a good job, which I still have. That was five years ago; I've been alone for six years now. At first I had to worry about survival, but I'm surviving comfortably these days. I can't throw money around but we're eating, and I can afford to buy Teddy a ten-speed bicycle if that's what he wants. I'm always overextended financially, but not to the point where I can't catch up with myself. What's more, I know I can live this way comfortably as long as I need to. I feel like I have roots. I enjoy my home. My son is doing extremely well. This is the first time I feel secure with what I have, that it's *mine.* It's the first time I haven't had someone hand me *any*thing, where I'm really doing it on my own, and that feels fantastic. Every time I've been married, I've lost everything I've ever had: my furniture, my clothes, my identity—everything. Now I've established my own identity. Nobody gave it to me, and nobody's going to take it away. I'm happy with my life.

I do find it kind of hard being alone with a child. It's not like Teddy has a father to pick him up on weekends and take him. In my case, he hasn't even seen a father, and he wants one. When a man comes in the house—any man: If Hitler walked into my house, Teddy would adore him. It doesn't matter who comes in, he just wants a man there. I have had men spend the night—I don't do that on a steady basis where there's a flow coming in and out of the house, but I have been in relationships with men who have stayed—and he has absolutely no problem with that. In fact, he's thrilled if they're willing to give some attention to him. And that's all right, except I don't want to see him get locked into something that's not going to be. Because he'll really grab on.

For Gail, it's been an ongoing struggle to find a balance between being herself and being a mother; taking care of Teddy's needs and taking care of her own:

I feel guilty in that I don't necessarily want the same things he wants. Actually, he's pretty independent, but then, he's had to be. I love my child and I know that he loves me. But I'm not going to be den mother or get down on the floor and play games and that kind of stuff. For a while, he and I were having problems, and it was spilling over into problems at school, so he's been seeing a counselor. And in the time he's been going there, things have been terrific. We get along much better. He's becoming more open with me. And it's been helpful for me, too, because the counselor tells me I shouldn't feel guilty for how I'm leading my life. Still, I sometimes get stuck on notions of how it "should" be. Like I *should* be home with him instead of out for dinner with friends. But if I *am* home when I don't want to be there, I get resentful and take it out on him anyway. I've found it's much better to be honest with him and say, "I need my adult friends, and I don't want to be home tonight. Just like the times you want to be with your friends and don't want me around."

Even though things are much better between us, I think he'll always be angry with me because of the father business. He still wants a father but I don't want a husband at this point, and it's *my* life. And you can't be a mother and father both, you can only do the best you can in whatever role you're in; there are limits to what I can do.

I'm looking forward to the next phase of Teddy's life, to his high school and college years. I'm looking forward to his being on his own. And I don't ever want him to feel responsible for me because I'm alone.

Actually, I've found I don't have to be alone if I don't want to be. I've made a lot of good woman friends since I've been back in Cincinnati, who have been very supportive. There's always somebody available to have dinner with or go to the movies, or whatever. Occasionally I do get lonesome and wish maybe I had a date if it was somebody kind of interesting. And then I'm on a date, and it's a bore, and I think, "Why did I bother?" Besides, I enjoy being with women friends. They're easy to be with. They're really not demanding. They more or less do their own thing. With a man, I'm always game- and role-playing. With a woman, I can be honest, so we can have a giving relationship.

But I do have men friends as well as women friends. I like men. Sex just really isn't that important to me right now, but if I want to go to bed with someone, there are men I can call and say, "Let's go have dinner," and I know where that evening is going to end up. I have learned that you don't have to be in love with them—which was also a big thing to overcome. All your life you've learned that you can't have intercourse with someone unless you're in love with him. That's just dirty, dirty, tacky, tacky. Well, you can. It's more pleasant if you *do* have good feelings for someone, but you don't have to.

Right now, I'm feeling pretty secure. Even if something happened to my job, I feel sure that I could get another one. I *know* that I can take care of myself. If I didn't know that, I might be searching and panicky like some single women I know who feel they've got to have a man to take care of them. I think if I went into a relationship now, it would be for the right reasons. It certainly wouldn't be out of panic or desperation or great need. I would never marry again for security purposes the way I married Joe.

LUCILLE

Lucille, a fifty-five-year-old black woman, carries her tall frame with grace and ease. She is a music teacher who has moved from the classroom into teacher education. At fifty-five, she has never been married:

One of the reasons I never married was not from a desire to remain single, but because I had a mother who was dependent on me, and I saw that as a responsibility that I didn't want to share with a husband. I came home from music school to take care of her when I was in my early twenties, and we lived together until she died five years ago.

Another reason for not marrying was that I've always had an interest in continuing to develop my musical ability, and in going to school to study, and somehow a husband just didn't seem to fit into those plans. I could see myself with a husband who would say, "No, you can't go to school this summer," and I couldn't deal with that. I wouldn't want that kind of control over my life.

I think the thing that happens—or happened to me—is that the longer you're single, and the longer you're free to do what you want to do, the more you want to stay that way. You begin to enjoy it. I liked having the freedom to come and go without having to answer to anybody. I went through my twenties and early thirties thinking I would marry eventually. I guess I was somewhere in my late thirties or early forties when I began to feel comfortable with the life-style of an unmarried person, and really to fear losing that freedom.

Of course, there are some things I don't like about remaining single. One is that everyone thinks you ought to be married; friends, relatives: everybody's after you all the time, and I find that difficult. Another is the loss of old friends who married and had children and moved into such a different life-style that we don't seem to have much in common anymore. Here I am still going out and dating, and they're concerned about their children.

Still, having intimate relationships has never really been a problem for me. There was a time when I felt I didn't *want* close female relationships because I felt they wouldn't be as rewarding as relationships with men, so I didn't encourage any. But in the last, say, ten years, I've found friendships with women to be just beautiful! I think my reluctance was due more to my own immaturity than anything else. I felt I would be jealous and competitive with women friends, and that I couldn't trust them around my men friends. But then, I was very insecure when I was younger. As I've grown in security over the years, I've stopped feeling that way and now I have very close, dear women friends.

I have one single woman friend in particular that I spend a lot of time with. She is almost like a sister to me. I feel I can count on her for almost anything at any time. That's another thing about married friends: you can't call them in the middle of the night if you need something. There are a lot of things they can't give because their time is given to their family and children. And as far as men are concerned, I have both close friendships and intimate relationships with men. Some relationships last a year or two, but some have lasted much longer. And there are several men I work with who are very good friends, with whom there's never been any romantic involvement. Of course, I find it easier to have that kind of relationship with men now than when I was younger.

People wonder how I feel about not having had children myself. I guess I did think about it sometimes, but it really didn't affect me that much. As a teacher, I worked with children so closely for so many years. And I taught Sunday School, and gave music lessons in my home on Saturday. So my life was immersed in children. Other people's children, yes, but still children. Oh, there are times now when I look at my friends' children who are at interesting ages doing exciting things, and I wish I had one that age. But I never really felt a desperate need to have a child of my own.

Lucille's responsibility for her mother was very long-term, and affected a great deal more in her life than the decision to postpone marriage. But she took on that responsibility willingly, although she admitted:

There were times later on in our relationship when I felt very put upon. I felt that she tried to hold me too closely. I was willing to give to her, but when I found I couldn't break away in any respect, then I really did begin to develop some resentment. At the time I guess I would have left and set up separate places for me and for her, except that financially that wasn't possible . . . and I resented that too. But eventually, we both learned to accept one another more, and the last few years of her life, we got along much better.

I remember when I used to come home at night after she died, I knew a great loneliness. There were so many times I wanted to share things with her and she wasn't there. But I didn't find living alone as difficult as I thought it would be. I didn't end up in a miserable, depressed, crying heap. I found I was strong enough to handle it, and that was kind of a pleasant surprise for me.

Actually, I started feeling stronger and more capable as a person in my mid-forties, when I went back to school and got a master's degree. It was an amazing experience for me; I learned a great deal about myself. I went from being a shy, sensitive, timid person to being able to ask for what I wanted and feel sure of myself. In fact, it was then that I began to break away from the old patterns in my relationship with my mother, and it was then that we started to get along better.

I think in general, my relationships have improved since then. I've learned that I mustn't let other people's expectations for my relationships—especially my relationships with men—influence me too much. I have to do what I think is good for me, and not let family or friends who want to be protective direct my life, or put their values on me. That's something I think single women have to guard against.

I also think single women must be careful of married men who want to use them in different ways. If a woman wants to have an experience with a married man just for the heck of it, that's fine. But that's different from being used. Sometimes a married man wants to tie you up permanently and have you be there for him, but he's not there for you because of his responsibilities to his wife and family. You can have a great deal of pleasure with men if you do the choosing and you draw the limits and end it when you want.

I've also learned that women have to be honest with themselves about what they want in relationships. If it's sexual pleasure you're seeking, then you should admit it, and not think you want to marry the man. Sexual pleasure for the moment is not the same thing as wanting someone for a husband. Or if you've got a friend who wants to do something, but tonight you want to be alone, say so. When you're single, you sometimes feel loneliness, and you're dependent on friends, and there's a fear of losing them. So you do anything sometimes to hold onto them. But when you're doing things you don't want to do, you end up feeling resentful, and you begin not to like that person. So in the long run, I've found it's better to be honest; better for the relationship, and better for me.

Realistically, I know there's less likelihood of my marrying at this point, but since I have never made a decision not to marry, I still think of it as a possibility; it's still in the back of my mind. I'm not actively seeking a husband, though; I enjoy living the way I do. At one point, I did long for that one and only, wonderful, long-term relationship, but I'm not going to die if I don't have it. I've found that there are a lot of other ways to get satisfaction. I find the older I get the more exciting and wonderful and interesting I find men to be. I don't know how much longer I'll have men as sexual partners, but I plan always to have them as friends. I like men. Probably expecting to have sexual partners at sixty-five isn't realistic, but then, I thought that about being fifty, and it certainly isn't true. Some of the most satisfying sexual experiences I've had have been in recent years. Most of my present relationships are with younger men, as much as ten or more years younger.

I try not to think too much about the future, but when I do think about ten years from now, it bothers me. I enjoy my work, and I can work past sixty-five if I want to, but right now, I don't think I want to. So I say to myself, "What are you doing *now* to enable you to retire and do the things you want?" And I'm not doing enough, I know. I've never managed to save much money, but around eleven years ago, I bought a house. That's the only security I have other than retirement benefits. When I'm sixty-five, it will be paid for, and maybe then I'll sell it, and move to some place smaller and cheaper—that will give me a little money.

There are a lot of things I'm looking forward to doing when I retire and have time. I've thought about moving to Mexico, where it's warmer and less expensive to live. I like the idea of getting away from the demands of city life. And when you're single, you have the freedom to make a choice like that.

BARBARA

Forty-nine-year-old Barbara, from Houston, Texas, has been a widow for ten years. She is a calm, self-assured woman with a deep, compelling voice.

When I was first widowed, I was overwhelmed with two feelings: one was the sense of loss. After having been in an intimate relationship for eighteen years, the loss caused a deep sense of grief. I could let myself have the feeling of grief and that overwhelming sense of loss, but I tried to avoid thinking about my other feeling, which was *fear.* I was really afraid, and for a long time I didn't let myself identify what I was afraid of. I guess I thought if I let myself admit to the fear, I would have to recognize that I was alone, and I didn't want to do that. I wanted to deny it. When I first began to acknowledge my fear, my first question was, "How am I going to raise my four children?" My two older ones were pretty independent, but I still had two younger ones. And then I began to understand that the fear wasn't just about not having help in raising children, but about the fact that I, myself, was alone.

In my marriage, I had put so much emphasis on being close to one person, and now I had lost that one person. I couldn't even begin to think of other ways to have intimacy. I was typical of women of my time in that I had put all of my energy into that one relationship. When it ended, I was bereft. Looking back, I think it took me three years to get through that fear.

I didn't always get the understanding that I needed from friends. People who were trying to be helpful would say, "You're going to have to pull yourself together. You'll just have to deal with this and get over it." I did function okay outwardly then. I carried on the function of being a parent and did a lot of things with the children. But inwardly, I withdrew. To me, my friends' good intentions were meaningless. I felt I was lacking my total identity— like an arm had been cut off, and friends were saying, "Don't bleed!"

When I first started to think about having other relationships, I had a fantasy of a white knight who would come along and rescue me. As time passed, I realized more and more that what I needed was not to replace Howard, but to establish my own identity. When I began to understand that about my grief, I could accept the loss of Howard. What I was grieving for most was the part of me I thought he took with him. And I had to regrow that part of me by myself; no one else could come along and make it all better.

Since the children were there, I didn't have the total loneliness of a woman who is left living alone. And the children had friends coming in and out of the house so that was another source of people around. Then there were my parents—my mother is still living, and my father was alive then—we spent a lot of time with them, going to the farm on weekends. And I also had a neighbor who was not working, and who was home all the time. I would go over to her house and spend a lot of time sitting and talking. She was a very important source of support for me in those early days.

After a while, I began to develop a lot of friendships with women. But I was still programmed to think that a relationship with a man—any man—was more important. I started looking for male relationships, and I was discriminating to a point, but not terribly discriminating. I would even go so far as to break a date with a woman if a man called me.

The business of going out with any man who'd ask me lasted only a short while. Then I began to ask myself what I really wanted; what I was doing, and why. I realized I had always believed there were things I couldn't enjoy unless I was with a man. Of course, that has nothing to do with the actual sensation of enjoying something. For instance, "Nobody likes to eat alone." That's nonsense. People eat alone, and do enjoy it. Watching a sunset, enjoying a movie, listening to music—these are all pleasures in their own right. Yet many women believe it's better to be with a man they can barely tolerate than to read a good book alone. I had to consciously reject those ideas about having to be with a man to enjoy something before I could take pleasure in doing things I loved again. That's when I really started to rebuild myself.

It was at around this time that I was also able to look back honestly at how I had related to my husband. I stopped idealizing his memory, and was able to remember what his bad and good qualities were. That really helped in dealing with the loss of him—I was no longer magnifying the loss. Doing this also helped me to think about what I wanted in a relationship. What was I asking of a male? If this is what I wanted in a man, what about me? How would I like to be in a relationship? So I began to do a lot of soul-searching. I tried to separate out what it was I really liked about myself. What do I value? What kind of people do I like to be with?

But getting things sorted out did not come easily. After I stopped wanting to be rescued by a white knight, I went to the other extreme of wanting to be totally independent: "I don't need a man to fill my needs; I can meet them myself." I began to look for sexual partners, fully knowing that sex was all I wanted out of the relationship. But I didn't like the way I was being. It was doing something demeaning to me. Again, I had to stop using other people that way, and face up to what I really wanted. And what I've found is that I like being discriminating about who I go to bed with. I'd like them to be sensitive and passionate and intelligent. But basically, I have to respect them or the experience is not that satisfying for me. It seems to be demeaning for me if I try to put aside all the qualities of the person and only relate to them sexually.

Learning to understand feminism helped me to be

able to respect myself enough to choose only to be with people I want to be with, and to be able to say, "No, this is not for me." Valuing myself as a woman helped me to value myself as a person. As my own self-respect has increased, I'm more able to present myself as someone who deserves respect— and I get it. I realize that I do need people, and I look for them, men and women. But I have different kinds of ideas now. If it's a man, it doesn't have to be someone I'm going to wind up in bed with. I've established a lot of different kinds of relationships. Also, I've really gotten away from thinking that it's preferable to be with a man. I can spend the evening with a woman and have a really good time. And I'm relating to all sorts of different people, different ages. With men, I've gotten away from thinking, "If I'm a forty-nine-year-old woman, then I've got to date a fifty-four-year-old man, who has a certain kind of education," etc. As I've opened my mind, I've broadened my possibilities.

At the same time I was trying to understand what I wanted in my relationships, I knew I also needed to start making decisions about my future. For a while I clung to the illusion that somehow someone was going to come along and take care of me. It's easier to hold on to the illusion than it is to take responsibility for your own future. But finally, I began to think about what I wanted to do economically for the rest of my life. I decided there was no way I just wanted to work, just go out and find any kind of job. I had had part-time jobs, and had done some work that I knew was "just for money" work, and I didn't like that. I wanted to get into something I really enjoyed. So I went back to school at a local community college and took a course to become a paralegal. And now I have an interesting job with a law firm. It was a long haul, but it was worth it; I make enough money to meet my expenses, and I get a lot of satisfaction out of what I'm doing.

About the time I went back to school, I realized that my house—which is very big—was not only my one asset, but my biggest expense. So I started taking people in. We've always had a very casual attitude about visitors; my children have always felt free to bring anybody home. Sometimes their friends who have had trouble with their parents have stayed with us for a while. So having extra people around wasn't anything new. But when I began doing this, it was a "boarder-landlady" arrangement, and that was very uncomfortable for me. I found that people were acquiescing a lot, and I didn't want that, so we made it into more of a communal situation. They were helping out or paying, and then we just kind of fell into habits of doing different chores. We don't formally set up jobs or anything, like, "you do this and you do that." It just all gets done. We take turns shopping, and people come and go a whole lot, so there are no scheduled meals or anything. People cook or they don't cook. The important thing is we like each other and we're there for each other.

Most of the people who live in my house are people I met when I went back to school, but several of them have been young people who were friends of my children who needed an inexpensive place to stay. They've usually been pretty creative people who have been interested in music and art. And I find I get very interested in what all these people do. A woman who is living here now is interested in library science, and she also does needlepoint, and is very much interested in the women's movement, and reads, reads, reads. So we have a lot to talk about. In fact, she turns me on to a lot of really good books.

So having these people around helps financially, and it helps to keep me from being lonely. And doing the kind of work I want to do is tremendously important to me too; it gives me a focus in my life. I find that I don't think about marriage. I think about having a relationship—maybe. It would all depend, because I know that I've gotten terribly independent, and I really like *not* accounting for my time. I'm much more secure in my identity, and because of that, I'm much more self-confident with women and men.

MARGARET

Margaret is an imposing figure—a six-foot-tall, thirty-nine-year-old woman with short, tousled, auburn hair. She grew up in Wisconsin; her parents were first generation Americans who dreamed of a bright future for their four children—and expected a lot from them. "There was a certain aura of German perfectionism in our house," she says. "It's strange, all four of us grew up lacking confidence. No matter how competent we became, I think we all felt as though we didn't quite measure up. I'm sure our background had something to do with it; no matter what we did, Dad always thought we could do better."

To look at and talk with Margaret now, it is difficult to imagine her lacking confidence. She has a presence—an aura of strength that is readily apparent. She freely discusses how her sense of herself has changed in the last few years:

I was brought up to be the family nun. I was the first daughter, was not very social, and I was smart. When I was a senior in high school, I was tempted to enter the convent. I remember thinking that would give me a purpose in life, I'd be respected and wouldn't have to worry about making my way in the world. No hassles about money, Saturday night dates, or catching the proper husband. The idea of service was appealing, but I finally decided that if I were to go into the convent, it would be for the wrong reason—to escape. I had to prove to myself that I could make choices for myself; I couldn't run away from life, although part of me desperately wanted to be protected and taken care of.

I went off to college with little idea of what I wanted to get out of it. I majored in English. And, like so many girls who graduated in the early sixties without a diamond on the fourth finger, left hand, I became a teacher.

As the years went on, I began to take my career seriously. It wasn't just something to do until marriage. It was becoming clear to me that I was going to be a career woman whether or not I married.

Margaret returned to the university and took a master's degree in student personnel work, and by the time she was thirty-three, she had established herself as the dean of students at a small women's college in the Midwest. She was respected by faculty, administration, and students alike. She recalls:

I should have felt competent and good about what I was doing, but I didn't. No matter what I did, I still didn't feel as though I could count on my own ability to survive and thrive. And I still hadn't found a place where I felt settled.

After two years in the dean's job, I knew I had to get out. For the first time I started thinking seriously about my age. I was thirty-five, and I felt it was now or never. I knew as long as I stayed near home, I'd always feel that I wasn't quite making it. I didn't fit into either of the molds I was expected to —religious, or wife and mother. I was depressed at the thought of my life stretching out before me— just a series of makeshift apartments with no focus, no continuity. I had to find out who I was and what I could do. I decided that I wanted to see where I came from to understand the mixed European heritage that was part of me. So I left my job, put my furniture in storage, packed my bags, and took off. I bought a three-month Eurail pass, and for the first time in my life I had absolutely no idea where I'd be or what I'd be doing from one week to the next. I did have a friend, Laura, who traveled with me part of the time, but she was on a Fulbright so, unlike me, she had a certain amount of structure to her life. I had my guitar with me, and with Laura's prodding, I'd take it out in various places and play and sing American folk music.

When I arrived in Italy, I was immediately caught up by the place. Italy was totally different from me and from my German and Lithuanian background. But for some reason it just felt right to be there—so I stayed. After my Eurail pass ran out, I literally lived hand to mouth, supporting myself with odd jobs, tutoring, and folk singing. I lived with a Signora in Genoa; I paid her a small amount of money for a very small room and had to resist her attempts to make me into a baby-sitter.

The folk singing was my main meal ticket. It's funny, I never would have done that here. My age would have gotten in the way, if not with others, certainly with myself. My image of a folk singer here is someone very young—not a thirty-five-year-old woman. It may be okay to be

Judy Collins and be forty, but to be starting out singing in little cafes and auditoriums—well, I just wouldn't have done that in the States at that age. But in Italy it was different. My age meant nothing there. I was so different from the Italians in looks, language, in culture—there's no way I could fit into a mold there. And maybe that's what freed me up.

Margaret spent a whole year in Genoa, singing, doing odd jobs, and traveling whenever she had the money and the urge to wander. Although she didn't see Laura a great deal, she knew that she could count on bumping into her every once in a while, and that she'd be there if Margaret ever needed her. As Laura's year of study came to an end, Margaret faced the decision of whether or not to stay in Italy. Laura, her last link with home and the past, was leaving. Margaret had no permanent job, and although she had made friends, none of them were really close. She didn't want to come back to the U.S. but she had no real reason to stay. So she decided to create a reason.

She told everyone that she was ready to settle down in Genoa with a real job. She knew she had to sell herself. She stopped being modest when she described her abilities. She checked out every lead she got, and with each contact she made, she asked for the names of others to call. Eventually word of Margaret reached the board of an international school that was looking for a new principal. After going through a relatively brief interview, she was offered the job. Her first response to the offer was "No." This was an elementary school, and her only administrative experience had been on the high school and college level. And besides, she didn't know if she could cope with all the complications of running an international school with financial problems, staff vacancies, and parental discontent. Five minutes after her refusal of the offer over the phone, she called back and said, "Okay, I'll do it."

Once again I felt my age breathing down my neck, and I think I decided then and there that I had to take another risk. Also, I told myself—you are thirty-six years old. You have ten years of experience. You've been in messy situations before, and you've gotten out of them. Besides, I started thinking about all the incompetent people I've had to work with over the years, and with each one I thought of I started feeling more competent myself. Anyway, I jumped in the water, and three years later, I'm still swimming.

I've become an officer in the international schools association, have taken additional graduate courses, and I have colleagues I'm in contact with all over the Continent. I've even done a television series— singing in Italian, no less. Most importantly, I've made a home for myself. I've taken care to fix up my apartment so that it truly feels like *my* place. I've collected some art, and I have a garden. I've made friends here who are like a family; we celebrate holidays together, have fun, and can count on each other. I'm on my own, but I'm by no means alone. I'm coming to terms at thirty-nine with the fact that I will probably miss one of life's most basic experiences—having and raising a child. But the life I'm leading feels so right to me now. I set my own pace, make my own decisions, and to tell you the truth, I wouldn't have it any other way.

12   Older Woman/Younger Man

Until fairly recently, relationships between older women and younger men were likely to evoke smirks and jokes and snickers. They brought to mind images of gigolos, women desperately trying to recapture their youth, exploitation, and unresolved Oedipus complexes—anything but honest, mutual attraction. And yet, it makes good sense for women to look to younger men as partners: women live longer, we peak later sexually, and there are more available older women than men. Why, then, has there been so much social disapproval of such an eminently sensible arrangement?

For the most part, the negative interpretations have stemmed from a double standard of aging, one that has deemed women "desirable" for a much shorter length of time than men. The double standard has been so prevalent in this society that we have tended to accept without question relationships in which the man was considerably older, but were often suspicious or amused when the woman was even slightly older. "It was treated as a big secret in our family that my mother was two years older than my father," one woman recalled. "I grew up thinking that was somehow inappropriate, an embarrassment." Another woman told this story: "I went home recently for my grandmother's funeral. At the service, the minister was talking about what a rich, full life she had led for eighty-two years, when a tiny old lady in the back called out, 'Eighty-six! She was eighty-*six* years old!' It turned out that for over sixty years, she had lied to everyone about her age so no one would know that my grandfather was four years younger than she!"

The double standard flourished in an era when men were brought up to place the child-woman on a pedestal, to value women mainly as decorative objects and child-bearers, and were, therefore, unlikely even to find themselves attracted to mature women. Nor, for that matter, did women's upbringing incline them toward looking to younger men. Helpless, dependent "girls" that we were, we felt we needed someone older, wiser, more powerful to take care of us.

That era may be passing, but the double standard has been the accepted norm for so long that it is not easily discarded. We have come to think of it as "only natural" that a man would prefer younger women; that younger women *are,* in fact, "preferable." Yet, anthropologist Estelle Fuchs says, "What is attractive or stimulating to a man is so often the result of what he has learned to believe is a desirable female. The tremendous value placed on the young, the firm and the fair in American culture, for example, is so strong as to make it appear 'natural' that men be attracted physically to such women. But compare this emphasis with that of other societies . . . to whom young, firm and fair are simply skinny, pale, and juvenile."[1] In short, the double standard is a subjective, learned standard, and as such, is subject to change.

And as a matter of fact, there are clear signs that it *is* changing, largely because mature women are no longer so willing to acquiesce to it. As we have, in recent years, changed the way we define and value ourselves as women, we have begun to see more choices for ourselves, including the choice of being with a younger man. And, as sex-role stereotypes begin to break down, more *men* are seeing the option of being with women who are older, more experienced, perhaps even more successful than they.

So, while there are still a great many more *men* who have younger partners, it is becoming much more common—and "acceptable"—for women to have them as well. It is a trend that the press has paid a lot of attention to especially when famous women are involved, but it is a phenomenon that extends far beyond the world of celebrities. Indeed, a growing number of women in their middle years, more confident and independent, are now entering relationships with men quite a bit younger than they.

In our survey, we asked women how they felt about the possibility of an intimate relationship with a younger man, and found that, despite past prohibitions about such an alliance, over two-thirds of all women thought it was fine, over three-quarters of the unmarried respondents.[2] Most of those who responded positively thought that the younger man could be at least five years younger, while the average acceptable age difference was seven years. Some, however, said they would consider a man as much as twenty years younger, and one woman in her fifties reported that she had for several years been in an extremely good relationship with a man twenty-eight years her junior. Not surprisingly, the acceptable age difference was greater when the woman herself was older, since a ten-year difference would, for example, mean one thing to a thirty-five-year-old, another to a fifty-five-year-old.

But although the idea was appealing to most, the reality was seen as having both advantages and disadvantages. The disadvantages for some still included worrying about the younger man's motives. ("He might be looking for a mother figure, or someone to support him.") The idea of going through his early career struggles—or, for that matter, his early developmental struggles—was seen as a major disadvantage ("I've already *been* through that; who needs to go through it all again?"), as were concerns that a younger man might eventually be threatened by the older woman's self-confidence, experience, or status. ("I'd have to really keep the lid on so I didn't overwhelm him.") A number of women feared what the younger man's reaction to their aging body would be (though, as one woman countered, "This 'aging body' knows more than any young stud has learned yet!"), and many wondered whether such a relationship would be lasting. ("But then," they added, "there's no guarantee that *any* relationship will be lasting.") "Younger men," said one woman scornfully. "All they're good for is to go to bed with."

Among the *advantages* women saw to relationships with younger men was the practicality of such an alliance. ("Older women fit better with younger men, since we live longer and have more sexual desire after thirty.") Many women also stated that it would give them a real ego boost to attract a younger man, to be the "mentor," and that it would be fun and more satisfying sexually. ("Younger men would relieve the frustrations I've acquired from older men.") Other advantages included the belief that a younger man would be "more tender," "less hung-up about machismo," more "energetic," "open," "honest," and "free." But the most frequently expressed advantage was that a younger man was likely to be less sexist, "less rigid about sex roles," and more willing to "allow me to be my own person."

When we interviewed women actually in relationships with younger men, it was clear that there were, of course, as many ups and downs and varieties of style in this as in any other kind of relationship. Yet several common themes did emerge. It was not unusual, they said, for problems to arise over whether the older woman could or should have children, or over partners having different values and interests because of being at different stages in life. Many women stated that their biggest concern at the outset had been how the outside world (her friends, his friends) would view the alliance. But they found, for the most part, that the anticipated disapproval never materialized, or that when it did, it seemed unimportant if the relationship itself were good.

One woman who was divorced some years ago and has lived for the past four years with a younger man found that "it was just plain easier to meet younger men. They're out there in greater numbers. Besides," she said:

> I didn't want to be in the position of being attracted to an older man who had a family. Younger men are not only more available, they're usually more flexible. When I was fairly young, I married someone much older, an established, settled businessman. I spent years trying—unsuccessfully— to fit into his life-style. After the divorce, I took my four children and moved to another part of the country and started over. I established the kind of life-style *I* was comfortable with. When I met Tim, who is six years younger, I already had a set and solid life: a home, a center, something that had meaning. I think that was part of what attracted him to me. And he was free and willing to move into my life: my home, kids, pets, bikes, everything. I think that would have been much harder for an older man who was more established.

Another woman, age forty-four, who lives with a man eight years younger explained:

> Being involved with Cliff is something I never would have considered earlier in my life. Even if I had, I would not have been strong enough to go against the rules. I was convinced I needed a man

to be older and stronger and smarter—to be superior in every way, and to take care of me. Now I'm with a man who doesn't want the role of being my superior or my caretaker, and I no longer want to be "taken care of." We consider each other equals. In order to be this way with Cliff, I had to first discard the idea that I needed a "father figure," and doing that has been such a good thing for me. I get enormous satisfaction from the life we have together. It's ironic; Cliff could have been any age. But being able to take a stand and *choose* to be with a man who is younger is a result of the strength and maturity I've gained as I've grown older.

Chris, a forty-year-old lawyer, is very much aware of both the joys and concerns of being in a relationship with a younger man. She wrote:

Having lived almost six months with Michael, a man who is nearly ten years younger than I, I find that I am no longer concerned with what other people think, or how the relationship is perceived. The relationship actually works beautifully— amazingly so—but I have a sense of foreboding that it is somehow temporary. I have adopted a marvelous day-to-day attitude which means there is no pressure—I never mention marriage or try to pin him down and he doesn't mention it either. We do talk about future plans—vacations, buying a new car, investing in property—so to some extent there is an assumption that we will stay together. Indeed, there is no basis for assuming otherwise. But I have had several nightmares in which he announces he is leaving. In the dreams my reaction is to coldly tell him he is a fool—that if he only knew what I know, he'd understand what an extraordinary relationship we had, and that he will never do any better—I am angry at his inability to recognize and value a good thing when he's got it. So while one part of me is anxious that he will leave, another part of me can't understand how he would be foolish enough to do it.

In any case, I do not ask for any commitment. I realize he's at a point in his life where commitment is a frightening concept—so I let it go. In my most rational moments, I trust my instincts that this is indeed the best thing that has happened to me and that could happen to him, and we are extraordinarily lucky and therefore it will last, and I needn't worry: Something that good has to work. At those times I am quite calm about needing to be sensitive to his stage of life and be supportive and encourage him to express his worries about his future. I try to make him understand or feel that my certainty is something solid he can rely on and won't be shaken by his doubts (the doubts really aren't about me—but about commitment in general). At my most irrational moments, I think that I will be left alone at forty-plus, and no one will want me and I'll have wrinkles and it's not fair —because I would have given him my best years and gotten him launched properly on his life, and then he'll go off and share all that with someone else.

It was a relief to meet his mother and discover she had gray hair and looked older than I—like a mother.

A year later, Chris wrote to us again:

Michael and I have been together now for a year and a half. He tends to say "a couple of years," which is nice. A friend of his came over one night recently, and talked about seeing Michael right after we met, and how Michael said he was in love and it was chemistry, and so on, and that made me feel pretty nice—but I don't even need that now. Time has indeed cured me of my worries . . . or rather, the relationship works, and if it's right, it's right, and the difference in age isn't going to hurt it.

I used to worry that because I can't have children, Michael would eventually need to find a person to have kids with. But that was more anticipated than real. It just doesn't come up. We have Elizabeth [Chris's daughter from a previous marriage] and she provides that family focus, emotional content, one gets from children: the excitement, love, warmth—and she manages to do all that without the burden. I can't imagine now that Michael would want to be tied down with kids, to be limited. He likes our life-style—not that we're swingers, but Elizabeth is fairly self-sufficient, and we live without an enormous sense of obligation and responsibility, except for work.

In the past year, I've taken better care of myself. I've lost weight, started running, improved my tennis . . . not really from a sense that I had better keep in shape, but because it was companionable. We like to do the same things: soccer, running, tennis. We have a lot of common interests; we spend good time together. This could be true at any age, of course. Maybe a forty-year-old man would do all these things too. Who knows? Anyway, it works for us.

Our common interests include work: we're both lawyers, in different fields, though, so there's no competition. In fact, we learn from each other. That also could be true at any age, but maybe the difference for us is no competition. I've been at it longer, so naturally I make more. Still, there's a sense of his being the breadwinner. My attitude is old-fashioned. . . . I don't feel put down, and he doesn't feel not in charge. We have real respect for each other's careers.

Our friends are an odd mix—all ages—no fixed crowd, and that's good too. There's a good balance, a variety. We're not trappable by any crowd. We don't fit—or we fit everywhere. That has been a particularly positive part of this relationship.

Actually, in a word, forty is my best year. I've never felt better, been a better mother—everything. I know Michael gets a lot of the credit, but I don't know how much is due to the difference in our ages. I don't want to proselytize, but all the things I mentioned before seem to have a common factor: looser life, fewer burdens, fewer inhibitions, less rigorous expectations . . . yes, that's it; we have avoided the curse that dooms us all: disappointment, failure of expectations. An older woman/younger man relationship is not so heavy on expectations!

Marriage is not a problem; I don't feel the need. It would cost us a fortune in taxes, I'd keep my name anyway, and we can't have kids. It's not embarrassing not to be married. Indeed, we both refer to "husband" or "wife" when nothing else would make sense and it's not worth explaining. We talk around the subject—never focus on it directly. It's always oblique: "X asked if I were married," or "If we were married, it would be easier to fill out this form." And then it's dropped. I don't think either of us knows what to do about it; there is no expectation, so we don't talk about it. There doesn't seem to be any need to. But we're as inexorably bound up together now as we would be married. It just all *works*. Why change it?

Meg, a fifty-year-old woman from Baltimore, has three grown children and a grandchild. She has been involved in a relationship with Jon, who is twenty years her junior, for the past two years:

I don't feel I have to conform to "what I'm *supposed* to be for my age." I don't think anybody has to. I went through a divorce when I was young, at a time when it just wasn't acceptable. I lived in a lower-middle-class conservative part of town, and divorce was a big no-no. I was discarded by people who I thought were my friends because of it. Their attitude was: "You're not supposed to do that. How can you do that to your kids? You're supposed to make the best of it." But there was no way I could tolerate that marriage. And I had to go my own way even if it meant losing some people that I had spent a lot of time with. The pressures of that divorce were much worse than any pressure I would have by being with a younger man. It took much more guts for me to get that divorce and raise my three kids and work to support them. Let's put it another way. I've learned from experience to do what's right for me, and what goes along with experience is getting older. Every day I learn something more.

I met Jon through a friend—at her birthday party. We got to talking about things we have in common —about the other cities we had lived in. And he was very interested in my job and what I did. He talked to a lot of other single women at that party—but always kept coming back. He's a very considerate person which is very important to me and that came through the first time I met him. He definitely wasn't one of those types who puts out a "hey, babe, you and I know we're automatically going to jump in the sack." But I did know I was attracted to him; the vibrations were immediate for me.

I didn't see him then for a couple of weeks. One night, I was substituting for a friend as a bartender and who should walk into the bar but Jon. "My God, I've been trying to track you down," he said. "I forgot to ask you for your phone number." So we talked and he stayed around until we closed up. Then we went to get something to eat, and had some more drinks, and I wound up going to his apartment. It turned out he was hesitant to invite me in because it wasn't fully furnished. He didn't know how I'd react to that. He was afraid I would think he wasn't all put together and he was apologizing about it when he put his key in the door. I don't know; maybe it was because I was older that he felt that way; he didn't realize that I'm not impressed by what people own. We talked for a long time. He asked me about my friends, about my feelings about men and women, what women were really about—he is very interested in understanding women—what do women think about, how do they feel about themselves? We had that whole conversation, and then made love. Lovemaking was gentle—it was beautiful, it was great. It still is. It's even better. The next morning the alarm went off and I jumped straight out of bed and thought, "Oh my God, did I really do this?"

That was Saturday. Sunday I had to go to a family party. I couldn't get him out of my head. There was no way to call him, and he didn't call Monday. Tuesday, I got a card from him. It was funny; we were on the same wavelength, I had shopped for a card for him and sent it Monday. So he called on Tuesday, and we were like two little kids. And I was thinking—now where do we go from here?

We started to spend time together, at least a couple of nights a week. I started taking him around and introducing him to friends, people at the office, to my boss. He was fairly new to the city and didn't know many people. We got mixed reactions everywhere we went. Sometimes we met with open hostility, sometimes curious looks because there is an obvious age difference. But we ourselves felt very comfortable with that. I've never felt at any time in our relationship like saying, "Hey, I'm ashamed to be seen out with you publicly." And he doesn't have any qualms about being seen with a woman twenty years older either. He comes from a family of twelve kids, he has a brother and a sister who are older than I am. He's one of the younger ones on the end, so I think that helped him a lot in that the age difference wasn't a traumatic thing, and it still isn't.

At one point they were going to have a party in his office, and he said "I want you to come to it with me." We both knew our obvious age difference would raise eyebrows. We talked about it and he said, "It's not that I'm asking you whether or not you can deal with it, I know you can. Obviously I don't have a problem about inviting you or I wouldn't have, because I didn't even have to tell you about this party." That was true and I knew it. He asked if I was willing to deal with it. And I said, "Why not?" That's the way I felt about it. And some nasty comments were made—not of course by his immediate superiors, but they did come from the truckers and some of the crew. A couple of times when he and I were just standing there rapping some of the young office women would pull him away to talk. His boss who was tuned in to the whole thing was immediately there at my side. He was my age—and I knew that had to be difficult for him. And it was. That came out in the conversation later on when one of the things he said to me was, "Don't you find it difficult, a woman your age, to be going out with a younger man?" And I said, "Do you date younger women?" He said, "Yes, but that is accepted." And I said, "Guess what, it's accepted for older women to go out with younger men now." He understood what I was saying, and he just kind of grinned, "Well, okay." As the evening progressed they all started relating to me. It was like "Hey, you're okay." And then they were very curious about me as a person—before they hadn't been.

Meg and Jon made a conscious decision not to live together, but they spent a great deal of time with one another, and developed a relationship that Meg described as "warm, good, and very pleasant." She told us:

Jon's a thoughtful, intelligent man. We share an awful lot. It's not unusual for us to get on the phone and talk for hours and hours. I guess what's interesting about the relationship is that we're operating on a couple of levels. We're not only lovers, but the friendship has been building and going on at the same time. And I think that's very unusual. I can't tell you about another relationship with a younger man because I have not had one before, and I don't know if that's a normal thing that happens when there's an age difference. All I can say is that in our relationship that's the way it grew. I happen to be pretty lucky.

Six months ago, Jon was transferred to Pittsburgh by his company.

I knew it would happen, eventually—he's on his way up in the corporation. But still, it was hard news to hear.

Now since he's been there we talk a lot on the phone. Last Saturday morning we talked for two hours—he said, "I got my phone bill, it was $286." I said, "You could have been back and forth forty-five times for that." But that isn't the point. We get on the phone and we'll rap, and then there will be a silence, and I know he's there and having strong feelings for me—and I feel the same way. I can feel him with me through the phone—I hardly know how to explain that. All I know is that because of the times we have spent together—in the physical sense—that electricity happens on the phone between us—especially when there's no conversation going on. It's very intense. Then he'll say, "Hey, how are you right now?" It's very special.

We have no plans for what will happen in the future, but he's coming to see me next weekend, and I can't stop smiling.

Julie, age thirty-eight, has for two years been in a very happy second marriage to a man nine years younger than she. It has not, however, been entirely smooth sailing—nor has she been without some doubts:

When Sam and I started thinking about marriage, I questioned him very intensely. I said, "Are you sure this is what you want to do? You could be marrying someone nine years younger instead of nine years older. How do you know you're going to be in love with a person who is so much older than you all your life?" I think I questioned him more severely than I questioned myself. However, I also thought to myself, "Well, what's it going to be like to live with a man who is a lot younger throughout the rest of my life?" I guess I had the feeling that our age difference would actually mean less as we got older, and I still think that that is true. Sam, on the other hand, had lived for twenty-six years as a bachelor, and he had known many, many women and he had absolutely no doubts that he was doing the right thing.

When we are together now we never think about our age difference. It's sort of interesting to other people, who meet us for the first time—but I don't think most of our friends ever think about our age either.

One benefit of his younger age is his willingness to go along with what I call women's movement-type ideas—more, I think, than an older man might be. He's really tuned in to women having equal rights, and he's very sympathetic to women wanting to have all the same breaks that men have, and to sharing work around the house, and sharing time with my kids. He wants me to have a career as much as he wants to have his own career—that's one big difference I find: his attitude toward me as a person. My first husband considered his career far and above the most important thing that was happening in our family, and saw the things that I did as kind of meaningless. He thought all my fulfillment in life should come from him and the kids. It may be individual differences, but I tend to think a sense of male-female equality is more likely to come from a younger man. I also think in some ways people in Sam's generation are more open to communication than people a decade or two older. He talks openly about what he's feeling. He's less judgmental than I, and that's partly because of growing up in a different time when there was more of a climate of acceptance of all kinds of people. And as a sexual partner—he is great.

In the beginning, I was really afraid that I would lose a lot of friends who had known me as half of a couple, with my first husband. But I have discovered that the people who were my friends and who just liked me for what I was remained my friends, and the people who had shallow relationships before and who really didn't mean that much to me didn't continue. So that fear also turned out to be unimportant.

Another thing concerned me at first: I thought, "What will happen when Sam takes me to a party with a bunch of young friends? Are they going to look at me and say 'who's the old lady?'" But I usually forgot about it after I got there. And when we've had his friends over for cookouts and things, I've really enjoyed them.

It was interesting meeting and getting to know Sam's parents. They are fifteen years older than I am, so I'm kind of in the middle between them and Sam. I must admit that when I first met them I felt very uncomfortable—but, then I think anybody feels uncomfortable at meeting their lover's parents for the first time. I've gotten to know them better since then—this year we spent a week with them hiking in the mountains. I really think in some ways they understand my concern with my daughters better than Sam does, because they have brought up kids themselves. It must have been a strange thing for them to have two adolescent grandchildren suddenly appear in their lives. But they are very nice to the kids—they always send them birthday cards and Christmas presents.

My parents, on the other hand, almost seem like Sam's grandparents, but my mother liked Sam right away. She liked his sense of humor and his directness. He really calls a spade a spade, and she appreciates that. And my father thinks I'm lucky to have such a good relationship—Sam's age isn't really an issue for either of them.

The major disadvantage to the relationship is financial, because I don't earn that much money and he is not nearly as far along in his career as my first husband was. But luckily we have enough money to have a house and food, my daughters are going to a good school, and we've worked it out so we have the things we need to carry on life. We have refused to let our lowly state of finances prevent us from doing the things we really want to do. If we want to go hear a concert or something like that, we just do it. It also bothers me much less than it used to because I've just decided to cope with it. My values have become clear to me in the last few years. I feel I've been very lucky to be with Sam. Money problems are bothersome, but not terribly important compared to other things.

Another drawback could be that I look older than him. When I ask Sam if he feels badly about my aging body, he says "well, my body is aging too, you know, just as fast if not faster." And that's the kind of thing that he constantly says to me when I express worries about getting older. He says "we're all getting older, you're not the only one."

He rejuvenates me—he will do things on the spur of the moment—things that I might pass off with a "well, maybe it would be fun." He'll say "Come on, let's go for a midnight swim," or something like that, and I end up glad we went. His energy level is higher than most people my age. Although sometimes it's hard to keep up, other times I think if I weren't married to him I would miss out on a lot of fun. Because he is so eager to enjoy what life has to offer, I'm getting a second chance to enjoy more.

In the final analysis, many of our survey respondents, as well as the women we talked to, seemed to agree with the woman who said, "Whether or not I have a relationship with a younger man would depend on the person—on his interests, his personality, his values. I know immature older men, and mature younger ones. Age should not be a factor of such importance if two people can build a deep, satisfying relationship."

Indeed, the point is not that women "should" be with younger men any more than that they "should" be with older ones; it's that any such obiter dicta are unnecessary and limiting. It makes sense to abandon taboos surrounding relationships with younger men, and open ourselves to new possibilities; to take an active role in deciding what we want and what feels right, and leave unreasonable restrictions behind.

13 Friendships: Woman to Woman

Friendships have always been important to women: from that first "very best" friend with whom we shared absolutely everything, to the other young mothers in the neighborhood with the same problems as our own, to the woman at the next desk at work juggling the same impossible combination of roles, women have traditionally looked to one another for a special kind of understanding, support, and affirmation.

Not that a woman's friends are always female, or in the same circumstances or even the same stage of life that she is. Indeed, as the preceding chapters have illustrated, "friendship" is often viewed as one important dimension of a broader relationship: women frequently described husbands, children, parents, siblings, lovers as "good," even "best" *friends.* But beyond that, a theme that emerged very clearly from both our questionnaires and interviews was the great value most women in the middle years place on friendships with other women.

Often these friendships were described as being "fewer

in number" than earlier in life, but "deeper," "richer," and "more meaningful" than ever before. "As I get older," wrote one forty-three-year-old, "I feel more committed to my friendships. I value them and want to nurture them. And I am much more responsible and giving in them." Women on their own especially stressed the importance of close friendships with other women.

In part, this emphasis on friendships between women is a reflection of the times. As the stability of marriage declines, and increased mobility makes it less likely that we will live near our parents or grown children or other family members in our middle years, friends often play a greater role in our lives. They may be more like extended family for us: a source not only of caring and intimacy, but of stability and continuity. We find ourselves turning to friends to provide the feeling of acceptance and connection we all seek. And most of us discover that we can make that "connection" in a very special way with other women. One forty-six-year-old we interviewed put it this way:

These days, I actually get a lot of my best "stuff" —support, understanding—from my women friends. It's not that I have a bad relationship with my husband and children; I don't at all. But there are always such complicated emotional involvements with your family. With my closest friends, there are no holds barred. I can let my hair down in a way I can't do even at home and know that I'll still be accepted. Of course, my friends don't have to put up with me day to day; they don't have to *live* with me. But—I don't know—we make *sense* to each other; we can be silly and angry and outrageously honest about ourselves and our lives and count on one another to understand in a way only another woman could possibly understand. We laugh together and cry together; I guess maybe you could say we keep life in perspective for each other.

Occasionally I feel a little guilty about how much I turn to my friends, you know? Because I grew up with the idea that my relationship with my husband was supposed to be the only one I really needed. And now my first impulse is often to share some bit of news or feeling—good or bad—with a friend. And as I'm sharing it, I'll realize that I'm telling her before I've even told my husband. Of course, the other side of the coin is that having that kind of closeness with other women takes a lot of pressure off what I expect from my marriage, so it probably helps more than it takes away. Anyway, I feel very blessed in my friends.

While it is certainly nothing new for women to turn to one another, to depend on one another, there is definitely a new consciousness about the value of relationships with other women. A professional woman in her early fifties is typical of many who described this change in attitude. She recalled having been "the prototypical woman who at parties talked only with men and thought women were very boring," and told us:

I couldn't relate to them, and for that matter, I didn't particularly want to. I preferred to work with men too, and I always made a point of avoiding women's groups and organizations. I just considered time spent with men to be much more valuable— more important and productive and so on—than time spent with women.
In the last four or five years, though, I have practically done a complete turnabout. I find myself meeting and working with many more capable, exciting women. When I go to a party now, the most interesting people in the room, the ones I gravitate toward and most enjoy talking to, are generally *women.* I don't know how much that represents a

change in *me,* and how much it's because women have changed in recent years: have gotten more involved and interesting and take each other more seriously; it's pretty hard to separate the two. But I do know that in establishing more close friendships with women, I have discovered something wonderful that I didn't even realize I was missing all those years I was a woman operating in a man's world. And it's not just that the relationships themselves are rewarding; it's that valuing other women helps me to value myself more.

Quite a few women we heard from described a new respect for their friendships with other women. There was a growing realization that they were sharing strengths, not just needs; that women had begun to serve as a *network* or *resource* for one another in a way men have long done or been in a position to do. Describing this "new girl network," a psychologist in her late thirties reflected:

I think women have always been drawn to each other, but now we're valuing one another in new ways. The women I work with give each other a lot of recognition in a way I suspect wouldn't have happened ten years ago. We don't just orient around men any more; we're starting to look at one another as individuals who really have something to offer, and approval from each other carries weight.

As we get older and more of us are moving into positions where we have some clout, the issue of friendship and competition comes up. Women have always competed for men, but now more of us are competing in the workplace. There aren't many models yet for blending power and friendship, but I see a lot of women supporting and helping each other, looking out for one another. Women seem to be feeling less resentment about working for other women too; that's been one real problem in the past, probably because no one wanted to work for someone others perceived as powerless. But as we get more entrenched and gain more power, we're going to have to work out the conflicts that inevitably arise between friendship and competition.

The primary emphasis women have traditionally placed on friendship and loyalty is being sorely tested in the work setting where the greatest premium is on performance and accomplishment, on "getting ahead." Many women report feeling a growing pressure to produce and achieve; to keep up with—or surpass—other women. But they also find themselves looking more at other women not just as competition, but as role models, as mentors. Women are encouraging and inspiring one another to reach out and try new things, to "take the plunge," and go back to school or seek advancement or change directions. There is the dynamic of "If *she* can do it, *I* can do it." Moreover, in the male dominated work place, women also look to one another for a particular kind of confirmation and empathy. "I can't emphasize enough," said one forty-four-year-old account executive, "how important it is for me to be able to talk to another woman who knows what it's like to be the only female at the conference table, or understands the way I felt last week when I had to be out of town on my youngest son's birthday." Women are able, in this sense, to validate one another's experience in a way that is supportive, and that gives their friendships an added dimension.

At the same time, however, the move away from traditional roles to more active involvement outside the home means that women have less time to be with friends, less time to devote to keeping relationships going. A woman in her early forties who had gone back to work told us about the problems she's had since she started working full-time:

> I find that if I don't make a special effort, I really start to lose touch with women I care a lot about, and some friends I enjoy have just fallen by the wayside. But then, I've also found that I don't feel tied to my friends in quite the same way. Oh, the caring and commitment are still there, even without the same time investment. But I can't—and don't really need to—maintain my friendships on the same level I used to. Friends who are just as involved as I am understand; we don't have to make apologies for not calling regularly or checking in, and when we do get together, each of us has new energy to bring to the relationship. The greatest problem is with friends who aren't so involved, the ones whose lives used to be very similar to mine and are now very different. With them, there's been a kind of . . . letting go. And yet, there are a few old friends who, no matter what direction our lives take, no matter how many demands there are on our time, there's just so much history and caring, we know we'll always be there for each other.

There is often, as this women points out, something we especially value about a long-term friendship, one with a "history," one that has endured—and grown—over the years. Even though new friendships can be tremendously satisfying and exciting, there is a special bond born of sharing a lifetime of important events and small moments with that special friend we couldn't wait to tell "I bought a bra!" "I got my period!" "I've been accepted to college!" "I'm in love!" "I got the job!" Whether the friendship dates from childhood or early adulthood, there is often a depth and a sense of continuity that make it particularly precious to us. And there is, too, an element of nostalgia for "the way we were," for the times we shared, that we keep alive for one another. A Boston woman in her early forties described one such relationship:

Sarah and I met in 1960, when each of us had only recently moved to Chicago. A mutual friend invited us over to meet, thinking we would have a lot in common since we were both married to graduate students, had very young children, and were struggling to make ends meet on various part-time and piecemeal salaries. But the immediate liking I had for Sarah went beyond all of those circumstances. I don't know whether it was because I identified with her irreverent way of looking at the world, or whether it was because she seemed to be "right there," really hearing and being interested in what I was saying, but I do remember feeling slightly euphoric after our first meeting. I had found a kindred spirit after having spent six lonely months in a new city without one. And, as it happened, Sarah felt the same way. When we were leaving our friend's house that day, it was she who broke the final barrier of newness and caution by saying, "Wonderful! I've found a friend!"

And we did have a close, intense friendship for the five years I lived in Chicago. We rarely socialized as couples because our husbands were so different, but I have warm memories of our time together: the fun we had playing folk songs; the exchanging of baby-sitting and recipes; the work we did in civil rights and political movements. But my most vivid memories are of the cold Chicago winters when we had long talks in each other's kitchens while the children played in the next room. We talked about everything: sex, marriage, old boyfriends, new ambitions. We felt that we could tell each other anything. Being able to talk so openly about our feelings helped us to understand a lot of things that were going on inside us. We saw each other through some of the toughest parts of being married to graduate students too pressured to be very interested in our lives, or to help with the frustrations of early child-rearing. It was Sarah who pinch-hit when I had to work and the baby-sitter couldn't come, and it was with Sarah that I could let myself fall apart after a solid month of cranky children and chicken pox.

Of course, Sarah and I had our bad times too. We could have the most incredible arguments about the smallest things. And I remember feeling particularly excluded and hurt at one point when she got to be close friends with a woman I thought was much smarter and more interesting than I was. I was sure I was being replaced, and I was very bitchy about the woman. But eventually, I realized that my reaction was a holdover from some adolescent notion about "best friends," whereas the truth was I had other friends too. And when I got that straight in my own head, I was able to relax and have a much better perspective on our friendship, and what it did and didn't "have" to be. In the long run, I think the bad times made our relationship stronger, because we found out we could come through rough times with each other.

Then my husband finished school and took a job that brought us here to Boston. I was very lonely the first year. I met people, but I missed Sarah. For a long time, I kept potential friends at a distance, partly, I think, because I was angry at the move that was foisted on me, and partly because I didn't want to let Sarah get replaced.

It's been nearly fifteen years now since we left Chicago. Sarah and I get together when we can: she and her family vacation in the East, or I stop in Chicago when I am traveling in my job. And even though our visits are relatively few and far between, the friendship has continued to grow. The most amazing and wonderful thing is how easy it is for us to pick up where we left off. Within no time, the two of us are laughing over old stories, or sharing confidences we wouldn't dream of sharing with anyone else. Our lives have evolved very differently: I'm still married and work for a large corporation; she's an artist who's been divorced twice and leads a much less conventional life than mine. But we have such a strong connection after almost twenty years that the differences offer a kind of fascination. I'm proud of her accomplishments and she's proud of mine, and we love finding out what new experiences and adventures the other is having.

Last summer, our families got together, and it occurred to us that our oldest daughters were just about the same age we were when we first met. It was a little sobering to realize how fast the time had gone by, but watching the two of them talking and laughing together, looking so much the way we used to look, and yet developing a friendship in their own right, gave us an incredible sense of continuity.

In many ways, our friendship has remained every bit as close and special as it was during those years in Chicago. We both know we can always count on each other, not only for support and understanding, but for the good times that are enhanced by shared memories, and by the changes time brings. And that's a very good feeling.

As women thought about their friendships, old and new, they kept talking about all they had *gained* from these relationships. But they also talked about what they had to *give* to their friendships, not only with women, but with men, family, colleagues. And most felt that as mature women, they had more to offer others than ever before: more understanding and acceptance, more perspective and experience, and a greater appreciation of the value of a caring relationship.

14 Hitting Our Stride

When we started this project nearly three years ago, we had no idea we'd be at it so long. Our plan was to begin with a simple survey, interview about fifty women in person, and read the limited literature available on women in middle age. It all seemed quite reasonable at the time. But, little by little, our horizons expanded, and our task became more complex as well as more intriguing.

To begin with, our "simple" survey turned out to be anything but simple. The longer we thought about the issues of the middle years, the more we wanted to know; and the survey we eventually designed broke the cardinal rules of questionnaire writing. It was *too* long, *too* complicated, and was expected by several of the researchers we consulted to yield a low response rate. Well, our respondents broke the rules too, by surprising us with an unusually high rate of return and an eagerness to go into detail about their experiences with maturing. Their enthusiasm for our project, their insights and specific suggestions, inspired us to explore additional topics, and to contact still more women.

And when we did our interviews in person, those women, too, were not only generous about sharing their time and thoughts with us, but they also urged us to keep going, to be sure to include this or that particular topic, to interview "this interesting woman I know." After talking with over two hundred women instead of our intended fifty, we reluctantly forced ourselves to call a halt. But we did so with a new appreciation of just how many dynamic, middle-aged women there are, and of how much they have to offer one another.

As we got further into our work, we noticed that more and more information about middle-aged women was becoming available. Every few weeks we discovered yet another newly published article about women in the middle years: from the latest research in academic journals on menopause, the empty nest, and mid-life marriage, to the popular magazine pieces on "The New Mature Film Heroines," and "Older Women and Younger Men." We saw that middle-aged women were not only becoming increasingly visible in our society, but that they were becoming a more viable force as well. We saw the creation of the National Action Forum for Older Women, an organization devoted to improving the quality of women's later years.[1] We saw the Older Women's Caucus of [the] National Women's Political Caucus step up its lobbying efforts, and we saw the development of programs and publications geared specifically to the needs of middle-aged divorcées and widows and women reentering the job force.

We kept extending our deadline and changing our focus so we could include our new insights and the new information bombarding us. With a growing sense of irony, we found ourselves writing about relationships with children while constantly telling our own, "I can't talk to you now; I'm busy working on the book." And as we wrote late into the night week after week, we thought of calling the chapter on sex "Remembrances of Things Past." We began to think we would *never* finish—and so did everyone else we knew.

But in spite of the frustration of dealing with a subject that "wouldn't hold still," we realized it was this very sense of *change* in middle-aged women and their emerging position in society that made our work so exhilarating.

As we immersed ourselves in the issues of the middle years and in the voices of all the women we heard from, the three of us were touched in a very personal way. While doing our interviews, we had gotten into the habit of seeking out middle-aged women all the time, of striking up conversations with them on airplanes, cornering them at parties, always in search of a good story. But even after we vowed not to do another interview, the habit stuck. We found ourselves continuing to gravitate toward other middle-aged women with the expectation that they would be stimulating to talk to, and that we would have something to share. More than anything else it is that positive sense of shared experience and support from other women, as well as the sheer pleasure of getting to know so many of them, that has affected our own feelings about being middle-aged.

The focus of this book would have been very different if it had been written ten, or even five, years ago. The women's movement, whether we have actively participated in it or not, has affected all of our lives. It has opened up new opportunities, challenged our ideas about relationships, provided us with information about the development of our minds and our bodies, and has stimulated us in our attempts to create a productive, satisfying life-styles for ourselves. Its effects have been felt more and more by older women in the last few years, giving us a far more positive sense of who we are and what is possible for us in mid-life. It is, however, only a beginning.

Betty Friedan, a founder of the current feminist movement, has called on middle-aged women to pick up the banner and carry on with the achievements that have been made in the past decade—to continue to carve out social change and to create our own futures. It is up to us, she has said, "to create new patterns of intimacy and growth, love and work in the third of life that most women ... now hope to enjoy after fifty.[2] She could not have issued a more exciting challenge. We feel that this generation of women is more than equal to the challenge; that with our collective energy and power we have already begun; that we truly are hitting our stride.

APPENDIX A

Two versions of the questionnaire were sent out. They were, for the most part, identical, but several items (usually the open-ended questions) appeared only on one form in order to keep the questionnaire from being too lengthy. The questionnaire below includes all the items except those asking for demographic data.

1. Health (Put the number of your answer in the blank.)
   1) Excellent   2) Good   3) Fair   4) Poor
2. How often, if at all, do you think about getting older?
   1) Very often   2) Frequently   3) Occasionally
   4) Rarely   5) Never
3. How old are you?_____
4. You just wrote down your age. Do you think of yourself as: (Put the number of your answer in the blank.)
   1) Younger than that age 2) About that age   3) Older

   SEVERAL TIMES THROUGHOUT THIS STUDY, WE WILL BE

ASKING YOU TO DESCRIBE *YOUR* EXPERIENCES AND FEEL-
INGS. WE ARE, OF COURSE, INTERESTED IN COLLECTING
DATA, BUT WE'RE EVEN MORE INTERESTED IN YOUR DE-
SCRIPTION OF YOURSELF IN YOUR OWN WORDS. PLEASE BE
AS COMPLETE AS POSSIBLE, AND USE THE BLANK PAGES
PROVIDED AT THE BACK OF THIS BOOKLET FOR CONTINU-
ING YOUR LONGER ANSWERS. BE SURE TO NUMBER THEM.

5. There is often a discrepancy between people's real age and the
age they think of themselves as being. If you feel this discrepancy, please tell us what it means for you.

_____
_____
_____
_____
_____

6. How do you feel about telling people your age? Why do you feel
that way?

_____
_____
_____
_____
_____

7. Please describe in detail one thing you consider a *benefit* of being
the age you are. If possible illustrate with an anecdote.

_____
_____
_____
_____
_____

8. Some women report they have experienced the following as benefits of being older. Please circle the number which best describes how much YOU ARE EXPERIENCING the following AS
BENEFITS of being older. (Circle your answers.)

	Not at all	Very little	Moder- ately	Very much
1) More motivation to achieve	1	2	3	4
2) More self-confident	1	2	3	4

3)	Looking more attractive	1	2	3	4
4)	More adventurous	1	2	3	4
5)	More aware of my own needs	1	2	3	4
6)	Less dependent on approval of others	1	2	3	4
7)	More inner peace	1	2	3	4
8)	Greater financial security	1	2	3	4
9)	Have more impact— more able to "make things happen"	1	2	3	4
10)	Being taken more seriously by others in my work	1	2	3	4
11)	More competent in my work	1	2	3	4
12)	More physical energy	1	2	3	4
13)	Better health	1	2	3	4
14)	Don't have to worry about getting pregnant anymore	1	2	3	4
15)	Satisfaction of passing on experience to younger generation	1	2	3	4
16)	Feeling good about life choices I've made	1	2	3	4
17)	Less prone to feeling depressed	1	2	3	4
18)	Children leaving home	1	2	3	4
19)	More free time	1	2	3	4
20)	More companionship	1	2	3	4
21)	More zest and enthusiasm	1	2	3	4
22)	Improved relationship with children	1	2	3	4
23)	Improved relationship with parents	1	2	3	4

24)	Improved relationship with spouse	1	2	3	4
25)	Feel more desirable sexually	1	2	3	4
26)	More sexual activity	1	2	3	4
27)	Satisfaction of fulfilling dreams	1	2	3	4
28)	More sense of purpose	1	2	3	4
29)	Becoming more physically fit	1	2	3	4
30)	Other_____	1	2	3	4

9. You have just rated benefits that you are experiencing as a result of being older. Now select 5 from this list that you think will be the greatest benefits *ten years from now,* and record the numbers from the above list in the next 5 spaces.

_____
_____
_____
_____
_____

10. Think of something that you do now that you wouldn't have tried when you were younger. What is it and what did you have to overcome or develop to do it?

_____
_____
_____
_____
_____

11. We frequently hear the statement that "men age better than women." Do you think this statement is generally true or false?
1) True   2) False

12. Whether or not you think this statement is true, how does this general societal attitude that "men age better than women" affect your feelings about getting older?

_____
_____
_____
_____

13. Please describe in detail one thing about growing older that particularly worries or concerns you now. Illustrate with an anecdote if possible.

_____
_____
_____
_____
_____

14. Some women report they have experienced the following concerns as a result of being older. Please circle the numbers which best describe how much _you now_ are experiencing the following as concerns.

		No concern	Little concern	Moderate concern	Large concern
1)	Less motivation to achieve	1	2	3	4
2)	Less self-confident	1	2	3	4
3)	Looking less attractive	1	2	3	4
4)	Less adventurous	1	2	3	4
5)	Less sure of what I want	1	2	3	4
6)	More dependent on others' approval	1	2	3	4
7)	Death	1	2	3	4
8)	More financial worries	1	2	3	4
9)	Less impact—less able to make things happen	1	2	3	4
10)	Diminishing opportunities in the work world	1	2	3	4
11)	Less able to keep up with the competition in my work	1	2	3	4
12)	Decline of physical energy	1	2	3	4
13)	Poorer health	1	2	3	4
14)	Too old to have a (or another) child	1	2	3	4

15)	Feeling "irrelevant" to younger generation	1	2	3	4
16)	Being trapped by my past choices	1	2	3	4
17)	More prone to feeling depressed	1	2	3	4
18)	Children leaving home	1	2	3	4
19)	Too much time on my hands	1	2	3	4
20)	Loneliness	1	2	3	4
21)	Decline of zest and enthusiasm	1	2	3	4
22)	Dependency of aging parents	1	2	3	4
23)	Less satisfying relationship with children	1	2	3	4
24)	Less satisfying relationship with spouse	1	2	3	4
25)	Feel less desirable sexually	1	2	3	4
26)	Decline of sexual activity	1	2	3	4
27)	Realization that I won't fulfill my dreams	1	2	3	4
28)	Less sense of purpose	1	2	3	4
29)	Becoming less physically fit	1	2	3	4
30)	Other_____	1	2	3	4

15. You have just rated the concerns that you are experiencing as a result of being older. Now select 5 from this list that you think will *be your greatest concerns 10 years from now* and record the numbers from the list above in the next 5 spaces.

    _____
    _____
    _____
    _____
    _____

16. Have you ever given up an activity because *others* told you that you were too old?
    1) Yes   2) No

17. If so, please tell us what the activity was, who applied the pressure, and how you felt.

_____

_____

_____

_____

18. Have you ever given up an activity because *you* yourself thought it wasn't appropriate for a woman your age?
    1) Yes   2) No

19. If so, please give us a specific example and tell us why you thought you were too old to do the activity.

_____

_____

_____

20. If there are new things that you would like to try but would hesitate to try because you think you are too old, what are they and why would you hesitate?

_____

_____

_____

_____

_____

21. Do you feel that men have fewer restrictions as a result of growing older than women?
    1) Yes   2) No

22. If yes, how? _____

_____

_____

_____

23. In our society, it is common to see relationships between older men and younger women, but the reverse (older women and younger men) is not nearly so common. How do you feel about this?

_____

_____

_____

_____

_____

24. We want to find out how women feel about having an intimate relationship with a younger man in this society. Assuming you wanted a relationship with a man, would you feel comfortable if he were younger than you?
    1) Yes   2) No

25. If yes, how many years younger than yourself could this man be?

    _____

26. What advantages, if any, would you see in having an intimate relationship with a younger man? (Circle those you see as advantages and add others of your own.)
    1) I see no advantages.
    2) It would make me feel good to attract a younger man.
    3) He's likely to be a better sexual partner.
    4) He'd be likely to be more interesting.
    Add others: _____
    _____
    _____

27. What disadvantages, if any, would you see in having an intimate relationship with a younger man? (Circle those you see as disadvantages and add others of your own.)
    1) I see no disadvantages.
    2) I'd be apprehensive about his motives for being interested in me.
    3) I'd fear his reaction to my aging body.
    4) I'd fear what my friends (and/or his friends) would think.
    Add others: _____
    _____
    _____

28. What aspects of your experience as a sexual person have changed as you've gotten older?
    _____
    _____
    _____
    _____
    _____

29. If you have a primary sexual partner, what is this person's age?

    _____

    Duration of relationship:

_____ years

or

_____ months

30. If you have a sexual partner of long duration, do you think your partner's sexual pleasure has changed over the years?
1) Yes 2) No
If so, how? _____

_____

_____

_____

_____

31. How would you compare your enjoyment of sex now with when you were younger?
1) I enjoy it *much less*.   4) I enjoy it *somewhat more*.
2) I enjoy it *somewhat less*.   5) I enjoy it *much more*.
3) It's about *the same*.

32. If you engaged in sexual activity ten years ago, how would you compare your *desire* for sexual activity now with ten years ago?
1) I desire sex much more often.
2) I desire sex somewhat more often.
3) It's about the same.
4) I desire sex somewhat less often.
5) I desire sex much less often.

33. How would you label your sexual preference?
1) Heterosexual   3) Lesbian   5) Other ———
2) Bisexual   4) Asexual

34. If a relationship with a male partner ends (or has ended), would you consider having a sexual relationship with another woman?
1) I would never consider it.
2) I would consider it, but have not yet done so.
3) I have had a relationship with a woman, and *would* consider it again.
4) I have had a relationship with a woman, but *wouldn't* consider it again.
5) I'm currently having a relationship with a woman, but don't necessarily prefer it.
6) It's now my preferred choice.
7) Other (please specify) ———

35. If you were without a partner, how would you (or do you) cope with sexual desires: (Circle as many as apply.)

1) Masturbation
2) Abstinence
3) Affairs with men
4) Affairs with women
5) Other (please specify) —————

36. When you think about your parents, which one had the greater influence on your attitudes toward growing older?
   1) Mother   2) Father
37. In general, was this parent's attitude:
   1) Positive   2) Negative
38. What do you remember about this parent's feelings about getting older? Please share any vivid images or recollections with us.

   _____
   _____
   _____
   _____
   _____

39. How has this parent's attitude toward aging affected your attitudes toward aging?

   _____
   _____
   _____
   _____

40. Was there a particular time or situation when you became especially conscious of growing older? If so, please tell us the age and the specific incident or situation involved.
   Age ——————
   Situation or incident: _____

   _____
   _____
   _____
   _____

41. In general, how well are you able to cope with stress and problems now compared with when you were younger?
   1) I'm more able to cope.   2) I'm about the same.
   3) I'm less able to cope.
42. If you are either LESS or MORE able to cope, describe what you think has caused the change in your ability to cope?

   _____

43. Are you . . . (Put the number of your answer in the blank.)
   1) Not yet in menopause   2) In menopause
   3) Through menopause

44. How has menopause affected you most OR how do you think it will affect you most?

_____
_____
_____
_____
_____

45. Do you have a woman at least ten years older than you whom you consider a role model?
   1) Yes   2) No

46. If yes, who is this person? What are her qualities that make her a role model for you?

_____
_____
_____
_____
_____

47. In what way has this person affected your own feelings about getting older?

_____
_____
_____
_____
_____

48. Has the media (use of women in TV, films, advertising, cartoons, etc.) influenced your feelings about growing older?
   1) Yes   2) No

49. If so, how? _____

_____
_____
_____
_____

50. What change, if any, would you like to see in the media in regard to their portrayal of older women?

_____

_____

_____

51. Has the women's movement influenced your feelings about growing older?
1) Yes   2) No

52. If so, how? _____

_____

_____

_____

53. Have you begun a career or made a change in your career in the last five years?
1) Yes   2) No

54. Do you plan to start a career or make a career change in the next five years?
1) Yes   2) No

55. If you have answered "yes" to Question 53 or 54, what was (or will be) the change, and why did (or will) you make it?

_____

_____

_____

56. Have you ever felt your age was held against you in an employment situation? (Put the number of your answer in the blank.)
1) Yes   2) No

57. If yes, how did you react and what did you do?

_____

_____

_____

58. If you could go back to being yourself *as you were* at some younger age, would you? (Put the number of your answer in the blank.)
1) Yes   2) No
If yes, what age? _____ (fill in age)
And why? _____

_____

_____

59. If no, why not? _____
_____

60. Has the *importance* of the following changed over the last ten years for you? (Circle your answers.)

	Decreased	Same	Increased
1) Spiritual beliefs	1	2	3
2) Friendships	1	2	3
3) Altruistic causes	1	2	3
4) Political causes	1	2	3
5) Intellectual pursuits	1	2	3

61. Choose one of the above that is particularly meaningful to you and describe what it's meant to you in relation to growing older.

_____
_____
_____
_____

62. Is there anything we haven't covered that you'd like to add about what it means to be a woman growing older in this society? If so, please tell everything you have the strength left to write after this long questionnaire. We thank you.

_____
_____
_____
_____
_____

APPENDIX B

What follows is a brief report on how women responded to our survey. The data no doubt reflects the bias inherent in all self-report studies. Women who find the process of filling out a particular questionnaire *confirming* in some way are, of course, much more likely to complete and return it. And even on anonymous questionnaires, there is a tendency for respondents to represent themselves in a positive light. Moreover, such surveys capture a woman at one moment in time. Rather than an analysis of observed behavior, we are presenting what middle-aged women have told us their experience is like today. With the size and composition of our sample and the extensiveness of our anecdotal data, however, we do this with the conviction that we are allowing a reasonable cross-section of middle-aged women to speak for themselves.

We used the questionnaire in part as a means of discovering what issues are most important to women. Their answers helped us to clarify our focus, and were often a catalyst for further exploration through personal interviews. Some of the questions in the survey evoked a great many anecdotal responses and requests that we "cover this topic" in our book. Others that had seemed important to us at the outset proved to be of little significance to our respondents. Many of the findings presented here were not highlighted in the text, but may be of interest to the reader.

Since there were two forms of the questionnaire, all questions were not asked of all respondents. Therefore, percentages given are *adjusted frequencies;* that is, they are not always percentages of the total sample, but of those who answered that item.

Forty percent of the women in our sample were under forty years of age; 29% were between forty and forty-nine; 31% were fifty or older. The average age was forty-five. Sixty-eight percent were currently married; 82% had children; 88% were Caucasian. Thirty percent lived in urban areas; 43% in suburban; the remainder in small cities or towns or in rural areas. In general, the women in our sample were above average in income and education. At the time of our study, the median family income was between twenty and thirty thousand dollars, although one-third had a total family income under twenty thousand. Twenty percent of the women had a high school education or less, but more than half were college graduates. Over 90% considered themselves to be in good or excellent health.

The majority of women (54%) reported that they thought about getting older "occasionally." Only 5% said they thought about it "very often," and approximately one-third of those were in the fifty- to fifty-nine-years-old age bracket. Nearly three-quarters of our sample thought of themselves as being younger than their age; only 1% thought of themselves as older. One quarter of the respondents had no particular feelings one way or another about telling people their age. ("It's not an issue," or "Why not? I am what I am.") Forty-four percent expressed positive feelings about telling others how old they were. Interestingly, most of the 16% who expressed very negative feelings about telling their age were between thirty-five and thirty-nine.

The six most highly rated *benefits* of being older ("moderately" or "very much") were: "more aware of my own needs" (93%); "more self-confident" (92%); "less dependent on the approval of others" (88%); "more competent in my work" (82%); "feeling good about life choices I've made" (81%); and "more inner peace" (80%). These held true for all age groups, although there was a slight decline in feeling more competent in one's work after age fifty-five (to 74%), and a slight increase in "inner peace" from age forty on.

Overall, women rated the benefits of being older much higher than they rated the concerns. The six issues of greatest concern to our respondents were: "becoming less physically fit" (44%); "death" (43%); "decline of physical energy" (39%); "more financial worries" (36%); "poorer health" (35%); and "looking less attractive" (35%). There was somewhat more variation by age for concerns than for benefits. Concerns about health, fitness, and energy jumped considerably after age fifty-five, while "more financial worries" was of greatest concern to women thirty-five to thirty-nine.

Seventy-two percent did not feel that the statement "men age better than women" was true, and yet, only 48% said that they had been unaffected by this general societal attitude. Forty-one percent felt that men had fewer restrictions than women as a result of growing older. (As several pointed out, "Their restrictions are merely different, that's all.")

Fewer than 5% had ever given up an activity because *others* had told them they were "too old." Seventeen percent reported that they had given up an activity because they *themselves* thought it "wasn't appropriate for a woman their age." Not surprisingly, it was usually some strenuous physical activity that was relinquished. (Skate-boarding and skiing were the most common replies!) Very few expressed any particular regret, however. The 17% were distributed evenly across all age groups, with a slight decrease between fifty and fifty-four, and a slight increase over fifty-five.

Nearly 70% said they would feel comfortable about having a relationship with a younger man. It was felt that he could be anywhere from two to twenty-five years younger, with the median being ten years, and the average acceptable age difference seven years. Forty-three percent saw no particular advantage to having a relationship with a younger man, but 31% said it would make them feel good to attract someone younger; 23% thought a younger man would be a better sexual partner; and 13% thought a younger man would be likely to be more interesting. On the other hand, 35% expressed some apprehensions about a younger man's motives; 31% worried about how a younger man might react to their "aging body"; 21% were concerned about what friends might think. Twenty-seven percent of our respondents saw no disadvantages to a relationship with a younger man.

Over 65% of those asked said they were *enjoying* sex "somewhat" or "much" more than when they were younger; 17% said they were enjoying it about the same; fewer than 18% said they were enjoying it less. Approximately 70% of those between the ages of thirty-five and fifty reported that they were enjoying sex more or much more. After fifty-five, the percentage declined, but the majority (57%) still reported enjoying sex the same or more than when they were younger. When women in our sample were asked to compare their present *desire* for sexual activity with their desire ten years ago, 80% between the ages of thirty-five and fifty said they desired sex as much or more, and so did 50% of those who were over fifty.

Ninety-five percent of our sample described themselves as heterosexual, but 14% of those said they would consider having a sexual relationship with another woman. Over half the women said they would masturbate and/or have affairs in the absence of a regular sexual partner; 47% said they would be abstinent.

In considering parental influence on their own attitudes about growing older, 69% felt that their mothers had the greater influence; 26% their fathers, and 5% made it a point to say both parents had been equally influential. Fifty-nine percent felt their parents had influenced them in a positive way. ("I admire her attitude—she has helped me view aging in a more positive way.") Eleven percent saw parents as having been negative models with regard to growing older. ("I have all the same fears she does," or "I'm so afraid I'll be like that."). Another 15% responded in ways suggesting that they were, in a sense, "rebelling" against parental attitudes. ("I've resolved to be very different!" and "I'm determined to have a much more positive outlook than she had.") Fewer than 7% felt that their parents had no influence at all on their own feelings about aging.

Over two-thirds said that, in general, they were *more* able to cope with stress now than when they were younger; only 7% felt they were *less* able to cope. The reasons offered by the overwhelming majority of those who felt more able to cope with stress were *experience* and *perspective* ("I've gone through plenty of rough spots; I know I can do it"; "I'm more flexible now—I know that everyone has problems and that they pass.")

Forty-one percent felt that there was a woman at least ten years older than they whom they considered a role model. Sixteen percent of those said that role model was their mother; 7% mentioned public figures. For most, it was a teacher, friend, or colleague who had inspired them or shown them what was possible for older women. ("She has made me aware of my potential power, and relaxed about knowing that I still have the opportunity to 'make my mark,'" wrote one forty-nine-year-old of her role model. Another woman in her late thirties wrote that her role model conveyed "most dramatically a sense that growing older means continued growth and satisfaction, rather than a diminution of satisfaction.")

Forty-two percent indicated that the women's movement had influenced their feelings about growing older. Almost 90% of those said that influence had been a positive one, either specifically with regard to aging, or to life in general. Roughly 37% reported that their feelings about growing older had been affected by the media (use of women in advertising, TV, films, etc.), but of those, only about one-third saw that effect as having been a positive one.

Nearly 50% of the women in our sample were working full-time; another 21% were working part-time. Half the women said they had begun a career or made a career change in the *last* five years, and roughly 45% were planning to start or change careers in the *next* five years (nearly 30% of those were over forty-five). Approximately 18% of our respondents felt that age had never been held against them in an employment situation; 41% of those were over fifty. Nearly 69% of the women who were *not* currently employed said they planned to look for work in the future. Forty-three percent said they were actively involved in volunteer work.

Approximately three-quarters of the women in our sample said they would decline the chance to go back to being as they were at some younger age, and the great majority of those said they felt that way because they liked themselves better now. ("I'm happy with who I am and where I am now!") But of those who *would* go back, the two most commonly expressed reasons were: the desire to repeat a particularly fun, fulfilling time of life; and the desire to "do it differently," to explore the road not taken the first time around.

For the majority of our respondents, the importance of *spiritual beliefs, altruistic causes,* and *politics* had remained essentially the same over the last ten years. But *friendships* had increased in importance for over 53% (decreased for 8%), and *intellectual pursuits* had increased in importance for 56% (decreased for 7%). When asked to elaborate on one of the five that was particularly meaningful to them, the greatest number (40%) focused on the importance of friendships.

Indeed, issues about friendships and relationships in general emerged in open-ended questions as themes of major importance to women, and became a primary focus of this book.

NOTES

CHAPTER 1 THE VOICES OF WOMEN

1. Susan Sontag, "The Double Standard of Aging," *Saturday Review of the Society,* Vol. LV, September 23, 1972, p. 29.

2. Exactly what constitutes "middle age" is open to interpretation. It depends on the criteria one selects: chronological age, physical condition, roles, or attitudes. We use the term here to refer to that broad span of time when one is no longer struggling with the issues and tasks of youth, and not yet dealing with the realities of old age.

3. See demographic information appearing in Appendix B.

4. Leo Srole and Anita K. Fisher, "Generations, Aging, Genders and Well-Being: The Midtown-Manhattan Follow-Up Study." Presented to the Eastern Sociological Society Annual Meeting, Philadelphia, PA, Revised, April 11, 1978.

5. Betty Friedan, "Feminism Takes a New Turn," *The New York Times Magazine,* November 18, 1979, p. 98.
6. Harold Dupuy as quoted in Caroline Bird's article, "The Best Years of a Woman's Life," *Psychology Today,* Vol. XIII, June 1979, p. 26.
7. Gail Sheehy, "The Happiness Report," *Redbook,* Vol. CLIII, No. 3, July 1979.
8. *Ibid.,* p. 59.
9. *Ibid.,* p. 210.
10. *Ibid.,* p. 54.

CHAPTER 2 DID YOU EVER GET THE FEELING YOU WEREN'T RAISED TO BE OVER FORTY?

1. In *Women, Work, and Volunteering* (Boston: Beacon Press, 1974), Herta Loeser gives a complete review of the changing state of volunteering including the "volunteer-to-career concept" and ways of locating suitable volunteer jobs for the stage of life and situation a woman may be in.
2. U. S. Department of Labor, *New Labor Force Projections to 1990* (Washington, D.C.: GPO, 1975), p. 5.
3. Eileen Gray, *Everywoman's Guide to College* (Millbrae, CA: Les Femmes, 1975), p. 6.
4. In *Everywoman's Guide to College,* Eileen Gray describes the many options and special services that are available to mature women in institutions of higher education. She includes everything from how to get college credit for previous learning and life experience to descriptions of financial aid, to ways to make the transition to school easier and more successful.
5. U.S. Department of Labor, Bureau of Labor Statistics, as quoted by National Commission on Working Women, Spring 1979.
6. Alternate work patterns are flexible variations and changes in the traditional nine-to-five, forty-hour work week. They include flexitime (an eight-hour

day, but with flexible, not fixed hours); permanent part-time (a shortened work schedule); and job sharing (splitting one job for two or more persons or pairing two people to take equal responsibility for divided full-time coverage). Groups that have information about such programs include: The National Council for Alternative Work Patterns, Inc., 1925 K St., N.W. Suite 308A, Washington, D.C. 20006; Options for Women, Inc., 8419 Germantown Ave., Philadelphia, PA 19118; New Ways to Work, 457 Kingsley Ave., Palo Alto, CA 94301; Job Sharers, Inc., Box 1542, Arlington, VA 22210; Flexible Careers, Inc., 37 S. Wabash Ave., Chicago, IL 60603; and The Women's Center, Community College of Denver, Red Rocks Campus, Golden, CO 80401.

7. Two recent books on this topic are *Networking* by Mary Scott Welch and *Women's Networks: The Complete Guide to Getting a Better Job, Advancing Your Career, and Feeling Great as a Woman Through Networking* by Carol Kleiman.

8. "The Age Discrimination in Employment Act of 1967, which became effective June 1968, prohibits discrimination in employment against persons *forty- to sixty-five*-years-old by employers, employment agencies, and labor unions. It is of particular importance to women who reenter the work force after an extended period of full-time family responsibility." (Marilyn R. Block, et al., *Uncharted Territory: Issues and Concerns of Women Over 40,* p. 136.)

9. Daniel J. Levinson, *The Seasons of a Man's Life* (New York: Alfred A. Knopf, Inc., 1978), p. 7.

10. Bernice L. Neugarten, Ph.D., "Time, Age and the Life Cycle," *The Journal of American Psychiatry,* Vol. CXXXVI, No. 7, July 1979, p. 887.

11. Carol Gilligan's article "In a Different Voice: Women's Conceptions of Self and Morality," which appeared in *Harvard Educational Review* (Nov. 1977), presents a

provocative case for the expansion of adult developmental theory to include the female experience.

12. In *The Managerial Woman* (New York: Doubleday, 1977), Margaret Hennig and Anne Jardim discuss the importance of the mentor relationship.

13. F. Scott Fitzgerald, "Notebooks," in *Crack-Up*, ed. Edmund Wilson (New York: New Directions, 1956).

14. Gail Sheehy, *Passages: Predictable Crises of Adult Life* (New York: Bantam, 1977), p. 496.

15. Neugarten, "Time, Age, and the Life Cycle," p. 887.

CHAPTER 4 PHYSICAL ISSUES OF THE MIDDLE YEARS: AN ACTIVE APPROACH

1. Taking the initiative to seek medical care and actively participating in medical decisions are important ways for women to take care of themselves. Unfortunately, the organization of our health-care system and the mystique that surrounds the medical profession often deter women from getting the care they need. Women who are poor, who live in rural areas, or are uneducated, are unlikely to have access to high-quality medical services. And even women who do have access to physicians are often faced with the difficulty of establishing a relationship that is satisfactory—both personally and medically. Most physicians in this country are trained to treat disease, rather than to maintain health. Many of them know little about nutrition, exercise, sexuality, or psychological distress. Yet, the physician, especially the gynecologist, is the person we usually turn to for advice in these areas. Doctors are often overworked and pressed for time. Too often women are treated paternalistically by physicians; they are frequently discouraged from asking questions, requesting a second opinion, or disagreeing with the doctor's viewpoint. Demeaning and patronizing attitudes toward women still abound in

medical textbooks, and medical students report that off-the-cuff sexist remarks or jokes by lecturers are not yet a thing of the past.

A lucid and concise analysis of the American health-care system as it affects women can be found in the Boston Women's Health Collective's *Our Bodies, Ourselves.* The chapter on "Women and Health Care" is an excellent resource for women who are interested in organizing and developing alternatives to the current system. It includes an extensive bibliography and specific suggestions for women as individual consumers and as group activists.

CHAPTER 5 "HOT FLASHES": THE GOOD NEWS
ABOUT MENOPAUSE

1. Robert A. Wilson, M.D., "A Key to Staying Young," *LOOK,* Vol. XXX, January 11, 1966, p. 69.
2. *Ibid.,* p. 70.
3. David Reuben, M.D., *Everything You Always Wanted to Know About Sex but Were Afraid to Ask,* (New York: David McKay, 1969), p. 41.
4. Leonard R. Sillman, M.D., "Femininity and Paranoidism," *The Journal of Nervous and Mental Disease,* Vol. CXLIII, No. 11, 1966, p. 166.
5. Carlos M. F. Antunes, Sc.D., *et al.,* "Endometrial Cancer and Estrogen Use: Report of a Large Case-Control Study," *New England Journal of Medicine,* Vol. CCC, No. 1, January 4, 1979, p. 13.
6. Estelle Fuchs, Ph.D., *The Second Season: Life, Love and Sex—In the Middle Years* (New York: Anchor Press/Doubleday, 1977), p. 159.
7. Bernice L. Neugarten, Vivian Wood, Ruth J. Kraines, and Barbara Loomis, "Women's Attitudes Toward the Menopause," *Middle Age and Aging,* ed. Bernice L. Neugarten (Chicago and London, University of Chicago Press, 1968), pp. 195–200.

8. *Ibid.,* p. 200.
9. The Boston Women's Health Book Collective, *Our Bodies, Ourselves* (1976 revised edition), p. 335.
10. There are reports of numerous groups in this country and in Europe devoted to the topics of physical and health issues of middle-aged women. Jane Page's *The Other Awkward Age: Menopause,* and Rosetta Reitz' *Menopause: A Positive Approach* provide helpful information and describe the menopause workshops these women conduct in Seattle and New York respectively.

CHAPTER 6 SEX: BETTER THAN EVER

1. Dr. Beverly Hotchner, sex therapist and director of the Center for Human Concern, St. Louis, Missouri.
2. For a sound perspective and helpful information on these issues, see the chapter on "Rethinking Sexual Goals" by Lonnie Barbach in *For Yourself: The Fulfillment of Female Sexuality* (New York: Anchor Books, 1976), p. 123f.
3. *Ibid.,* see pp. 76–82. See also Nancy Friday, *My Secret Garden: Women's Sexual Fantasies* (New York: Pocket Books, 1974).
4. Judith Bardwick, *In Transition* (New York: Holt, Rinehart and Winston, 1979), p. 91. See also Linda Wolfe, *Playing Around: Women and Extramarital Sex* (New York: William Morrow and Company, 1975).
5. James Leslie McCary, *Sexual Myths and Fallacies* (New York: Schocken Books, 1973) pp. 52, 54. See also Kinsey, et al., *Sexual Behavior in the Human Female* (New York: Pocket Books, Simon & Schuster, 1953).
6. When women in our sample were asked to compare their present desire for sexual activity with their desire ten years ago, 80% between the ages of thirty-five and fifty said they desired sex as much or more; so did 50% of those who were over fifty.

7. Approximately 70% of our respondents between the ages of thirty-five and fifty reported that they were enjoying sex more or much more than when they were younger. After fifty-five, the percentage declined, but the majority (57%) still reported enjoying sex the same or more than when they were younger.

8. The majority of women through age fifty-four consider "feeling more sexually attractive" a benefit of age, although there is a slight downward trend with increasing age.

9. Lance Morrow, "In Praise of Older Women," in *Time,* Vol. CXI, No. 17, April 24, 1978, p. 99.

10. Ruth and Edward Brecher, eds., *Analysis of Human Sexual Response* (New York: Signet Books, 1966), p. 252.

11. Carol Tavris, "Sexual Lives of Women Over 60," in *Ms.* Magazine, Vol. VI, July 1977, p. 65.

12. Helen Kaplan makes an interesting point about this in Iris Sangiuliano's *In Her Time* (New York: William Morrow & Co., Inc., 1978), p. 208.

13. Joseph LoPiccolo and Julia Heiman, "Cultural Values and the Therapeutic Definition of Sexual Function and Dysfunction," in *Journal of Social Issues,* Vol. XXXIII, No. 2, 1977, pp. 166–183.

14. Lillian Rubin, *Women of a Certain Age: The Midlife Search for Self* (New York: Harper and Row, 1979), p. 98.

15. William H. Masters and Virginia Johnson, *Human Sexual Inadequacy* (Boston: Little, Brown and Co., 1970) p. 326.

CHAPTER 8 "HAPPILY EVER AFTER": MARRIAGE IN THE MIDDLE YEARS

1. In *Passages: Predictable Crises of Adult Life* (New York: Bantam, 1977), p. 285f., Gail Sheehy describes this as "Switch Forty."

2. Florine B. Livson, "Coming Out of the Closet: Mar-

riage and Other Crises of Middle Age," in Troll et al., *Looking Ahead: A Woman's Guide to the Problems and Joys of Growing Older* (Englewood Cliffs, NJ: Prentice-Hall, Inc., 1977), p. 84.
3. Judith Bardwick, *In Transition,* p. 102.
4. *Ibid.,* p. 103.

CHAPTER 9 LETTING GO: RELATIONSHIPS WITH CHILDREN

1. Written by Deborah Reese, after an article by John Leonard, appearing in *The New York Times,* Wednesday, December 1, 1976, p. C14.
2. Livson, in *Looking Ahead,* p. 88f.
3. Lillian Rubin, *Women of a Certain Age: The Midlife Search for Self,* p. 24.
4. *Ibid.,* p. 15.
5. *Ibid.,* p. 23.
6. Bernice Neugarten, "Time, Age and the Life Cycle," p. 889.
7. Pauline Bart as quoted in Margaret H. Huyck, *Growing Older* (Englewood Cliffs, NJ: Prentice-Hall, Inc., 1974), p. 71f.
8. Livson, p. 88.

CHAPTER 11 ON OUR OWN

1. *Statistical Abstract of the United States,* 1978, published by the United States Department of Commerce, p. 41.
2. Rae Lindsay, *Alone and Surviving: A Guide for Today's Widow* (New York: Walker and Company, 1977), p. 2.
3. It has become so prevalent a problem, in fact, that the federal government has designated "displaced homemakers" a specific target group, and has allocated funds for centers to aid them.
4. See, for example, Walter R. Gove, "The Relationship

Between Sex Roles, Marital Status, and Mental Illness," in *Social Forces,* Vol. LI, September 1972, pp.
34–44. See also Bardwick, *In Transition, pp. 106–109.*

CHAPTER 12 OLDER WOMAN/YOUNGER MAN

1. Estelle Fuchs, *The Second Season,* p. 7.
2. A solid majority of women in all age groups responded in the affirmative, but there was a slight decrease after the age of fifty-five.

CHAPTER 14 HITTING OUR STRIDE

1. The National Action Forum for Older Women has or-
   ganized to accomplish the following goals:

   * To establish a network and central resource exchange for all people with interests in the issues
   which affect women in mid-life and late-life,

   * To encourage the development of support services
   and community resources designed to benefit women
   in the second half of their lives,

   * To conduct and stimulate research relevant to the
   health and well-being of older women and to widely
   disseminate the results,

   * To increase public awareness of the status of older
   women and to act as advocates in their behalf.

   For further information contact Jane Porcino, Co-
   Director, School of Allied Health Professions, The
   State University of New York, Stony Brook, New York
   11794, or Nancy King, Co-Director, Center on Aging,
   University of Maryland, College Park, Maryland
   20742.
2. Betty Friedan, "Feminism Takes a New Turn," *The
   New York Times Magazine,* November 18, 1979, p. 102.

BIBLIOGRAPHY

Antunes, Carlos M./F., et al. "Endometrial Cancer and Estrogen Use: Report of a Large Case-Control Study." *New England Journal of Medicine*, Vol. CCC, No. 1 (January 4, 1979), p. 13.

Astin, Helen S. *Some Action of Her Own: The Adult Woman and Higher Education.* Lexington, MA: Lexington Books, 1976.

Barbach, Lonnie G. *For Yourself: The Fulfillment of Female Sexuality.* Garden City, NY: Anchor Press/Doubleday, 1976.

Bardwick, Judith M. *In Transition.* New York: Holt, Rinehart and Winston, 1979.

Bart, P. "Depression in Middle-Aged Women." *Women in Sexist Society: Studies in Power and Powerlessness,* eds. Gornick and Moran. New York: Basic Books, 1971.

Belliveau, F., and Richter, L. *Understanding Human Sexual Inadequacy.* Boston: Little, Brown, 1970.

Bensman, Joseph, and Lilienfeld, Robert. "Friendship and Alienation." *Psychology Today,* Vol. XIII (October 1979), pp. 56–66; 114.

Bequaert, Lucia H. *Single Women: Alone and Together.* Boston: Beacon Press, 1976.

Bernard, Jesse. *The Future of Marriage.* New York: World Publishing, 1972.

Bird, Caroline. "The Best Years of a Woman's Life." *Psychology Today,* Vol. XIII (June 1979), pp. 20–26.

Block, Marilyn R.; Davidson, Janice L.; Grambs, Jean D.; Serock, Kathryn E. *Uncharted Territory: Issues and Concerns of Women Over 40.* College Park, MD: Center on Aging, University of Maryland, August 1978. (Outstanding resource book with comprehensive bibliography.)

Bolles, Richard Nelson. *What Color Is Your Parachute? A Practical Manual for Job-Hunters and Career Changers.* Berkeley: Ten Speed Press, 1972, 1973.

Bolles, Richard Nelson. *The Three Boxes of Life and How to Get Out of Them.* Berkeley: Ten Speed Press, 1977.

Boston Women's Health Book Collective. *Our Bodies, Ourselves: A Book by and for Women.* 2nd Ed. New York: Simon and Schuster, 1976.

Boston Women's Health Book Collective. *Ourselves and Our Children: A Book by and for Parents.* New York: Random House, 1978.

Brecher, Ruth and Edward. *Analysis of Human Sexual Response.* New York: Signet Books, 1966.

Caine, L. *Lifelines.* New York: Doubleday and Co., Inc., 1978.

————. *Widow.* New York: William Morrow and Co., Inc., 1974.

Catalyst Publications. *Catalyst Report on Flexitime.* New York: Catalyst, 1978.

Catalyst Publications, Self-Guidance Series: *G.1—Planning for Work; G.2—Your Job Campaign; Education Opportunities Series; Career Opportunities Series.* New York: Catalyst, 1973. (Catalyst, 14 East 60th Street, New York, N.Y. 10022.)

Chodorow, Nancy. *The Reproduction of Mothering, Psychoanalysis and the Sociology of Gender.* Berkeley: University of California Press, 1978.

De Beauvoir, Simone. *The Second Sex.* New York: Alfred A. Knopf, 1953; Bantam Books, 1961.

Delaney, Janice; Lupton, Mary Jane; Toth, Emily. *The Curse: A Cultural History of Menstruation.* New York: New American Library, 1977.

DeRosis M.D., Helen A., and Pellegrino, Victoria Y. *The Book of Hope.* New York: Bantam Books, 1977.

Fader, Shirley Sloan. *From Kitchen to Career.* New York: Stein and Day, 1977.

Firestone, Shulamith. *The Dialectic of Sex.* New York: Bantam Books, 1970.

Fitzgerald, F. Scott. "Notebooks." *Crack-Up,* Edmund Wilson, ed. New York: New Directions, 1956.

Francke, Linda Bird, et al. "Going it Alone." *Newsweek,* Vol. XCII (September 4, 1978), pp. 76–78.

Frank, Ellen; Anderson, Carol; and Rubinstein, Debra. "Frequency of Sexual Dysfunction in 'Normal' Couples." *The New England Journal of Medicine,* Vol. CCXCIX, No. 3 (July 20, 1978), pp. 111–115.

French, Marilyn. *The Women's Room.* New York: Harcourt Brace Jovanovich, 1977.

Friday, Nancy. *My Mother/Myself.* New York: Delacorte Press, 1978.

—————. *My Secret Garden: Women's Sexual Fantasies.* New York: Pocket Books, 1974.

Friedan, Betty. "Feminism Takes a New Turn." *The New York Times Magazine* (November 18, 1979), pp. 40; 92–106.

Fuchs, Estelle. *The Second Season: Life, Love and Sex—In the Middle Years.* Garden City, NY: Anchor Press/-Doubleday, 1977.

Gilligan, Carol. "In a Different Voice: Women's Conceptions of Self and Morality." *Harvard Educational Review,* Vol. XLVII (November 1977).

Gornick, Vivian, and Moran, B. K. *Women in Sexist Society.* New York: Basic Books, 1971.

Gould, Roger. "Adult Life Stages, Growth Toward Self-Tolerance." *Psychology Today,* Vol. VIII (February 1975), pp. 74–78.

Gove, Walter R. "The Relationship Between Sex Roles, Marital Status, and Mental Illness." *Social Forces,* Vol. LI (September 1972), pp. 34–44.

Gray, Eileen. *Everywoman's Guide to College.* Millbrae, CA: Les Femmes, 1975.

Gray, Francine de Plessix. "Friends: A New Kind of Freedom for Women." *Vogue,* Vol. CLXVIII (August 1978), pp. 190–191; 257.

Greenberg, Joel. "Adulthood Comes of Age." *Science News,* Vol. CXIV, No. 5 (July 29, 1978), pp. 75–79.

Harris, Janet. *The Prime of Ms. America: The American Woman at Forty.* New York: G. P. Putnam's Sons, 1975.

Hartmann, Susan M. "The Dimensions of 'Woman's Place' in American History." *Journal of Contemporary Business* (Summer, 1973), pp. 69–82.

Hennig, Margaret and Jardim, Anne. *The Managerial Woman.* Garden City, NY: Anchor Press/Doubleday, 1977.

Hite, Shere. *The Hite Report: A Nationwide Study of Female Sexuality.* New York: Dell Publishing Co., Inc., 1976.

Howe, Louise Kapp. *Pink-Collar Workers.* New York: Avon Books, 1978.

Hubbard, Ruth; Henifin, Mary Sue; and Fried, Barbara, eds. *Women Look at Biology Looking at Women: A Collection of Feminist Critiques.* Cambridge, MA: Schenkman Publishing Co., 1979.

Huyck, Margaret H. *Growing Older.* Englewood Cliffs, NJ: Prentice-Hall, Inc., 1974.

Janeway, Elizabeth. *Man's World, Woman's Place.* New York: Morrow, 1971.

Kahnweiler, Jennifer Boretz. "Developmental Concerns of Women Returning to School at Mid-Life Based on a Concept of Mid-Life Transition." (A doctoral dissertation.) Florida State University, College of Education, June 1979.

Kinsey, A.C., et al. *Sexual Behavior in the Human Female.* Philadelphia: W. B. Saunders and Co., 1953.

Kleiman, Carol. *Women's Networks: The Complete Guide to Getting a Better Job, Advancing Your Career, and*

Feeling Great as a Woman Through Networking. Lippincott and Cromwell, 1980.

Klemesrud, Judy. "The Last Taboo." *St. Louis Post-Dispatch* (Sunday, April 15, 1979).

Kreps, J. *Sex in the Marketplace: American Women at Work.* Baltimore: Johns Hopkins University Press, 1971.

Lederer, Muriel. *Blue-Collar Jobs for Women.* New York: E. P. Dutton, 1979.

Le Guin, Ursula. "The Space Crone." *The CoEvolution Quarterly* (Summer, 1976), pp. 108–110.

Le Shan, Eda. *The Wonderful Crisis of Middle Age.* New York: David McKay, 1973.

Lessing, Doris. *The Summer Before the Dark.* New York: Random House, 1973.

Levinson, Daniel J. *The Seasons of Man's Life.* New York: Alfred A. Knopf, 1978.

Lindsay, Rae. *Alone and Surviving: A Guide for Today's Widow.* New York: Walker and Company, 1977.

Loeser, Herta. *Women, Work, and Volunteering.* Boston: Beacon Press, 1974.

Lopata, Helena Z. *Occupation Housewife.* New York: Oxford University Press, 1971.

LoPiccolo, Joseph, and Heiman, Julia. "Cultural Values and the Therapeutic Definition of Sexual Function and Dysfunction." *Journal of Social Issues,* Vol. XXXIII, No. 2 (Spring, 1977), pp. 166–183.

Loring, Rosalind, and Wells, Theodora. *Breakthrough: Women Into Management.* New York: Van Nostrand Reinhold, 1972.

Lowenthal, Marjorie F., and Chiriboga, David. "Transition to the Empty Nest." *Archives of General Psychiatry,* Vol. XXVI (January 1972), pp. 8–14.

Maccoby, Eleanor E., and Jacklin, Carol Nagy. *The Psychology of Sex Differences,* 2 vols. Stanford, CA: Stanford University Press, 1974.

Masters, William H., and Johnson, Virginia. *Human Sex-*

ual Inadequacy. Boston: Little, Brown and Co., 1970.

Masters, William H., and Johnson, Virginia. *Human Sexual Responses.* Boston: Little, Brown and Co., 1966.

Matthews, Esther E.; Feingold, S. Norman; Weary, Bettina; Berry, Jane; and Tyler, Leona E. *Counseling Girls and Women Over the Life Span.* Washington, D.C.; National Vocational Guidance Association Monograph, 1972.

Mayer, Allan J., et al. "The Graying of America." *Newsweek,* Vol. LXXXIX (February 28, 1977), pp. 50–69.

Mayer, Nancy. *The Male Midlife Crisis.* New York: Signet Books, 1979.

McCary, James L. *Sexual Myths and Fallacies.* New York: Shocken Books, 1973.

McCoy, Vivian Rogers; Ryan, Colleen; and Lichtenberg, James W. *The Adult Life Cycle,* Training Manual and Reader. Adult Life Resource Center, Division of Continuing Education. The University of Kansas, Lawrence, KS, 1978.

McEaddy, Beverly Johnson. "Women in the Labor Forces: The Later Years." *Monthly Labor Review,* Vol. XCVIII (November 1975), pp. 17–24.

Moreland, John R. "Some Implications of Life-Span Development for Counseling Psychology." *Personnel and Guidance Journal,* Vol. LVII (February 1979), pp. 299–303.

Morrow, Lance. "In Praise of Older Women." *Time,* Vol. CXI, No. 17 (April 24, 1978), pp. 99–100.

Neugarten, Bernice L. *The Psychology of Aging: An Overview.* (Master Lectures on Developmental Psychology) Abstracted in the JSAS Catalog of Selected Documents in Psychology, 1976, Vol. XI, No. 4, p. 97. American Psychological Association, Washington, D.C.

———, ed. *Middle Age and Aging.* Chicago: University of Chicago Press, 1968.

———. "Time, Age and the Life Cycle." *American Jour-*

nal of Psychiatry, Vol. CXXXVI, No. 7 (July 1979), p. 887.

New Research on Women and Sex Roles at the University of Michigan. Ed. by Dorothy G. McGuigan. University of Michigan, Center for Continuing Education for Women, Ann Arbor, MI, 1976.

New Ways to Work: A Booklet of General Information About Job Sharing. San Francisco, June 1977.

O'Brien, P. *Woman Alone.* New York: Quadrangle, 1973.

Page, Jane. *The Other Awkward Age: Menopause.* Berkeley: Ten Speed Press, 1977.

Parlee, Mary Brown. "Psychological Aspects of the Climacteric in Women." *Psychiatric Opinion,* Vol. XV, No. 10 (October 1978).

Parlee, Mary Brown, and the eds. of *Psychology Today.* "The Friendship Bond." *Psychology Today* (October 1979), pp. 43–54; 113.

Reitz, Rosetta. *Menopause: A Positive Approach.* Radnor, PA: Chilton Book Co., 1977.

Reuben, David, M.D. *Everything You Always Wanted to Know About Sex but Were Afraid to Ask.* New York: David McKay, 1969.

Rivers, Caryl; Barnett, Rosalind; and Baruch, Grace. *Beyond Sugar and Spice.* New York: G. P. Putnam's Sons, 1979.

Rubin, Lillian. *Women of a Certain Age—The Midlife Search for Self.* New York: Harper and Row, 1979.

Rush, Anne Kent. *Getting Clear: Body Work for Women.* New York: Random House, 1973.

Sangiuliano, Iris. *In Her Time.* New York: William Morrow and Company, Inc., 1978.

Schlossberg, Nancy K., and Waters, Elinor B. "Shifting the Balance from Problem to Possibility: Counseling Mid-Life Women." Paper prepared for the House Select Committee on Aging, U. S. House of Representatives (June 1978).

Seaman, B. *Free and Female.* New York: Coward, McCann and Geoghegan, 1972.

Sheehy, Gail. *Passages: Predictable Crises of Adult Life.* New York: Bantam, 1977.

Sheehy, Gail. "The Happiness Report." *Redbook,* Vol. CLIII, No. 3 (July 1979), p. 29.

Sillman, Leonard R. "Femininity and Paranoidism." *The Journal of Nervous and Mental Disease,* Vol. CXLIII, No. II (1966), p. 166.

Slater, Philip E. "Sexual Adequacy in America." *Intellectual Digest,* Vol. IV (November 1973), pp. 17–20.

Smith, B. K. *Aging in America.* Boston: Beacon, 1973.

Sontag, Susan. "The Double Standard of Aging." *Saturday Review of the Society,* Vol. LV (September 23, 1972), pp. 29–38.

Srole, Leo, and Fisher, Anita K. "Generations, Aging, Genders and Well-Being: The Midtown-Manhattan Follow-Up Study." Presented to the Eastern Sociological Society Annual Meeting, Philadelphia, PA. Revised (April 11, 1978).

Stein, Ruthe. "Myth of the Empty Nest." *San Francisco Chronicle* (Tuesday, August 22, 1978), p. 17.

Steinem, Gloria. "Why Do Women Work, Dear God, Why Do They Work?" *Ms.* Magazine, Vol. VI (March 1978), p. 45.

Strouse, Jean, ed. *Women and Analysis.* New York: Grossman, 1974.

Tavris, Carol. "The Sexual Lives of Women over 60." *Ms.* Magazine, Vol. VI (July 1977), pp. 62–65.

Tavris, Carol, and Offir, Carole. *The Longest War: Sex Differences in Perspective.* New York: Harcourt Brace Jovanovich, 1977.

Tavris, Carol, and Sadd, Susan. *The Redbook Report on Female Sexuality.* New York: Delacorte Press, 1975, 1977.

Terkel, Studs. *Working: People Talk About What They Do All Day and How They Feel About What They Do.* New York: Pantheon Books, 1974.

Troll, L., Israel, J., and Israel, K., eds. *Looking Ahead: A Woman's Guide to the Problems and Joys of Growing Older.* Englewood Cliffs, NJ: Prentice-Hall, Inc., 1977.

U.S. Department of Labor. *Statistical Abstract of the U.S.* Washington, D.C.: GPO, 1978, pp. 40, 41.

U.S. Department of Labor. *1975 Handbook on Women Workers,* Bulletin No. 297. Washington, D.C.: GPO, 1975.

U.S. Department of Labor. *Women Workers Today.* Washington, D.C.: Women's Bureau, 1976.

U.S. Department of Labor, Bureau of Labor Statistics. *New Labor Force Projections to 1990.* Washington, D.C.: GPO, 1975.

U.S. House of Representatives 95th Congress Select Committee on Aging, and the Subcommittee on Retirement Income and Employment. *Women in Midlife—Security and Fulfillment* (Part I and Part II). A Compendium of Papers, 1978, 1979.

U.S. News and World Report. Vol. LXXXV. "Working Women—Joys and Sorrows." January 15, 1979.

U.S. Women's Bureau. *A Working Woman's Guide to Her Job Rights,* No. 55. Washington, D.C.: GPO, 1974.

Vaillant, George E. *Adaptation to Life.* Boston: Little, Brown and Co., 1977.

Washington Opportunities for Women: A Guide to Part-Time Work and Study for the Educated Woman, ed. by Reyna Weisl, Jane Fleming, and Mary Janney. Washington, D.C.: Robert B. Luce, Inc., 1967.

Wax, Judith. *Starting in the Middle.* New York: Holt, Rinehart and Winston, 1979.

Welch, Mary Scott. *Networking.* New York: Harcourt Brace Jovanovich, 1980.

Wilson, Robert A. "A Key to Staying Young." *LOOK*, Vol. XXX (January 11, 1966), p. 69

Zimmeth, Mary. *The Women's Guide to Re-Entry Employment.* Mankato, MN: Gabriel Books, 1979.

INDEX